PASSIONATE POLITICS

Other books edited by Charlotte Bunch:

*International Feminism: Networking Against Female
  Sexual Slavery*
Learning Our Way: Essays in Feminist Education
Building Feminist Theory: Essays from Quest
Lesbianism and the Women's Movement
Class and Feminism
Women Remembered: Biographies of Women in History
The New Women: A Motive *Anthology on Women's
  Liberation*

ESSAYS

PASSIONATE

1 9 6 8

POLITICS

1 9 8 6

FEMINIST THEORY IN ACTION

CHARLOTTE BUNCH

ST. MARTIN'S PRESS
NEW YORK

Library of Congress Cataloging-in-Publication Data

Bunch, Charlotte, 1944–
  Passionate politics.

  1. Feminism—History.   2. Feminism—United States—
History.   I. Title.
HQ1154.B86   1987   305.4'2'0973   87–4433
ISBN 0-312-00667-5

Design by JOHN FONTANA

10 9 8 7 6 5 4 3 2

For Roxanna, Nancy, Shirley, and my mother Marjorie

CONTENTS

ACKNOWLEDGMENTS

For a selection of essays that covers so many years of my life, there is not enough space to acknowledge all the people I would like to thank. But naming names is important. This book is not a solitary endeavor for it reflects many working partnerships and group projects, during which friends have sustained me both as a source of ideas and comfort as well as by challenging me to keep moving. Each person mentioned supported me at one or many times when it really mattered, and without them, these essays would not exist.

Several people were especially important in giving final shape to this collection. Jackie St. Joan commented on drafts of the Introduction and pushed me to write by publishing my speeches through her creation, Antelope Publications. Kay Whitlock consulted on what to include here while also providing humor and perspective on making it through the publishing process. Rima Shore read through all the articles helping me to place the pieces in context. Renate D. Klein wrote comments, proposals, and letters that prodded me to complete the project. Mary Ellen Capek, Phyllis Chesler, and Mary Farmer offered suggestions from their experiences in the publishing world and helped me through some crucial decisions. My agent, Frances Goldin, gave invaluable attention and advice even after my file lay dormant for several years, and Michael Denneny's supportive approach as my editor made the process of turning this over to St. Martin's Press easier than I had expected.

Over the years many others have discusssed my doing such a collection and encouraged my writing in various ways including Nancy K. Bereano, Rita Mae Brown, Bertha Harris, Joanne Parrent, Sandra Pollack, Arlie Scott, Jacqui Starkey, Kate Stimpson, Jim Weeks, Liz Wood, and both Joanne Edgar and Gloria Steinem of *Ms.* magazine. Shirley Castley was particularly helpful in the early stages of preparing this book and shared in the work and discussions that led to many of the essays.

My life as an organizer and activist lies at the heart of this book, and in this, I have drawn sustenance from various quarters. Many whom I first knew in the student Christian movement of the '60s remained allies as we each explored what feminism meant for our lives; particular thanks goes to Peggy Billings, Peggy Cleveland, Judy Davis, Sara Evans, Ruth Harris, Ann-Catrin Jarl, Elmira Kendricks, Nelle Morton, and Dick Shaull. The Institute for Policy Studies enabled much of my earlier writing, by supporting my work with D.C. Women's Liberation and *Quest: A Feminist Quarterly.* My political direction took shape during the thirteen years I worked on various projects in Washington, D.C. where my ideas were developed with friends too numerous to mention but including Joan E. Biren, Carol Blum, Sharon Deevey, Helaine Harris, Nancy Hartsock, Ellen Malcolm, Mary Helen Mautner, Linda McGonigal, Sydney Oliver, Coletta Reid, Lee Schwing, Cynthia Washington, and Arthur Waskow. Special mention must be made of Alexa Freeman, Beverly Fisher Manick, and Juanita Weaver who deeply influenced me both as close colleagues and as part of my feminist family.

My activism was not confined to Washington, D.C., and for many years the National Gay Task Force and especially its women's caucus and its previous directors, Jean O'Leary and Lucia Valeska, provided a supportive context for my national activities. I also benefited from long-distance collaboration with Dolores Alexander, Jean Crosby, Karla Dobinski, Frances Doughty, Sally Gearhart, Roma Guy, Mary E. Hunt, Ginger Legato, Barbara Love, and Ginny Vida.

In New York, the women of the International Women's Tribune Centre have been a continuous source of information and encouragement for my work on global feminism: Anne Walker, Vicki Semler, Joanne Sandler, Vicky Mejia, Vanessa Davis, Alice Quinn, Martita Midence, and Mildred Persinger have all gone out of their way to assist me. Many other women have also helped me to develop a global perspective but special thanks go to Anita Anand, Peggy Antrobus, Claudia Hinojosa, Rosa Dominga, Liz Fel, Caren Grown, Ied Guinee, Sara Lee Hamilton, Ruth Lechte, Ana Maria Portugal, Rosemary Pringle, Elizabeth Reid, Diana Russell, Julie Thompson, Virginia Vargas, Joyce Yu, the women of ISIS and of the Pacific Asian Women's Forum.

There are four women who I want to remember here who are no longer alive, but each was influential in my life at different moments: Nanci Weldon, Carol McEldowney, June Arnold, and Barbara Deming. I hope that this book carries forward some of the feminist spirit and determination that they gave to me and others.

Finally there are those who have been essential to my life and hence to this book especially in recent years. Lori Ayre and Mallika Dutt have been not only my assistants but also thoughtful advisers who kept me in touch with a younger generation of feminists. Dorothy Lyddon has provided financial aid at critical moments. Jean Millar has helped me keep focused on what really matters to me. Betty Powell has been my close friend and collaborator sharing with me ideas and events as well as the agonies and exhilarations of a movement life. I have benefited enormously from working closely with Roxanna Carrillo, whose personal support and keen political mind have expanded the scope of my work and my life, as well as helped to put many finishing touches on this book. Nancy Myron, as my roommate for over a decade, witnessed how these essays finally got written, yet in spite of the frustrations of living with a writer has encouraged me in it. She, her niece—Nadine Myron—and our cats Violet and Sido, saw me through some of the thinner times in my life. And I want to thank my parents, Marjorie and Pardue Bunch, whose continuous support has strengthened my efforts to carry on the ideals they imparted to me at an early age.

A NOTE TO THE READER

n preparing the essays for this collection, I thought of how my work on feminism evolved. First, I had a file folder labeled women. Then the "women" files grew until they took over a drawer of my filing cabinet, and soon I had to get a new cabinet for them. As I developed more specialized interests within feminism, this process repeated itself. A file on lesbianism became a drawer full of files, as did one on feminist media and on global feminism.

Following these organic divisions, I organized this book around five areas: A Feminist Overview; Movement Strategies and Organizing; Lesbian Feminism; Media and Education; and Global Feminism. Within each section, the essays are in chronological order. While the topics are interrelated, this approach aims at providing a sense of how my thinking on certain themes evolved in relation to specific events in my life, the movement, and the world. I see this book not only as a body of feminist thought but also as an illustration of how theory develops in relation to activism.

I have selected essays and speeches that reflect important aspects of my development and that others have told me they found helpful. Since these pieces were originally prepared for a variety of purposes, there is some overlap. Yet even the overlap reflects the evolution of my ideas in different settings. In a few instances, I have removed repetitive passages, combined articles, condensed longer works, or clarified points. But generally, the works appear here as they were originally.

PASSIONATE POLITICS

INTRODUCTION

I have often been asked why and how I became a political organizer and writer. The short answer is that these activities most consistently engaged my imagination and energies over the years. They brought meaning and satisfaction to my life, and became what I needed to do to feel truly alive. Some call that a vocation, others call it survival or see it as a career. For me, it has been all three.

By describing the evolution of my life's work here, I seek to flesh out that short answer. I also hope to provide a context for this selection of essays drawn from the past eighteen years. This is clearly my story. But in a broader sense, it is also the story of a number of women of my generation who grew up in the movements of the 1960s and '70s and whose adult lives have been shaped by those experiences. For, like many, I have been both a creator and a product of the social and political forces sweeping through the world over the past quarter of a century. What was happening in movements for change at different moments affected why and how these articles and speeches were originally conceived.

For me, the decisive year was 1963. As an undergraduate, I participated in my first civil rights demonstrations in North Carolina, started reading *I.F. Stone's Weekly*—a newsletter that pro-

1

vided a view of the world besides that of the mainstream U.S. media—and learned about poverty working in an inner-city project in Philadelphia. I began to see how the problems of Northern urban slums and the blatant racism of the South were connected to the unacknowledged race and class divisions of the Southwestern town of my childhood. That was the year I first visited Harlem and Greenwich Village and that an enlightened director led my campus YWCA to discuss a recently published book, *The Feminine Mystique*, which confirmed my unarticulated suspicions about the prospects for "educated women."

In 1963 Martin Luther King, Jr. gave us his dream at the civil rights March on Washington, which I watched on TV, wondering if I should be there. Later that year, students wept over the assassination of John F. Kennedy, fearing that it meant the end of our hopes for a new era. It was the year that I first heard someone from the Eastern bloc (Czechoslovakia) talk about Marxist-Christian dialogue, met black South Africans whose stories made apartheid real to me, and saw a friend beaten by police during a peaceful protest. I turned nineteen that year and knew that I would never go home again. For during 1963, dramatic events and courageous people had ushered me simultaneously into adulthood and into a life of political activism. I saw the world through a new prism, which affected how I began to shape my life.

My family drove me across the country in September 1962 to begin my college education at Duke University in Durham, North Carolina, which we spoke of as "going East," not South. I had spent almost eighteen years in Artesia, a small "West Texas-like" town in southeastern New Mexico. My mother had been president of the local school board when Artesia was featured in *Time* magazine for having the first underground school that doubled as a bomb shelter. In the '50s, it was the kind of place where arguments raged over whether putting chlorine in the water was a Communist plot to destroy America. My parents were open-minded Methodists and middle-class professionals whose commitment to fairness and moderate politics often made them controversial. They were active in church and civic affairs and encouraged me, my two sisters, and one brother in many extracurricular activities. One year we were designated New Mexico's Methodist Family of the Year, but failed to make a national showing.

I was the third and most adventurous of the children and the only one sent East for an education. This was not only for my intellectual growth but also, as my father put it, because men there would be more willing to accept such an independent woman. His meaning escaped me since I saw myself as a "good girl." I did not imagine having trouble finding a husband when the time came for me to marry, even though I had only dated boys sporadically. As a child, my education, natural curiosity, and desire to explore the world were encouraged. I was rarely told that I should not do certain things because I was female. The idea that as a woman I would later be excluded from certain avenues of life was foreign to me. Nor did it occur to me that being female would be of any great significance to what I did with my life. When I left home for college, I was bright, optimistic, adventuresome, civic-minded, experienced in organizations, with a strong moral sense, but essentially apolitical and naïve.

As an undergraduate at Duke, I moved gradually but inexorably from morally opposing the unfairness of racism in the South to an understanding of such oppression as political and to personal outrage over many forms of injustice in the world. I went from a shy presence at "pray-ins" protesting segregation at the local church to a life full of movement activism. I organized locally with campus groups, participated in national demonstrations such as the 1965 Selma-to-Montgomery civil rights march as part of the National Council of the Methodist Student Movement, and joined protests against the Vietnam war at the Durham post office and then in Washington, D.C.

I also sought to satisfy my curiosity about the world and to understand social change through my academic work. I shifted my major from religion to psychology and then to history and political science. My senior history honors paper was on the role of women in the Chinese revolution, which I saw as an intriguing aspect of revolutionary change, not a feminist topic. I enjoyed combining what the university called the "life of the mind" with life as an activist. During several vacations, I smuggled dry cereal into the library stacks so that I could eat lunch while working to make up for time I lost going to meetings and marches.

As the prospect of graduate school approached, however, the word "choose" was written everywhere I turned. The female professor I most respected warned that my career would be hampered unless I curtailed my political activities, while movement heavies called the university irrelevant. Feeling that I had to choose, I did. I chose the movement as my career, and I wanted it then, not later.

When I graduated in 1966, I thought of myself as leaving academia and casting my lot with the movement. As we not so humbly put it, we were making history, not studying it. I moved to Washington, D.C., where I helped to start a community-organizing project in a black ghetto. Like many radical middle-class students, I saw community organizing as a way both to learn from living with the oppressed and to help mobilize people to take power over their lives and change society. Simultaneously, I was organizing nationally as the first president of the newly formed University Christian Movement (UCM), an attempt at radical Christian ecumenism that did not survive the '60s. My political identity was still linked to the radical wing of Christianity—influenced by the Southern black church—that sought to put the gospel into action for social justice.

In the spring of 1967, I married Jim Weeks, whom I had met at a National Student Christian Movement conference in 1963. He was a student in California then and we had courted across the country for several years until we both moved to D.C. to live and work in the same project. Our alternative wedding vows did not talk of obedience but were based on our decision to build a life together around our commitment to social activism. We did not think of it as feminist, but we saw our marriage as a partnership of two people whose work was of equal importance. We lived in a commune where household chores had been divided among couples and we continued to split ours. I was too busy with political work to spend more time on housework because I was married, and neither of us imagined that I should.

Politics was uppermost in all aspects of my life. I identified loosely as part of the "New Left"—a term that '60s radicals had adopted to distinguish ourselves from the "Old Left" parties that we saw as outdated, authoritarian, and sectarian. I was sympathetic to the ideals of socialism but had no hard and fast ideological positions. I was more interested in political action than political theory.

I was not in D.C. long before I realized that my role as a white radical was not to organize a black community. I turned to working against racism among whites and became acquainted with the Institute for Policy Studies (IPS), a progressive think tank in Washington. Under the direction of Arthur Waskow, I began a tutorialship there, studying a "depth education" project that we had launched in UCM in an effort to create an educational process that would lead people to action for social change. I wrote an ambitious prospectus consisting of seven pages of vital questions to explore. But that endeavor was cut short by my overwhelming discovery of sexism in this movement citadel of political-intellectual life.

My recognition of sexism at IPS probably had more to do with my evolving consciousness of myself as a woman than with any behavior unique to the Institute. Nevertheless, this was the place where I first confronted sex discrimination and patronizing attitudes toward women within social-change groups. I often felt invisible there, and was stunned by the prevailing attitude that women were not politically serious. When Marilyn Salzman Webb, who was also associated with IPS, suggested that we form a women's group, I was ready.

We had our first women's meeting in January 1968, immediately after the Jeanette Rankin Women's Brigade for Peace—a national antiwar march cosponsored by Women's Strike for Peace, church women, and others. I gave a speech on radical young women's views of imperialism at the rally, but while there I saw a New York group perform a feminist skit about men and warfare that fascinated me and shocked many. It was one of the early confrontations between feminists and peace women about women's priorities, relationships with men, and feminism. On the edges of the march, we met with women from the radical women's groups that had formed in New York and Chicago. I knew about them because my closest friend from college, with whom I had developed politically in those years, Sara Evans, was in the Chicago group. They described the excitement of women uncovering common problems and creating political directions for ourselves. These discussions enabled many of us to see women's liberation as a national phenomenon and laid the groundwork for the formation of such groups in more cities.*

*For more about the roots of the women's liberation movement in the movements of the 1960s, see *Personal Politics* by Sara Evans (New York: Alfred A. Knopf, 1979).

5

Our first Washington, D.C. group consisted of about eight women connected with IPS or the left generally. Calling ourselves a radical women's group, we spent months convincing ourselves that it was politically okay to meet separately as women and to focus on women's concerns. We felt somewhat more secure because we saw a parallel to the arguments of blacks who had been establishing their right and need to have their own space. Ultimately, however, the experience was so powerful that it justified itself. Most of us gradually changed our political work, embraced the term "women's liberation," helped start more such (later called consciousness-raising) groups, and initiated public actions aimed at making people aware of women's oppression.

A number of us went to Atlantic City for the first protest against the Miss America beauty pageant in September 1968. We took our own flyer, which the New York organizers would not let us pass out since it did not follow their precise line. Based on this and other conflicts, some of us felt a need for more national dialogue about our movement. We initiated the first national women's liberation movement conference and recruited representatives from groups in New York and Chicago to help us organize it in three months out of the basement at IPS. Over two hundred women from groups in some twenty cities came to talk about women's liberation at a YMCA camp outside Chicago at Thanksgiving, 1968. Snow and wind raged outside as verbal battles raged within. Arguments flew between groups defined as feminists and leftists, between advocates of reform versus revolution, between those labeled "politicos" and "life-stylists," whose focus was more personal. We debated interpretations of the sources of women's oppression and the consequent priorities for organizing. I often found myself in the middle feeling that there was some truth to many of the competing positions, and I tried hard—but not very successfully—to clarify the best ideas of each and to find ways to keep us working together. The conference forecasted the divisiveness that would plague the women's movement as it grew.

During this year of women's organizing, I started to write about women. Our experiences of consciousness-raising had been so powerful that we believed that describing the various forms of women's oppression and getting enough copies of "Why Women's Liberation" into enough hands would create the changes we sought. I wrote my first articles about the women's movement and cajoled the staff of *Motive* magazine—a liberal student publication of the Methodist Church that often published avant-garde work—into devoting an issue to the "woman question." Their lone woman editor Joanne Cooke and I conspired to produce an issue on the women's liberation movement itself. That edition published in March 1969 was one of the first women's liberation anthologies, and all sixty thousand copies sold out in a few months. It created more controversy in the letters to the editor than had any edition of *Motive* in thirty years. In 1970, we made revisions and it was published by Bobbs-Merrill as *The New Women.*

During most of 1969, I lived in Cleveland, Ohio, where I organized women's liberation with Carol McEldowney whom I had met at the Jeanette Rankin Brigade the year before. This was my first experience initiating women's groups among women in the left who resisted the idea. The Left generally labeled us divisive or trivial, but these women seemed particularly fearful of their men's rejection and had difficulty trusting that women could develop our own politics. Cleveland was then giving birth to the militant Weathermen faction of SDS (Students for a Democratic Society), which would later go underground. Faced with their sharp criticism of feminism, I found myself forced into a more vigorous defense of the importance of women's liberation. I also learned how to organize new female constituencies utilizing street theater, provocative pamphlets, and public forums to reach women not already active politically. I began to move away from the Left as well as to hone my own politics, which I increasingly defined as feminist and autonomous.

I had moved to Cleveland for my husband's education and found myself being identified, for the first time, in terms of him—being called Mrs. James Weeks. This made me so angry that I hyphenated my name to Bunch-Weeks. While this period was politically useful, I found Cleveland cold and depressing and often felt isolated there. Meanwhile, IPS had begun to recognize the importance of the women's movement and offered me a position as one of their first women "fellows." While my husband finished his degree in Cleveland, we tried a commuter marriage for six months, and I returned to D.C. where the women's movement had been expanding rapidly.

The next year was one of constant activity. By 1970 women's liberation had gained media attention and our groups were besieged with calls from women wanting to find out more about it. Projects proliferated and D.C. Women's Liberation set up a coordinating council of all groups called Magic Quilt. Here we tried to stay in touch with each other and cope with conflicts over political direction and internal structure. We opened a women's center in an apartment and organized ongoing orientation courses for women new to feminism. Some of us who were now "old" in the movement formed a closed collective called Daughters of Lilith, where we talked about what to do next and sought to create a sense of direction in a movement that was growing helter-skelter.

In the midst of this activity, the Mobilization to End the War in Vietnam invited me to participate in a trip to North Vietnam in May 1970. I was excited about representing the independent women's liberation movement, which was beginning to be recognized as an autonomous political force in the U.S. On my return, I helped organize a Women and Imperialism group that sought to develop a specifically feminist approach to these issues. We tried. But soon we found ourselves in the cross fire between feminists who thought we should only focus on women, so long neglected, and the peace movement, which was impatient with feminism. The pressures were so intense and the battles so debilitating, that I felt I could be more effective if I chose one area. After considerable frustration, I decided to concentrate on domestic feminism.

During this same period, D.C. Women's Liberation was trying to forge coalitions with other groups like the National Organization for Women. NOW defined itself as concerned with equal rights for women and had kept its distance from our radical brand of liberation. We too had kept our distance. But we joined in when NOW proposed major women's rights Marches for Equality in many cities on August 26, 1970—the anniversary of women's suffrage in the U.S. Our representatives to the coalition included Joan Biren and Sharon Deevey, who lived in the same commune with me and my husband, and who were in the process of coming out publicly as lesbians. They fought vigorously for antiracist and openly lesbian speakers and eventually got a black lesbian added at the bottom of the list for the local rally. We also held our first women's cultural festival and women's dance following that march. Through all of this, I was gradually discovering lesbianism both politically and personally.

Early in 1971, I left my marriage and came out as a lesbian. This was not a reaction against my husband but a response to the power of sexual self-discovery. There was a sense of excitement about lesbianism that compelled me forward. I saw this as politically, as well as personally, important and was public about my identity. Therefore, I never experienced the pain, the fears, or the safety of being in the closet. Soon my concern over the homophobia and antagonism toward lesbians in the women's movement superseded my other political work. Lesbians were demanding recognition of our existence, of our contributions to the movement, and of the political implications of heterosexism for feminism. Anger exploded throughout the movement as D.C. Women's Liberation experienced the "gay-straight" split. It was traumatic for everyone. I felt I was being torn asunder from a movement that had become my family—mother, sister, and daughter.

After several months of such confrontations within the women's movement, Rita Mae Brown and I decided to form a separate lesbian political group. We joined up with Joan Biren, Sharon Deevey, and Ginny Berson—who had been part of the first consciously lesbian feminist commune in D.C.—and others to establish what became The Furies collective.* The Furies withdrew from the organized women's movement and committed ourselves to developing a lesbian-feminist political analysis, culture, and movement. We were still concerned with the women's movement as a whole, but following the path of other oppressed groups, we concluded that we could influence it best by building our own power base and politics first.

I was accustomed to being in a political minority. But now for the first time, I belonged to a minority that was loathed, stigmatized, and feared for its very existence, by both society generally and the "progressive" movements to which I had committed my life since 1963. I had to know why the simple act of loving other women sexually, which had occurred for me as a natural extension of feminism, was so taboo and threatening to others. Thus, the development of a political analysis encompassing lesbianism and

*Eventually there were twelve women in The Furies collective: Ginny Berson, Joan Biren, Rita Mae Brown, Sharon Deevey, Helaine Harris, Susan Hathaway, Nancy Myron, Tasha Peterson, Coletta Reid, Lee Schwing, Jennifer Woodhul, and I.

9

heterosexuality not only fascinated me intellectually but became integral to my survival. The Furies edited a lesbian feminist issue of *Motive* magazine—which had become independent of the Methodist Church and died soon after. I turned to questions of theory with a sense of urgency that continued in my work on *The Furies* newspaper, which published ten issues in 1972 and '73.

Much of our time within The Furies group was spent in internal struggle over political analysis, over questions of leadership and collectivity (from whether toothbrushes should be communal to how to structure decision-making responsibilities), and particularly over class differences. Although we were an all-white group, we came from a variety of classes and ethnic backgrounds. It became one of our priorities to understand the effects of these as part of our effort to create a feminist analysis of differences among women, such as class and race, as well as sexual preference.

The Furies made important breakthroughs, but after a year, the positive intensity of our interaction threatened to deteriorate into self-destructive cannibalism. Due to both our politics and the insularity of our group, we had become isolated from other women—even other lesbians whom we had hoped to organize. We often took out our frustrations with the world on each other. The group's intensity had led to insightful analysis of conflicts among women, but we could not find a way to continue without tearing each other down. After expelling several members, we chose to disband the collective rather than continue this destructiveness. We had differing ideas about what to do next, but most of us felt the need to interact more with other women and wanted to create feminist institutions.

I spent the next year recovering from the collective experience and exploring how to continue the work begun there in broader ways. With Nancy Myron, who had also been part of The Furies, I rested and reflected in the mountains of New Mexico and met with lesbians in other parts of the U.S. Later that year, we traveled together to East Africa after I attended my last World Student Christian Federation meeting in Ethiopia—I was finishing a four-year term on its executive committee although I was no longer involved with the church. We observed and wrote about differences between women in capitalist Kenya and African socialist Tanzania. This reactivated my interest in developing a global perspective on women's lives.

10

In April 1973, I returned to D.C. and moved into an apartment by myself, living alone for the first time in my life. Gradually I became politically active again. By October I had joined a group of women who had been active in a variety of feminist projects in D.C. and we founded *Quest: A Feminist Quarterly.* We shared a frustration over the splintered state of the women's movement and decided to create a journal as a forum for the exploration of ideas and strategies from various feminist perspectives. We sought to address issues of class, race, and sexuality, as well as to explore questions of power, leadership, and organization. As activists concerned with what we called practical theory, we felt a need to connect theory to the experiences of movement organizers. We viewed *Quest* as a tool for expanding theory in order to develop more effective strategies, and we anticipated creating a new feminist organization based on those explorations.

Within a year, Beverly Fisher (Manick), Alexa Freeman, and I were working full time with a staff of volunteers—many of whom contributed money as well as time—to turn our idea into reality.* While we also organized a feminist theory course and a number of us participated in other projects, the task of producing the journal ultimately overwhelmed our other plans. We found ourselves part of a growing subculture of feminist media, but we never created a larger political organization as we had hoped to do.

Initially, *Quest* operated out of my office at the Institute for Policy Studies. After several years and many verbal battles, and with the unwavering support of a few male colleagues, I became the first tenured female fellow there. This gave me a politically stimulating environment and the economic freedom from which to pursue my work. However in 1977, there was a split within the Institute over questions of internal process and political direction. While I did not play an active role in this fight primarily between male factions, most of those who had supported me at IPS left to form the loosely affiliated and less economically secure Public Resource Center. I left with them realizing that I would now have to test my ability to financially support my political work. While

*During the years I was an editor, other *Quest* staff members were: Dorothy Allison, Jane Dolkart, Beverly Fisher-Manick, Alexa Freeman, Nancy Hartsock, Karen Kollias, Jackie McMillan, Mary-Helen Mautner, Emily Medvec, Sidney Oliver, Gerri Traina, and Cynthia Washington. Dolores Baugowski, Rita Mae Brown, and Juanita Weaver were also founders of *Quest.*

this was frightening, I also saw it as a challenge that would prevent me from becoming too dependent on IPS, which had been my primary employer as an adult. *Quest* then moved into an office of its own and began experiencing the burden of larger overhead expenses.

My work in the feminist media subculture during the mid-1970s was satisfying and productive. In addition to *Quest,* I edited three collections of articles from The Furies published by Diana Press and I consulted for Daughters, Inc.—two of the early feminist publishers. I helped June Arnold organize the first national Women in Print Conference held at a desolate Camp Fire Girls site in the dry dusty August of 1976 in Omaha, Nebraska. We argued over how to relate to the mainstream media, what to do about FBI informers, whether feminist material should be edited, and about vegetarianism. We agonized over the rising costs of paper (some even tried to make it more cheaply there) and the difficulty of distributing feminist works. The heat and grasshoppers were terrible and the debates fierce, but the energy of over a hundred women engaged in feminist publishing was intoxicating.

I became more involved in feminist education and taught feminist theory on a course-by-course basis at various universities in the '70s. At Sagaris, a feminist summer institute held in 1975 in Vermont, I taught feminist organizing and strategies. Controversies there led me to edit a book on feminist education initiated by Daughters, Inc. Eventually this book, coedited with Sandra Pollack under the title, *Learning Our Way,* was published by The Crossing Press in 1983.* I attended the founding conference of the National Women's Studies Association in 1977, and my ties with its burgeoning world grew.

During the United Nations' International Women's Year (IWY) in 1975, I plotted with Frances Doughty of the National Gay Task Force over how to get lesbianism raised at the nongovernmental Tribune that was part of it. While I did not go to the conferences held in Mexico City, I wrote an article trying to prepare U.S. women, helped raise money to send Frances, and followed the proceedings. Later that year, I was invited by Eliza-

---

*For additional information on Sagaris and the process of the book, see *Learning Our Way: Essays in Feminist Education* edited by Charlotte Bunch and Sandra Pollack (Trumansburg, N.Y.: The Crossing Press, 1983).

beth Reid, the women's adviser to the Australian government who had played a key role in raising feminist concerns in Mexico City, to be a resource person at the Australian National IWY conference. The issues raised in Mexico and the debates among feminists in Australia over their experiences with the progressive Labour Government made me aware of the importance of questions of government policy regarding women. I had tended to see these as liberal rather than radical concerns, but I was in the process of redefining my understanding of the relationship of radicals to reform activities. On this trip, I met with women from New Zealand and Fiji as well as Australia, and began an enduring connection to feminism in the South Pacific.

I had been elected to the board of directors of the National Gay Task Force (NGTF) in 1974—six months after its founding. At that point, they committed themselves to gender parity on the board and had to find more women quickly. I had little experience with the male-dominated gay movement, but I wanted to explore the potential of coalitions between feminists and gay men. While I did learn about the gay movement, I was more often one of the liaisons from NGTF to the women's movement. The women of the board formed a caucus active in national coalitions with women's rights groups such as NOW and the National Women's Political Caucus, as well as with older mainstream organizations such as the American Association of University Women.

The NGTF women's caucus connections proved most fruitful in 1977 when we organized the lesbian caucus for the National Women's Conference (the U.S. government-sponsored IWY event) held in November in Houston, Texas. Our goal was to have a sexual-preference (pro-lesbian rights) plank added to the National Plan of Action recommended by the conference. Lesbians all over the country participated in their state conferences— proposing resolutions on this issue, getting elected as delegates to Houston, and building local coalitions with other feminists. We worked as part of the Feminist Pro-Plan Coalition, which managed to get all of its twenty-five–point plan passed in spite of considerable right-wing opposition. It was perhaps the most unifying coalition effort of the U.S. women's movement and a high moment for feminists. However, it also alerted us to the intensity with which the Right was organizing against gay rights and the women's movement.

During this period I took an apartment in New York City with a friend and her teenage daughter. For two years, I commuted between D.C. and New York, enjoying the sense that I had the best of both worlds. But after a while, I felt that I needed to choose one or the other as home. In May of 1978, I left New York but Washington was no longer the same for me, and I began to wonder where I belonged.

In the last years of the '70s, the U.S. women's movement grew, and I tried to be everywhere at once. But after a while something went wrong. Based on the Houston Conference, I decided that it was time for more radical feminists to reach beyond the feminist subculture. I wanted to bring together the perspectives and power of the various sectors of the women's movement to meet the growing challenge from the Right and to advance our own agenda for fundamental change. But the more that I cared about unifying disparate forces, the more I realized how separate they were. More importantly, I recognized that many in each sector wanted to keep it that way. Whether because of political differences or for the personal ease of being with those most like themselves, I saw that many feminists did not feel the need to deal with our diversity.

I worked more with mainstream groups, which seemed politically important, but where I often felt on the margin. Meanwhile I had less time for the radical feminist subculture that was still home, but seemed too isolated to be as effective as it should be. Previously my life had been well integrated, but now it seemed fragmented. Often before I had felt that I needed to choose between competing things that I wanted to do. This time, however, nothing seemed quite right. I resigned from the staff of *Quest* in the autumn of 1978, feeling that it needed new leadership and I needed to refocus my work. I found myself unsure where I wanted to live, not in a primary personal relationship, without a job, and no longer central to the project that had been my base. I panicked.

I was experiencing what I now see as the midlife crisis of a movement organizer. Trying hard to figure out what to do, I began to feel that it did not really matter that much what I did next. I focused on how much had not changed in society and wondered if my efforts had been worthwhile. I began to wish that I had become a lawyer or a bookkeeper—something that the world recognized and rewarded financially. I found it hard to get up in the morning and took little pleasure in anything. My energy level was low, but I felt I had to continue with some political activities, if only to support myself. I struggled to keep writing, although that has not supported me and was difficult because it necessitated committing my ideas to paper, and I was no longer so sure what I thought.

Some very supportive friends encouraged me to talk about this crisis and to let go of the feeling that I had to have everything worked out. I discovered others going through something similar and organized what we, somewhat humorously, called a depression C-R group. I became interested in understanding midlife crisis as experienced by my generation. I read what I could find on the subject, talked to people, gave a few speeches about it, and took notes for an article that I never wrote. I saw that part of what we were going through was a common reaction to no longer being young and therefore having to face our own limitations. But our process was also unique as we had shaped our lives consciously around feminist presuppositions, often in opposition to society. We were therefore experiencing the limitations of feminism as well.

For just as we were individually facing midlife crises, the women's movement was also facing a crisis in its evolution. The past decade had been full of the excitement of consciousness-raising, with changes occurring in our lives rapidly. But now feminism was in the difficult process of confronting its own internal contradictions, of consolidating its gains while facing a backlash, and of realizing the full complexity of making structural change. I knew that it was not entirely coincidental that we faced these pressures at the same time that the economy was flagging and the right wing was in resurgence. Determined that the Right not benefit from our crisis, I paid more attention to what they were doing and to devising strategies to counter them.

I saw that my crisis also came from recognizing that I would never see the world change as much as I had hoped in my lifetime. I sought ways to adjust to that limitation without becoming cynical, giving up my visions, or no longer caring. I began to take more pleasure in what did succeed, however small, and to pay attention to the political activities that I enjoyed as well as felt needed to be done. I realized that getting through my midlife crisis was less about figuring out the next correct step and more about changing my perspective on what I did. It was also about finding areas of work that engaged me in learning anew, in thinking creatively, and in growing in my own understanding of feminism, while also providing a way that I could feel productive. I found this first in looking at the issue of midlife crisis for feminists and then in examining how to respond to the right wing. I was to find it more profoundly in exploring issues of global feminism.

As I looked beyond myself more, I observed burnout and midlife crises particularly among long-time activists who had been involved in building feminist institutions. In the late '70s, these had become hard to sustain financially. Many projects were collapsing as our dreams of an alternative world floundered. It was a time of great disappointments. Yet, our depression was also short-sighted. For those institutions had considerable impact on defining issues that were now being discussed on a larger scale. Further, as I looked beyond the subculture, I saw there was still much activism. If anything, a more diverse range of women were now defining feminism and seeking changes in their own lives as well as in society. There were more working women's groups— blue- and pink-collar as well as professional; there were increasing numbers of women of color—black, Hispanic, Asian, and Native American women—in the U.S. defining their feminist reality and visions; and there was a movement of women emerging globally. The forefront of feminism was changing and often groups once active were less so. But to see this as a decline of feminism revealed a race and class bias that we could ill afford. I began to broaden my perception of feminism and looked to these emerging forces for new insights.

In mid-1979, I moved from Washington to Brooklyn with Nancy Myron and her ten-year-old niece Nadine. Although Nadine went to live with her mother after three years, Nancy and I created a home where I have now lived longer than any place since childhood. I left D.C. because I felt that a change of locale would help me to make changes in my life more readily and I had come to find the omnipresence of the federal government depressing. I was not sure New York was the place to go, but it was different without being unfamiliar. It also seemed useful for exploring global feminism. I spent several months that year in Australia and New Zealand, reviving my involvement with feminism

16

there, and participated in an international feminist workshop in Bangkok, Thailand, that influenced the direction of my work.

The Bangkok workshop held in June 1979, sponsored by the Asian and Pacific Centre for Women and Development (APCWD), was to assess feminist ideology and structures in the first half of the Decade for Women, in preparation for the United Nations Mid-Decade Conference on Women held in Copenhagen in July 1980. In describing our national experiences and writing a global report, many of the fifteen participants became intensely involved in discussing feminism as seen by women in different parts of the world. I became excited about the possibilities for feminism in Third World countries and realized that I could play a role in relating that to the women's movement in the U.S. As a follow-up to this meeting, Shirley Castley of Australia and I organized another small international workshop in Stony Point, New York, in April 1980, under the direction of Peggy Antrobus of the Women and Development (WAND) unit of the University of the West Indies, a cosponsor with APCWD. This workshop resulted in a publication—"Developing Strategies for the Future: Feminist Perspectives"—and a videotape called *World Feminists* that we took to Copenhagen to raise issues about feminism there.

While organizing this workshop, I became acquainted with the International Women's Tribune Centre (IWTC), a communication and resource service for women in developing countries that had been founded as a follow-up to the NGO Tribune in Mexico City in 1975. From the IWTC office in New York, I then helped to organize a room at the NGO Forum in Copenhagen devoted to International Feminist Networking. Cosponsored by ISIS, an international women's communication and information service based in Geneva and Rome, this section of the Forum became a gathering place for feminists from around the world to exchange ideas and strategize together. It never caught the attention of the mass media that was only reporting on women in conflict in Copenhagen, which they often were. But our site hosted constructive feminist interaction among groups and individuals—many of whom made plans for future global cooperation. My experiences in Copenhagen convinced me further that the growth of feminism in the Third World was vital and that it was crucial to expand the understanding of feminism in the West.

As with the Mexico City and Houston conferences, I felt it was important that issues of lesbianism be addressed in Copenhagen. I joined with Frances Doughty and Betty Powell, whom I had worked with in NGTF, Claudia Hinojosa of the Lambda group in Mexico, and several European women to present low-key lesbian sessions at the NGO Forum. The discussions were good and much networking occurred. But the issue was so buried in the list of some two thousand disparate workshops that many women never realized lesbianism was discussed. Thus, while we had avoided the sensationalism attached to this topic in Mexico, we realized that this time we had been marginalized.

In organizing for Stony Point and Copenhagen, I had formed my own business, Interfem Consultants, which consisted primarily of me and Shirley Castley with whom I worked on both of these projects. We decided at the end of the Forum that Interfem's next major activity would be to organize an international meeting on trafficking in women and female sexual slavery. This concern had received widespread response at the Forum and women from many regions expressed interest in discussing it in depth. Collaborating with Kathleen Barry, we wrote a concept paper, formed an international advisory group, and began fund raising assuming that we could hold the meeting in 1981.

We soon found that most funders shied away from a topic that so directly confronted men's sexual abuse of women and how it interacted with economic injustice and militarism. But it was precisely these connections that convinced us of the global importance of the issue. Determined that our meeting not be just for those who had the money to go, we finally raised enough to bring thirty women from twenty-four countries—two thirds of them in the Third World—to Rotterdam, The Netherlands, in April 1983 for ten days. The story of this meeting and how we formed a global network is told in our book, *International Feminism: Networking Against Female Sexual Slavery.* The network has functioned as an informal communication link since, maintained out of the IWTC office, primarily by Mallika Dutt of India.

During 1981 and '82, I also continued to work in the domestic gay and feminist movements. I was excited by the civil disobedience actions of the Congressional Union and helped them create a militant response to the impending loss of the Equal Rights Amendment. As a consultant on women's programs at the National Gay Task Force, I participated in coalitions focused on countering the attacks of the right wing. Always trying to make connections between issues, I spoke on behalf of lesbians and gays at the June 12 Disarmament and Nuclear Freeze Rally in Central Park in 1982. I had spoken to large rallies before—perhaps the most exciting of which was the First National March for Lesbian and Gay Rights in Washington in October 1979. But the June 12 crowd, not all sympathetic to gays, was so large that it was impossible to see where it ended. This was a high point for me. But in general I was moving away from NGTF and those sectors of the mainstream gay and women's movement that were becoming more involved in electoral politics, which was not my major interest.

In 1983, Betty Powell and I went together to the Second Feminist Encuentro for Latin America and the Caribbean held in Lima, Peru. We had been impressed with the feminists from that region we had met elsewhere and wanted to experience firsthand the growing movement there. We teamed up again with Claudia Hinojosa who translated for us when my rusty textbook Spanish revealed itself to be inadequate for passionate feminist debate. We listened intensely and basked in the energy created by over six hundred women questioning patriarchy in Latin America in relation to nineteen topics. We applauded when special sessions were added on both racism and lesbianism.

As a result of this meeting, I was invited to Peru to teach a course on Feminist Theory and Strategies for the Women's Movement sponsored by Centro de la Mujer Peruana: Flora Tristan, in 1984. Thirty activists in Lima attended the course, which challenged me to crystallize my insights from over a decade of organizing and provided an opportunity to learn what was relevant cross-culturally. This also marked the beginning of my collaboration with the course organizer, Roxanna Carrillo of Centro Flora Tristan, in various efforts to develop cross-cultural feminist exchanges. In April 1984, with Ied Guinee of the Netherlands, we led a working group that met throughout the Second International Interdisciplinary Congress for Women in Groningen, the Netherlands, and analyzed how feminism was perceived there. Since that time, we have organized feminist workshops and courses in a variety of settings.

Within the U.S. in 1983 and '84, I consulted with the National

Congress of Neighborhood Women on creating a dialogue about women and community development. We brought sixty women—grass-roots working-class leaders and feminist professionals—together for five days to discuss a women's agenda for community change. Working to build coalitions across these class and race lines reminded me that the issues of diversity and development in the global movement have their parallel within the U.S. This reinforced my interest in not only learning what women were doing elsewhere but also connecting that to the movement back home. Much of my work since 1980 has focused on how to build transnational linkages and to find ways to operate with a global perspective on what we do domestically as well.

In 1985, my energies were focused on the NGO Forum and United Nations End-of-the-Decade Conference on Women held in July in Nairobi, Kenya. I wrote and spoke on how feminists—particularly in the West—should prepare for Nairobi in order to have the most productive exchanges there. As a member of the New York City Commission on the Status of Women, I helped organize two sessions for local women to prepare for and then to hear reports from those events. From my desk at IWTC, where I have worked off and on as a consultant, I kept in touch with Forum plans and coordinated several feminist efforts for it. I was particularly concerned with creating opportunities for cross-cultural dialogue on feminism and how it has developed in various regions. I also organized sessions for the network against female sexual slavery and on the use of media for social change as part of the Film Forum held in Nairobi.

The NGO Forum in Nairobi exceeded my expectations. There was so much feminist activity, much of it led by women from the Third World, that I could not possibly keep up with it all. The broader definitions of feminism as a perspective on all issues, not just a list of women's issues that many of us had argued for, were assumed from the start. Lesbian activity was constant, creative, and led by a diversity of women from various regions. The efforts to sensationalize and divide women around it were countered, and in the process, lesbians were more visible than we had been in Copenhagen. My only complaint in Nairobi was that I could not go to more sessions because there was so much happening and I was exhausted from taking on too many responsibilities. My only wish afterward was that the Forum would be repeated, and this time, I would go as a participant, not an organizer.

I left Nairobi convinced that the new day of global feminism had indeed dawned. I felt confirmed in many of my struggles over the past six years, although of course I also knew that the work had just begun. There can be no doubt that Nairobi was a landmark event for women globally, and I was happy that I had been there. At the same time, I knew that this meant that once again I would have to redefine my work, much of which I had organized around Nairobi. But this time there was anxiety but no panic. Even though I was not sure what to do next, I had gained a clearer perspective on both my successes and my limitations. I could see that I had survived over two decades of challenges and transitions since I had committed my life to political organizing. So, I knew that I would continue to find activities that engaged my imagination and energies and that mattered at least a little somewhere. As Nairobi faded into memory, I returned to a project I had set aside—putting together a book of essays from my life in the feminist movement.

I have been urged by a number of people to do a collection of my essays. While this has seemed a good idea, I never felt that the moment was right or that I was ready. I wrote a first draft of this piece in 1982 in Australia, but then put it aside. I am completing it now in Peru in 1986. For this book, like my life, has continued to evolve. Each time I approach it, it grows longer. As the beginning of a biography, I find that it leaves out too much. There is not space to include many of the conferences, projects, and people that have engaged my attention, much less all my articles and speeches. Eighteen years is a long time. And yet there is still not distance enough for me to be certain what is most important. In the end, I have made decisions according to what seemed most illustrative or what I felt had shaped me most at the time.

Like every writer and organizer, I have constantly had to make choices about which issues to pursue. Some of these were made consciously on political principle and others were determined as much by what opportunities came my way. Since I left my salaried position, I have also found that such choices are affected by what others are willing to pay me to do or whether I can raise money to work in a given area. There are many important feminist topics and discussions not addressed here. For example, while I have spoken about the problems of pornography, I have not played an active role in this debate in the U.S. Partly this is because I have not had time to develop my perspectives, which do not fit neatly into the existing camps, and partly because my primary focus in these years has been on feminism in the Third World, where this debate does not have the same prominence. Further, I feel that the acrimonious character of the debate has divided feminists and drained energy from the movement. Nevertheless, I consider the fundamental questions raised by it important and see finding more responses to them as a challenge to feminist theory and action.

I also find that I must speak to the issue of how to approach personal relationships in a work like this. For sex and passion have never been entirely separate from the political passions of my life. But what is the line between personal respect for the privacy of others and the personal that is political? I have opted for respecting the privacy of those whose lives have intertwined with mine, not because they have been unimportant to my work. On the contrary, the personal relationships of my life—both friends and lovers—have provided the sustenance and the challenges that have kept me growing. Without them, I would not have done what I have done. But ours is still a homophobic world, and I do not presume to determine for others when or how they will deal with that publicly. Some of the women mentioned here are openly lesbian, others are in the closet to varying degrees, and some are bisexual or heterosexual. I have mentioned names primarily in relation to work and leave the rest of the story for a later, hopefully safer, time.

Not long after Nairobi, my father died suddenly of a heart attack. In reflecting on this and spending more time with my biological family, I realized how much I had taken their support of my work for granted. As an adult, I have created a family of women with my friends, who have been crucial to my life and work. I have not been especially close to my original family in an everyday way. But they have never stood in the way of my personal or political development as have the families of many feminists I know. On the contrary, my parents encouraged me to follow my own path, discussed my work, and only commented gently if they felt I had gone too far. My two sisters share many of my interests and my brother has seemed to accept my life. I have been lucky in this and have drawn support for my political work from both my biological and feminist families.

In bringing this story to a close, I want to return to the work in this volume. For just as the political and the personal inter-twine, so too are theory and activism inseparable in my life. The analysis that I have written has been my response to concrete events and problems that were put to me at specific times. Each of the essays and speeches in this collection was written because I was concerned with, often obsessed by, a particular question—some issue of strategy or of how to build a more effective move-ment. They reflect not only my own thinking but also that of the women with whom I have worked and lived. I have sought there-fore to provide enough background information in this prologue to locate the work included here. For it is in this interaction of events and ideas, of group efforts and individual reflection, that I have lived over the years. In collecting these pieces, I recognize that they are mine and their limitations are my own. But they also reflect the ideas and experiences of many of the women of my generation who have committed our lives to feminism. Therefore I see this work as theory of and from that movement.

A FEMINIST OVERVIEW

his first section consists of three essays that provide an overview of how I saw feminism at several critical points during the years covered by this book. The first piece was written in 1969 for *The New Women,* a book I coedited that was based on an anthology of women's liberation writings, which I had helped to edit for *Motive* magazine earlier that year. This article defines the basic aspects of women's oppression as we saw them then, and goes on to discuss major strategies being adopted by the movement for liberation. The second essay was written in 1976 as part of *Quest: A Feminist Quarterly*'s reponse to a divisive time in the women's movement in the U.S. It approaches feminism as an independent world view neither automatically attached to nor in opposition to the Left. As such, feminism is presented as a new gestalt that must respond to all aspects of life—political, economic, cultural, and spiritual. The final essay in this section is condensed from one of three pamphlets I published on "Feminism in the 80s." Based on a speech given in 1982, it examines the advances and failures of the women's movement in the previous fifteen years and outlines an approach to the questions posed for feminism in the future.

A BROOM OF ONE'S OWN:
NOTES ON THE WOMEN'S LIBERATION PROGRAM

In the past two years, the women's movement has mushroomed from a sprinkling of groups in major cities to a movement of perhaps a hundred thousand women in over four hundred cities. In Ohio alone there are groups in some thirty cities, from Cleveland to Chillicothe. Regional and local conferences have taken place all over the nation, reflecting an excitement that this is a movement whose time has come.

Perhaps more important than its growth in size, the women's movement has grown rapidly in self-confidence, analysis, and program.* My first women's liberation group, which like many consisted of women active in the New Left, spent much of its first months struggling with our own fears and resistance. We were uneasy about whether we should be spending so much time on ourselves, whether our problems were really a common oppression, and whether other women would respond to us. Today,

"A Broom of One's Own: Notes on the Women's Liberation Program," was published in *The New Women,* edited by Joanne Cooke and Charlotte Bunch-Weeks and Robin Morgan, poetry editor (Indianapolis: Bobbs-Merrill, 1970).

*Even its name has been subject to careful scrutiny and change. Some groups now speak of the Female Liberation Movement, to show that all women of all ages are included, not just adults. We have assumed that the term "women" includes all females.

many of us work full-time with women's liberation; we have not resolved all the issues facing us, but we are confident about our priorities. Where once we felt alone, now we do not have enough time, energy, or resources to respond to the growing interest in this movement. Similarly, women everywhere are speaking out boldly—in the church, in senior and junior high schools, in traditional women's organizations, in black liberation groups, in professional associations, in labor unions, and many other places.

Women's liberation has touched off a resurgence of the women's struggle by giving public visibility and common analysis to an uneasiness and hostility that many women feel, but that had been confined until now to the personal sphere and thereby dismissed. Women are responding because, as one sister put it, women's liberation is simply organized rage against real oppression.

Over the past year, it has become clear that our opposition is not simply a result of chauvinist attitudes but is indeed deeply rooted in all the institutions of our society. Ours is a sexist or male supremacist society that assumes male superiority (and female inferiority) in all its day-to-day workings, creating a lower status or a caste for women. A woman is assigned to this caste by sex at birth, and it defines the boundaries of her life and the nature of her relationships with those outside her caste: men. The particular boundaries vary in different classes, but in each, women as a caste are at the bottom.

It is clear that capitalism in the U.S.A., as in many societies in the past, benefits from and perpetuates sexist ideologies for its own profit. It exploits us as cheap labor through unpaid work at home and as a threat to other workers in order to prevent strikes and keep wages down. Through the sacred concept of the nuclear family, it isolates women, defines us as secondary to our men (Mrs.), yet assigns us major tasks for maintaining life, keeping up their castles and their egos, raising children, and so on, all without pay. Further, by creating and exploiting sexual and psychological insecurities, profit seekers use our bodies as commodities and manipulate us into a highly profitable (for them) consumer's market.

All women in the United States are thus exploited economically, psychologically, and sexually. The most immediate forms of oppression vary according to class, race, marital status, and age.

Working women are most often oppressed by discrimination, degrading work conditions, and special problems, such as child care, that they encounter on the job. Housewives, especially young educated ones, are most frustrated by their dehumanized and trivialized environment. Welfare mothers are concerned with the immediate and daily economic and social pressures placed upon them. Single or divorced women may be fighting against their marginality and society's scorn, especially if they have children. Students encounter both sexual exploitation and society's attempts to train them for their "proper place"; they note that women in hippie and radical groups don't seem to have escaped male supremacy, as they serve as secretaries, cooks, and playmates for the movement.

Beginning with the daily experiences of many different women, we have just begun to probe the complexity and depths of our oppression. No existing explanations or ideologies adequately interpret our lives. We have therefore begun our own study of sexism, as it relates to other oppressions such as racism and as it works in various socioeconomic systems of the past and present. A more comprehensive analysis will grow out of our practical experiences and reflections as we struggle together and separately for our common liberation.

In this struggle, separations that have frustrated previous movements—separations between analysis and program and between personal and political life—are breaking down. Ending sexism means destroying oppressive institutions and ideologies and creating new structures and images to replace them. There is no private domain of a person's life that is not political and there is no political issue that is not ultimately personal. For example, a man who states that he supports women's liberation, but whose relationship to his secretary is oppressive, is politically a male supremacist, regardless of his rhetoric. A woman who has seen the care of her children as her personal dilemma discovers that her response to this situation is basically a political one.

As the women's liberation movement has grown rapidly in size, self-confidence, and analysis, so also it has grown in the development of program. Our programs must both confront the sexist system and enable us as women to struggle for our liberation. This involves three interlocking and reinforcing processes that must go on at once: raising consciousness, ending dependencies, and challenging sexist institutions.

RAISING CONSCIOUSNESS

Consciousness-raising is our term for the process by which women begin to discover ourselves as an oppressed people and struggle against the effects of male supremacy on us. It happens when we describe and share our individual problems so that we can understand the universality of our oppression and analyze its social roots. It is learning to take pride and delight in our femaleness, rejecting the need to follow the feminine mystique or to copy men as our models; it is learning to trust and love each other as sisters, not competitors for male approval. It is deciding and redeciding each day, individually and together, that we will take control over our lives, create and support each other in alternative ways of living, and struggle together for the liberation of all women.

A major goal of consciousness-raising, ending our isolation from each other and our silence about the fears and frustrations of our lives, is primarily accomplished through the small group. Pam Allen has described the process of her small group in San Francisco in four stages. First is *opening up*—each individual talks about her feelings about herself and her life, about why she came to a woman's group. Next is *sharing*—the group members teach each other through sharing experiences and build a collage of similar experiences among the women present. The third stage is *analyzing*—the group examines the reasons for and causes of the oppression of women, looking not only at their shared experiences but also at experiences of women in other situations in an effort to gain a sense of the whole. Finally, the group begins *abstracting*—the group removes itself from immediate necessity, takes the concepts and analysis it has developed and discusses abstract theory, drawing on the work of others as well.

While the small group is the most intensive process of consciousness-raising, it is clearly not the only method. Consciousness-raising includes all those ways in which women are brought to see their oppression as a group and are confronted with the question of what they will do about it. Susan B. Anthony stated it clearly in 1872:

I do pray, and that most earnestly and constantly, for some terrific shock to startle the women of the nation into a self-respect which will compel them to see the absolute degradation of their present position; which will compel them to break their yoke of bondage and give them faith in themselves; which will make them proclaim their allegiance to women first. . . . The fact is, women are in chains, and their servitude is all the more debasing because they do not realize it. O to compel them to see and feel and to give them the courage and the conscience to speak and act for their own freedom, though they face the scorn and contempt of all the world for doing it!

Many women's liberation activities, such as protests at Bridal Fairs and beauty contests, are created to produce that first shock. A WITCH leaflet at a Bridal Fair in New York proclaimed to young engaged women, "Always a Bride, Never a Person." Less shocking but equally important, most groups have courses and forums for new people dealing with all aspects of women's oppression. Courses range in size from five to two hundred, are taught everywhere from junior high schools to community YWCAs, and cover a wide variety of topics.

Increasingly important are women's liberation plays, like *How to Make a Woman,* produced in Boston, and media productions, such as "Look Out Girlie, Woman's Liberation Is Gonna Get Your Mama," an introductory slide and tape show prepared by Oberlin women. Skits, comic books, pamphlets, tapes, stickers that read "this exploits women" or "this woman is not for sale" to put on ads, newspapers, song books, journals are appearing everywhere. These startle women into a new awareness of their situation and introduce them to the movement for liberation.

But consciousness-raising is not simply awakening to one's condition. It must also be the process of finding the courage and confidence to move. Central to this process, then, is the development of a positive self-image for ourselves as women. Because we have been taught that men are superior and not so limited, most women, especially those who strive to "get ahead," look up to and identify with men, resulting in a dislike of other women and a hatred of ourselves as women. In order to change this self-image, groups can encourage each woman to develop a fuller sense of herself, helping her to take the time and energy to pursue her own identity and interests, and pushing her to develop previously thwarted talents and abilities. Through sharing and working together on projects and in discussion groups, women begin to see each other not as competitors or inferior companions but as sisters in a common struggle who can and must be loved and trusted.

> Our history has been stolen from us.
> Our heroes died in childbirth, from peritonitis,
> —of overwork
> —of oppression
> —of bottled-up rage
> Our geniuses were never taught to read or write.
> We must invent a past adequate to our ambitions.
> We must create a future adequate to our needs.
>
> *The Old Mole,* Cambridge, Massachusetts

As part of developing a new self-image, women are discovering the past history of women's struggles for freedom and self-expression. In Cleveland, women held a woman's culture evening, featuring our little-known artists; former suffragettes in Nashville are leading history seminars; women in Chicago and Washington, D.C., have written skits based on our past. Articles and journals are being written, courses taught, and our common history is coming alive again. As part of this consciousness, women held a variety of actions on March 8, 1970, International Women's Day, in honor of a women's strike in New York on March 8, 1908.

Consciousness-raising is not a mechanical act performed in any one way. It is an unending process for discovering ourselves as a group and making ourselves anew, both individually and as a movement, a process that permeates all women's liberation activities. In consciousness-raising we confront ourselves and every woman with our lives, offering alternative visions of what we might struggle to become and opportunities to begin that struggle as part of a group, and we demand that each woman make a conscious decision about her future and the future of her daughters.

ENDING DEPENDENCIES

We have all grown up in a male supremacist society that has made us dependent on men and caused us to neglect our growth in many ways: physically, politically, economically, and psychologically. The struggle before us requires that we begin to end these dependencies.

Most of us are afraid of men. We are out of shape and underdeveloped physically, and we do not have a sense of control over our bodies. Women's groups have therefore begun physical development and self-defense courses. On campuses, women are demanding these from the university. At the University of California, Berkeley, women invaded an all-male karate class, chanting, "Open it up or we'll shut it down—self-defense for women!" They charged discrimination since there was no class that women could attend. The result of these activities is both physical and psychological. New York women wrote of their class:

> As a result of karate, we are gaining confidence in our bodies and going through some fantastic changes in terms of our feelings of self-worth. Our confidence has increased not only in confrontations with "dirty-old-men" in the streets, but in nonphysical confrontations with our own men and society in general. We do feel as though we have more control over our own lives because of our new potential physical power.
>
> "Karate as Self-Defense for Women,"
> Susan Pascale, Rachel Moon, Leslie B. Tanner,
> *Women: A Journal of Liberation*

A major dependency common to all women is lack of direct control over the process of reproduction in our bodies. Almost every city now has an abortion counseling and/or birth control information center related to women's liberation. The newly formed center in Minneapolis states their purposes:

> The Woman's Counseling Service deals with the problems of insufficient medical facilities—antiquated abortion laws, inadequate dissemination of birth control, and the lack of readily available medical care—in two ways. Most women have very

little knowledge of the medical services available to them; therefore, one function of the Women's Counseling Service is to direct women to those services available to them in the areas of birth control, maternity care, child care, services for unwed mothers, adoption agencies, and venereal disease. . . . The Women's Counseling Service is a place where women can come and talk with trained counselors who are well informed of the "ins and outs" of different agencies, who can talk with women about the fears that they have, and who can give women the personal care and information that are lacking in most public agencies. A very important aim of the Women's Counseling Service is to create a solidarity between women which recognizes that the problems of each individual are the problems of all women—that our "personal problems" are political, exemplifying the status of women in our society.

What began as counseling and work to repeal abortion laws has expanded into a major emphasis on health care. Women are dependent on a white male medical establishment, not only for abortions, but for all our own care and that of our families. In many cities, women are challenging hospitals, doctors, and drug companies on their sexist, racist, and profit-making assumptions and demanding free and adequate health care for all, not just the rich and privileged.

Courses in mechanics and auto maintenance make women less intimidated by machines and technology. This increases our ability to provide for ourselves and to protect ourselves from fraud at the hands of various servicemen who assume we are ignorant suckers, especially when we are living or traveling alone. *Off Our Backs,* the Washington, D.C., women's newspaper, has a survival column that covers such fundamentals as how to change a tire.

Many women feel intellectually inferior to and politically dependent on men, since we have had little training or experience in political analysis, writing, public speaking, or leading meetings. Women's groups are experimenting with ways to discipline ourselves to overcome these inadequacies, while avoiding the authoritarian political styles of men. Most groups have role-playing and discussion sessions that develop every woman's ability to participate in a variety of political activities. Women in Seattle ran a six-week training workshop in public speaking; many groups are also experimenting with new styles that allow more group participation, like skits. Regular political education and strategy sessions also push women to take their intellectual work more seriously.

Psychologically, most women are still very dependent on men. We have real emotional needs for love, praise, comfort, approval, which we have been taught to fulfill through men, rather than through self-confidence and relationships with our sisters. This dependency on men can only be overcome as part of the total process of liberation, as we develop more skills, more self-confidence, and more ability to support each other in these needs. The small groups and some women's collectives have begun this job. From another angle, some seminary women plan to do women's liberation counseling addressed to this need and are demanding that the church provide them with resources.

Some groups have begun to tackle the problem of women's economic dependence on men by pooling their resources, sharing the burdens of housework, and helping each other to find good jobs. The problem of economic dependence can only be solved when we force society to pay us for the work we do in the home and to provide us equal job opportunities and pay outside. In the meantime, various communal and cooperative provisions for doing daily tasks, such as cooking and child care, help alleviate financial burdens and give women more time for other activities.

There are many other needs that women must fulfill in order to function more independently and effectively. Groups are beginning to respond to these through setting up women's houses and centers. A center in the San Francisco Bay area is scheduled to provide:

1. Informational and referral services:
   Employment counseling
   Medical and psychological referrals
   Legal referrals
   Child-care facilities
   Educational counseling
   Housing information
2. Library and research facilities
3. Educational programs and a speakers' bureau
4. Communications center
5. "Free space" for women who need someplace to go and be

While many of these services and activities are aimed primarily at individual needs, they are needs created by our common oppression that must be met for us to work together. As women's liberation encounters more ridicule and resistance, such training and serious networks of support will become even more essential. We must stay alive and grow in order to end the sexist system that has caused our dependencies and to create a liberated people in the future.

CHALLENGING SEXIST INSTITUTIONS

The third essential process involved in the struggle for liberation is confronting both the institutions that oppress us as women and the sexist ideology that supports those institutions. The first women's liberation actions at beauty contests and around the media focused primarily on the ideology—the images of femaleness and their perpetuation in our society. Over the past year women's groups have also begun to analyze institutional oppression, demanding change in those that perpetrate and profit from sexism, such as corporations and the health system. In the process, we have begun to define social structures for a humane, nonracist, nonsexist society, thereby projecting visions for the future and creating what we can now, where that is possible.

No single list of programmatic demands and projects has been agreed upon across the country. However, in addition to those activities mentioned in the two sections above, the following are some of the major areas of work: employment/civil rights; abortion/health; media; education; the family/child care.

Employment/Civil Rights

The department, to begin with, was situated like a harem. . . . Women were isolated in one corner of the shop, in one department. . . . The "specialness" of our department lay in the fact that the work we did had been recently reclassified by management from heavy work to light work; this is the way management distinguished "men's work" from "women's work." It was apparent that the designation had nothing whatever to do with heaviness or lightness, but only with rate of pay.

Olga Domanski, "Pages From a Shop Diary,"
Notes on Women's Liberation, Detroit, Michigan

Women's groups are involved in a variety of activities centering on employment, demanding equal pay for equal work, job security, equal opportunity in hiring, training, and promotion not only on the job but also in unions and professional associations, day care and maternity leave without loss of pay, and an end to sexual objectification on the job. Some are organizing or supporting unions of women making these demands in places like hospitals, telephone companies, and during the General Electric strike. For example, Detroit Women's Liberation Coalition is supporting a clerical workers' strike at the Fruehauf Trailer Company; the strikers are meeting great resistance since they are among the first clerical workers to organize a union.

Discussions about women's liberation have been initiated among women workers, especially around universities. For example, *Yale Break*, a newspaper for and by women, proclaimed a coalition of women employees, wives, and students against "male Yale." As one of its first articles states:

> A lot of anger is building up. Yale is an institution run by underpaid female labor—women work in the kitchens, at the brooms, at the typewriters, in the library stacks, and in the homes. Women work at one-third men's wages. Yale is a male dominated institution whose primary function is to produce the future male leaders of the male society.
>
> "Bow Down to the Kingman, Dear"
> *Yale Break*

Another approach is to challenge hiring practices. In Canada, women are attacking the Canadian Manpower Center for its role in perpetuating job discrimination; one of their strategies is to ask that "all women who file a federal income tax return should deduct by either withholding or requesting a refund, that amount of their tax money which will go to supporting Canada Manpower" ("Women against Manpower," *The Pedestal*). Throughout the United States, suits are being brought charging job discrimination. In San Francisco and Pittsburgh, suits ask that the Equal Employment Opportunities Commission enforce the 1964 Civil Rights Act by ending discrimination between male and female in help-wanted ads in newspapers. College women have begun to challenge the policies of placement bureaus on campus.

Free child care and more humane working conditions are increasingly important job issues. At several hospitals and universities, women have threatened to bring or have brought their children to the workplace. On campuses like the University of Washington in Seattle, uniting around the common project of child care for employees, students, and wives has brought student political groups and university staff together for the first time. Women are also demanding changes in the nature and conditions of their work. Women's liberation in Albuquerque picketed a downtown department store in support of a young Mexican woman who was fired for refusing the manager's heavy-handed sexual advances. In Nashville, women protested a Post Office dress code that permitted a committee of men to measure female employees' skirt lengths and to send them home if hems were more than four inches above the knee.

Further, women are demanding that our civil rights be upheld in all matters of law, business, and public services. Women have protested laws that give husbands control of a woman's property, expensive and humiliating divorce proceedings, "men only" restaurants and clubs, and real-estate policies that discriminate against single women with children. Some groups are pushing for an Equal Rights Amendment for women. The Congress to Unite Women in New York in November 1969 said, "While the Fourteenth Amendment guarantees equal protection under the law to all persons who are citizens, the Supreme Court has refused to rule on the issue of whether women are persons."

Abortion/Health

Today at noon the moon,
  Symbol of the female,
Rises to eclipse the sun,
  Symbol of the male.
From the Morgue to your door,
  Our mourning echoes long.
You have killed our sisters—
  In hell you belong!

> Hex for Abortion Demonstration in Detroit,
> The Day of the Eclipse of the Sun

Throughout North America, women have changed the tepid debates about abortion reform of two years ago into a hot campaign to repeal all abortion laws—a campaign pursued through the courts, hospitals, and legislatures. One of the most ambitious was a nationally coordinated "war on Ottawa" declared by Canadian women. Beginning on Valentine's Day, 1970, with demonstrations in Vancouver, women planned actions all over the country to culminate on Mother's Day, when thousands of women, some coming in a black hearse cavalcade across the country, gathered in Ottawa to demand an end to abortion laws in Canada.

In the process of challenging abortion laws, women have quickly realized that the issue is more comprehensive. Attempts at abortion reform have shown us the pervasive sexism and racism of the medical establishment. Where abortion laws have been abolished or significantly reformed, abortions are still difficult to obtain and still expensive. One group expressed its discovery of the nature of medical services:

> When we talked about contraception, we found out that we'd all received very haphazard care, that we'd been ignorant about how our bodies worked and about how contraceptives worked, that our visits to doctors and our discussions had often been surrounded by secrecy, embarrassment, and guilt. We had made many visits to doctors and spent a great deal of money yet had received very inadequate, often callous, care and advice. . . . What started out as discussion quickly became anger. We began by treating "Women and Health" as a discussion topic, and now we're considering what kinds of action to initiate.
>
> Women's Liberation Health Collective,
> New York City

Through broader alliances around health issues, we have realized that what is a problem for white middle-class women is twice so for poor and black women. They have even worse general health care, *no* access to safe abortions, and they fear forced birth control and sterilization at the hands of the white male medical establishment.

Women's groups have begun to demand more research on such

39

vital concerns as contraception and more adequate public health care for all, including the right of every woman to *total* control over her body, to bear or not to bear children. In Washington, D.C., women have challenged medical and state negligence in dispensing birth control pills and, with the ACLU, have brought a suit against the public hospital for its neglect of women's health needs, including abortion for indigent residents. At Bowling Green College in Ohio, women students are demanding that university health services provide more birth control information and better health services generally.

We have discovered that better sex education, including an end to sex hypocrisy, the double standard, and exploitative "free" sex, is essential to our liberation struggle. Handbooks on abortion, birth control, and sex in general have been published by women's groups and distributed widely, especially on campuses. In Bloomington, Indiana, a group took special training with a psychiatrist and has been conducting sex education seminars in women's dormitories. The overwhelming response to these efforts and to women's counseling services indicates the depth and breadth of health as a gut women's issue.

Media

Women's liberation has responded to the power and exploitation of the media today in two basic ways: first, by challenging and cajoling them to change, and second, by taking them over. One major issue is the sexual objectification of women. A group in New Orleans has articulated women's demands:

> We demand that the television, radio, and newspaper industries establish a new code of ethics, removing from advertisements, news shows, and commentaries all discriminatory allusions to females. Serials, cartoons, and stories which feed off the stereotyped images of the "empty-headed" woman, the "fickle" woman, the "bitch" and the "happy" housewife armed with the tools of household slavery, must be discontinued. Let's see as many men as women washing the clothes and dishes, cleaning the house (not as a joke, but seriously). Let's see women washing the car and pole vaulting. People identify with the models portrayed in the news media.
>
> Program of the Southern Female Rights Union,
> New Orleans, Louisiana

The variety of challenges to the media has overlapped with protests against other social institutions that perpetuate the same stereotypes such as beauty contests, Playboy Clubs, women's auxiliaries, and so on. Protest articles, guerrilla theater actions, boycotts, work stoppages within the communications industry itself have all been used to confront the media. Women within the industry have refused to type, write up, or participate in producing programs or stories that they think are exploitative or degrading to women. Women lawyers may bring a suit against a leading advertiser for defamation of character. Other women, refusing to have anything to do with the established press, have begun our own media: newspapers, journals, films, tapes, comic books, and maybe even a radio station.

Women in New York took over the *Ladies' Home Journal* offices and extracted an agreement for a special supplement to be written and edited by women's liberation groups. Underground papers have been attacked by women in many cities. Women on the *RAT,* a major movement paper in New York, took it over, stating:

> The takeover had to happen. It was long overdue. . . . When a woman can walk into the *RAT* office and say to the editor that she'd like to write for the paper, only to be told, "We've got enough female writers, what we need is a secretary to answer the mail and take the phone calls"; when two or three men out of a staff of ten or twelve people can slap together an issue at the last minute in total disregard for any political opinions the rest of the staff might have; when we who work at the paper have no notion of what each other's politics might be—then the paper is about to die of its own diseases. We *RAT* women want to create a revolutionary rebirth out of that death.

Women in San Francisco forced the "movement" men preparing a pornographic magazine, *San Francisco Review of Sex,* to abandon their plans. These are some of the ways in which women's liberation is working to defeat the overwhelming power of the media to distort our news and to poison us with degrading images of ourselves and our sisters.

> In my high school they had three curriculums: occupational, business, and college prep. The occupational curriculum had drafting, and several skilled trades courses. Not one single girl had ever been allowed into this curriculum. . . . They simply placed girls in the home economics courses as electives.
>
> Ester Serrano, "Barefoot and Pregnant,"
> *Notes on Women's Liberation,* Detroit, Michigan

The school system is another institution that discriminates against us and shapes our lives by its sex-role indoctrination and tracking. Women's demands on the educational system have two aims. First, equal educational rights must be guaranteed to all women, which means free and equal access and financial aid in all fields, an end to female tracking in courses and counseling services, and an end to discrimination against women for their marital status, children, or pregnancy. Second, sexist bias in curricula must be eliminated, which requires a vigorous program of critically examining the content of education, women's studies at every level, rewriting of textbooks.

These two thrusts are being pursued in many different contexts and at different levels of the school system from the nursery to adult education. In Durham-Chapel Hill, North Carolina, and in Bloomington, Indiana, women are writing nonsexist children's books. Nonsexist education is basic to all child-care collectives and other experimental projects as well. High schools are festering with oppressiveness and high-school women are organizing around women's liberation issues.

In colleges, women are confronted with academic discrimination, sexist courses, and social limitations. A women's liberation group at the University of Iowa got its impetus from a university-sponsored program entitled "Feminine Focus," which was aimed at educating them to the techniques and strategies involved in "being feminine." In San Diego, women asked for four and one-half faculty positions for women's studies, to which a male administrator suggested they get women volunteers from the community.

The social treatment of women in colleges reflects the status of women generally. Hours, dress codes, and housing restrictions, which women have begun to protest, put a woman under the supervision and protection (control) of men. Since she is not at home under her father's care and not yet in the control of her husband, the university must be her "protector." This situation is based on the notion that a woman's only "real" role is that defined in the family, as daughter, wife, and mother.

Family/Child Care

Much of women's oppression is rooted in the division of work and status in the home and the human relationships and attitudes developed by the nuclear family. Through the family, women's work at home, and hence on the market, has been devalued, and her economic dependency and isolation increased.

While, for many women, liberation means dividing up those responsibilities in new ways, so that they can get out of the home, women who prefer or must do housework full-time should be paid. Some homemakers in Stockton, California, are organizing themselves into a union of houseworkers to deal with these grievances. Many women are seeking to find ways of sharing monotonous and trivial housework and are demanding that these tasks be industrialized by the society, thus both paying people to do them and reducing the amount of human energies that they require.

While not necessarily advocating a total end to the family for all people, married and single women in women's liberation are involved in various living experiments. Such experiments include all-female communes, group marriages, cooperative houses, and extended families. Social barriers to these should be abolished, relaxing marriage and divorce laws, changing housing policies that prevent or discourage communal living, challenging social attitudes toward "illegitimate" children, unmarried couples, group living, and so forth. Only through experimentation can we discover what variety of social units meet different people's needs for love and security, without oppressing women, men, or children.

Regardless of living style, women's liberation views better child care as a basic responsibility of the society. Child care should be free, creative, available twenty-four hours a day, but noncompulsory, and run by both men and women. The society should provide all children with adequate food, medical care, clothing, and nonsexist toys. Women have begun to demand such services or the

43

space and money to set them up from employers, the government, and other public institutions.

Since these services do not yet exist and many of us do not want our children programmed by our present government and industry, women are also setting up our own child-care facilities. Forms vary from daytime play groups to cooperatives, communal living, and sharing of all responsibility for all children. Women are also demanding that colleagues within the movement, both male and female, become more responsive to the needs of children and mothers, in meetings, demonstrations, and travel. For example, women demanded that child-care facilities and emergency child provisions be set up for the Mobilization Against the War on November 15, 1969.

Child care is essential to the liberation of women, but as two women wisely point out, it is more than that:

> Day care is a people's liberation issue. Women, of course, will gain from a good day-care program, but in the final analysis women's liberation depends on an entire transformation of society, not just on one institution. However, that one institution, if radically structured, can help obtain that transformation of society. The way children develop is part of that transformation.
>
> Louise Gross and Phyllis MacEwan, "On Day Care,"
> *Women: A Journal of Liberation*

These are some of the ways in which women's liberation groups are building programs for raising consciousness, ending dependencies, and challenging sexist institutions. Many other issues and institutions are involved, but it is impossible to cover everything.

While our analysis and program have grown over the past year, we face many important questions for the future. Most women's groups have just begun to struggle with the questions of structure and leadership. We are asking how to have enough structure to build a mass movement, yet not become bogged down in stultifying bureaucracy. We are seeking ways of avoiding our society's cult of leadership; we want solid leadership without creating special elites. We are struggling with how to relate to other movements and organizations that share common concerns. Should we work as caucuses in other organizations? Should we remain independent? Should we form alliances and, if so, around which issues? Many of us feel that we must build a strong, autonomous women's movement, but we have only begun to define what that will mean and how to do it.

Politically, we have many unanswered questions before us. We have grown in our analysis of sexism, but we still do not understand well enough its relation to racism, imperialism, or class structures in our society. We must define more clearly the dynamic forces of our oppression, its roots, its symptoms, and how best it can be conquered. While these political questions can only be answered by our concrete experiences, we must keep them before us at all times.

In building a strong independent women's movement and defining more clearly its political direction, there will be many hard questions and times. Only as we develop sisterhood, develop the consciousness of our own oppression and the ability to love and trust our sisters, will we gain the strength to work together to end the dependencies of a male-supremacist ideology, to challenge our totally dehumanized sexist society, and to lay groundwork for a new society. This is a lifelong struggle that will itself reveal to us the issues and oppressions with which our daughters and sons must wrestle in the future.

BEYOND EITHER/OR:
NONALIGNED FEMINISM

T he time has come to reassess the experience of the women's movement, particularly with the Left, and to reassert a direction for feminism that is both radical and independent and that integrates the political, cultural, economic, and spiritual dimensions of women's lives. I have chosen to call this direction *nonaligned feminism.* Although the issues discussed affect all its segments, I am primarily concerned here with the radical portion of the women's movement—by which I mean those feminists who are critical of all patriarchal systems, including U.S. capitalism, who tend to feel alien to those systems, and who are not satisfied only with their reform. Much of my analysis is based on the ideas and experiences of both radical feminists and lesbian feminists, who have most frequently expressed this position in the United States. However, I have chosen a new term—nonaligned feminism—in order to avoid the limitations of existing labels and to suggest new grounds for defining a movement that incorporates the experiences of a wider variety of women.

The need for such a reassessment grows out of the increasing pressure that feminists (as individuals and as a movement) have

"Beyond Either/Or: Nonaligned Feminism," first appeared in *Quest: A Feminist Quarterly,* vol. III, no. 1 (Summer 1976).

experienced over the past few years to align ourselves—once and for all—either with or against the Left, either as "socialists" or as "reformists," since this mentality recognizes no other options. Even if we resist that dichotomy, we encounter another one: that between "political/economic" feminists and "cultural" or "spiritual" feminists. Presenting them as mutually exclusive options, this dichotomy distorts the function of each of these spheres and ignores their interrelatedness. As a result, many feminists have begun to feel that they do not quite fit anywhere, that there is little defined space for the pursuit of a feminism that is critical of the United States, very much engaged in politics, and yet independent of the socialist movement.

I have no intention of succumbing to these choices as defined by others. Although we are not organized around a single goal, I believe that many feminists feel limited and confined by pressures to conform to one or the other of those options. I believe that we must resist pressure for a final declaration of allegiance and continue to pursue the fullest implications of a nonaligned but committed and active feminism.

The pressure to choose one or another of these dichotomies does not come from only one side or any single source but is the result of many factors: our lack of answers in some situations, since a feminist analysis of patriarchy as it affects all aspects of life is still incomplete; women's doubts about our ability to create and effect a new political direction, which often results in either a retreat from politics or an acceptance of the older, better defined traditions of liberal reformism or socialism; legitimate but often immobilizing concerns about the race and class makeup of the movement, which paralyzes some white feminists with guilt; and finally the difficulties of survival for independent feminists—since white men, whether left, right, or center, generally control most of the resources in our society, if we align with one of them personally, or with their politics, or remain in what they define as women's spheres, we are allowed greater access to those resources.

Under these pressures, the radical portion of the women's movement seems to be fragmenting into three dominant and often mutually exclusive trends: socialist feminism, political reformism, and cultural or spiritual separatism. While each of these embodies important work, what is disturbing is their general tendency not only to denounce or ridicule the work of the others but also to deny the necessity for an independent feminist framework that would integrate aspects of each and go beyond them to create a synthesized feminist politics revolutionary in its implications for all aspects of our lives.

In this article I explore some of the questions raised by this situation, primarily in terms of pressure to be pro- or anti-Left. In particular, I look at the concept of nonalignment and how it can be useful to feminists; examine how feminists have dealt with this dichotomy over the past decade and how it is reemerging today; and describe how *Quest* functions as a nonaligned vehicle for political debate and analysis aimed at further developing a radical, nonaligned feminism.

THE CONCEPT OF NONALIGNMENT

The pressure to be for or against the Left is neither new nor unique to the feminist movement. It reflects the polarity dominating our world for at least the past thirty years: capitalism versus communism. In the 1950s, when this polarity was called the cold war between the "Free World" and the "Iron Curtain," many of the less powerful nations began to act to force open the vise squeezing them into allegiance to one or the other. In particular, leaders of some of the newly independent countries of Asia and Africa called the Bandung Conference in 1955, at which many of the "developing nations" worked together to establish their nonaligned status. As Indian Prime Minister Jawaharlal Nehru proclaimed: "For anyone to tell us that we have to be camp followers of Russia or America or any country in Europe is not very creditable to our new dignity, our new independence, our new freedom, our new spirit."*

The nonaligned nations were not always united with each other and did not create one single unifying ideology, but they did establish space outside the control of the two dominant poles (USA/USSR), give legitimacy to the concept of nonalignment, and eventually alter the perception of world forces through the concept of the Third World. These efforts, along with the seismographic crack between Russia and China, made new alliances and

*Prime Minister Jawaharlal Nehru, *Economic Review,* May 1955, as quoted in O. Edmund Clubb, *Twentieth Century China* (New York: Columbia University Press, 1964), p. 345.

new modes of development possible within nonaligned countries, allowing them more political flexibility without making them irrelevant, powerless, or totally unaffected by the controls of the major power blocs.*

My purpose here is neither to detail the debates surrounding the nonaligned nations nor to propose that feminists are in an identical position. Rather, I want to establish a historical context for a concept that can be useful to us. "Nonaligned" does not mean neutral; it does not mean uninvolved, inactive, separated, or disinterested. Nonalignment is not a withdrawal from politics. It simply means that one is not automatically attached to one of the dominant lines or factions; hence it does not preclude taking stands on issues, making coalitions around particular goals, or condemning or commending the actions of other groups or governments. In our context, nonalignment means simply that actions are taken according to an assessment of the particulars involved from an independent feminist perspective, rather than from an already stated and automatic decision for or against the Left in general.

Such a concept may sound simple, or to some, simpleminded. It is neither. To be nonaligned is difficult because it requires careful attention and debate to determine what actions are appropriate in each situation. Our positions are based on an emerging feminist analysis of particular issues and how they affect women's interests and long-term feminist goals rather than on preestablished approaches to each issue. For example, in the development of feminist theory, nonalignment requires that we study not only Marxism but many other theories critically, in order to learn where and how they can contribute to the development of a comprehensive feminist analysis. But we neither seek to force feminism into an existing (e.g., Marxist) framework nor reject a given ideology out of hand, as having nothing to offer.

Nonalignment is not solely a reaction to Left/anti-Left pres-

*While this polarity has diminished some in the past decade, its dominance is still evidenced in many world issues and was certainly a very present conflict at the United Nations International Women's Year Tribunal in Mexico City, Summer 1975. Feminists should study the experience of nonaligned nations. A recent conference in Washington, D.C., on "The Nonaligned Movement in World Politics Today" (Howard University, April 8–10, 1976), revealed that the concept is still evolving and has had varying degrees of political and economic viability in different contexts.

sures; it is a positive stance for feminists. It is an affirmation of our belief in the future, strength, and potential of our own analysis and movement. We do not approach it without a history, without principles, or without politics.

We start from an analysis of patriarchy (in America and elsewhere) and how it manifests itself in capitalism, imperialism, racism, and heterosexism. We start with commitments to develop new processes and to end the oppression of all women—commitments that require us to develop and support efforts that will lead to an end to all forms of oppression. Our greatest potential lies in taking ourselves seriously as a powerful though relatively new nucleus for profound change. Although we may work with and learn from other groups when it is appropriate, our primary purpose must be the expansion of our insights and our movement as feminists, for in that process, we will create new possibilities, new perspectives on ending all oppression. Our potential rests not in being absorbed into existing ideologies or groups but in actively creating new efforts toward reshaping the political, cultural, economic, and spiritual structures of our world.

OUR RECENT PAST

In the twentieth century, the term "radical" has generally been identified with "leftist" or "socialist." Every political group critical of any or all aspects of the Western capitalist/imperialist/racist/heterosexist patriarchy has been forced to confront its relationship to the most developed opposition: communist nations, socialist movements, and Marxist thought.

In my generation, which came of age in the 1960s, struggle with the question of the Left played a significant role in the civil rights, student, antiwar, and black militant movements. All of these began from an essentially nonaligned position—critical of America but aloof from the Old Left debates. Yet, as they became frustrated with the limitations of reformism in the United States, they discovered that the only alternative model for change seemed to be Marxism. Over time, they therefore became engaged in the issues of socialism. Many became intricately involved in the nuances and warfare of the Left; some rejected the Left entirely, either returning to work in the system or dropping out; and a few, most notably some black leaders, began searching for and developing other ideologies not primarily oriented around Marxism, such as Pan-Africanism. While this phenomenon requires more careful elaboration, it shows feminists clearly that many of our problems are not new and that we should seek to avoid mistakes made by other groups.

My own resistance to the socialist/antisocialist polarity facing feminists at present is not, therefore, simply a question of male versus female politics. Women *can* learn from the experiences of other movements, and particularly from the black movement's struggles with the questions of race, nationalism, and socialism. For example, we should discuss such questions as why the Black Panthers decided to enter electoral politics or how Angela Davis views her relationship to the Communist party. Certainly many of the issues raised by socialist critiques—class, the domination of monopoly capital, imperialism—are crucial to any movement for change. My resistance to this polarity comes from my experience in and analysis of the 1960s. It seems to me that the terms in which the pro- or anti-Left question were argued then did not prove adequate to and were often destructive of those movements.

Debate with the Left is not new to feminists. The women's liberation movement and much of feminism's rebirth in the 1960s came out of that debate. Women's caucuses in leftist organizations fought first for our right to exist and then joined with the more radical elements from mainstream women's groups such as NOW to create an autonomous women's movement, and hence established women's liberation and radical feminism. During this struggle, analysis of patriarchy as the root cause of female oppression developed and pointed the way toward theory and process that go beyond the confines of the capitalist/socialist polarity.

But feminist theory is still evolving toward a total analysis, and thus we are repeatedly subject to pressure that it be subsumed by some preexisting "larger, more complete" perspective. Consequently, in the early 1970s, after several years of experience with women's liberation, many feminists became impatient with our lack of complete answers. This impatience, combined with concern over the Vietnam War and our class and race privileges, led many to consider working with the Left again. At the same time, some leftist groups began concerted recruitment efforts to win back "their women" and tap a now-large women's constituency.

The resulting upsurge of socialist debate in the independent feminist movement took two primary forms: women's anti-imperialist study and action groups and attempted takeovers of women's centers and organizations by leftist groups, particularly the Socialist Workers Party. The takeovers, when perceived by independent feminists, led not only to resistance but also to resentment of the Left. The women's anti-imperialist movement (of which I was initially a part) included women of many political backgrounds but was dominated by strife between "socialism" and an emerging female separatism. Those tensions eventually led to splits in groups all over the country, symbolized in dramatic battles over the planning and execution of a North American Indochinese Women's Conference in the spring of 1971.*

Out of this resistance to the Left—in both its male and female forms—grew female separatism. In the early 1970s, female separatism was widely discussed and became the prevailing means for maintaining a feminist stance that was neither reformist nor leftist.** Simultaneously, lesbians, who were oppressed by radical feminists as well as by reform and socialist feminists, began to articulate lesbian feminist theory and separatism. By 1974, lesbian feminism emerged as the predominant separatist position and led not only to new feminist theory but also to a flourishing of feminist culture, enterprises, and communities. Separatism in both these forms represented the independent and radical posture previously articulated by women's liberation. This period paralleled a similar period in the black liberation movement in the 1960s—a time when establishing one's independence, identity, and ideology, and solidifying a base of power, were the priorities.

Separatism arose out of the instinctive need of feminists to

*The North American/Indochinese Women's Conference, held in two parts—in Toronto and Vancouver in the spring of 1971—grew out of contact that feminists had with North Vietnamese women in 1970. It was meant to be the first meeting between Indochinese (North and South Vietnamese, Laotian, and Cambodian) revolutionary women and feminists from Canada and the United States. The battles that ensued in the United States had primarily to do with who should organize and go to the conference and what should be presented as the content of feminism here. This international event interested many women and quickly embodied all the problems and conflicts among feminists in the radical segment of the movement in the U.S.

**Two important statements of female separatism were *The Female State,* a journal printed in Boston in 1970, and "Fourth World Manifesto," a paper written by women in Detroit in response to the North American/Indochinese Women's Conference.

remain nonaligned in order to maintain ourselves as a distinct interest group and create new political theories and strategies. But we learned that separatism has its limits. Perhaps inevitably, separatism seemed to lead to isolation and powerlessness rather than to the politically engaged but independent stance we had envisioned. Ultimately, women's interests are not totally separate from the problems being struggled with universally. We are affected by all systems and divisions (e.g., class, race) and by all the practical issues (unemployment, housing, welfare, and police surveillance) and have a stake in how these issues are resolved.

THE FEMINIST DILEMMA TODAY

Emerging out of feminist separatism over the past couple of years, I and others sought new approaches that would embody an independent radical but nonaligned feminist position. In that search I have become distressed by the movement's fragmentation, its widespread pessimism, introspection, and dogmatism. I want now to examine this phenomenon in terms of the dominant trends mentioned earlier: cultural and spiritual separatism, political reformism, and socialist feminism.

While cultural and spiritual feminism are not the same, they have in common a recent flourishing and seem to be the most independent of the Left/anti-Left debates. Yet many, although certainly not all, activities associated with both trends are increasingly detached from questions of political and economic change. Thus, the energy generated in both these areas, which if combined with a new feminist politics could be a powerful force for change, is instead becoming more "separatist"—that is, more isolated from other struggles. Culture and spirit are integral parts of all movements for change (culture, for example, reflects the best and the worst of what is happening politically), and a politics that does not express itself culturally and spiritually is necessarily weakened. Therefore, the growing polarization and hostility from *both* sides of the "political" and "cultural" camps is disastrous for feminism. The issue is not whether you work in the cultural, political, economic, or spiritual arena, but what perspective and analysis you bring to your work and how you understand its relationship to the other areas. The problem I perceive with both present-day popularized "cultural feminism" and "women's spirituality," is their tendency to embrace the most negative aspects of separatism and isolate themselves from other areas of struggle. This stance contributes to allowing the patriarchal status quo continued domination over most women's lives. While my primary focus in this article is not on cultural/spiritual feminism, I believe that the tendency to separate themselves from politics is related to the pressures from many politicos to define pro- or anti-Left as the sole political options for feminists.*

Independent feminists who are not primarily involved in cultural or spiritual activities seem increasingly divided among those who are moving toward traditional political reformism, those who are moving toward socialist feminism, and those who are not aligned with either. Again, the problem in radical feminists' involvement in reform activities is certainly not in the work being done—it is both useful and logical for radicals to engage in a variety of reforms, such as rape-crisis centers, legislative changes, credit unions, and the like. The problem is that in building feminist strategies around reform goals dependent on existing political and economic structures, feminists often come not only to accept the limitations of reform but also to *defend* existing institutions instead of working toward feminist alternatives.

This may occur when feminists' work becomes too dependent on funders or government agencies (e.g., rape-crisis centers, which are funded only through law-enforcement agencies), that their identities and political futures become tied to maintaining the establishment base for their work. This precludes developing a base for radical changes that might eliminate the need for their own feminist institution as well. Another cause for this shift in politics may simply be that working on any feminist reform or institution requires so much energy that longer-range questions get put aside in the struggle to survive. Whatever its causes, many once radical feminists seem to defend the system more and accept the argument that if you are not satisfied with socialism or the U.S. Left, then you must necessarily endorse capitalism. The pressure to say that if you aren't pro-Left you must be anti-Left, or vice versa, is coming not only from socialists but also from women

---

*Thanks to Bertha Harris and Beverly Fisher Manick for help with the ideas in the section on culture and spirituality. For more discussion of women and spirituality, see Peggy Kornegger, "The Spirituality Ripoff," *Second Wave,* vol. IV, no. 3 (1975): 12–18.

engaged in political reformism. While there are exceptions, the general trend is nevertheless so strong that we must examine what is happening to feminists engaged in reform activities and determine how to maintain radical politics and goals during the process. Otherwise, both political reformists and socialist feminists end up denying the revolutionary possibilities in feminism, including its potential to go beyond the old capitalist/socialist polarity.

This brings me to socialist feminism, which is having a resurgence even though generally the New Left in the United States is in decline. The problem again is not feminists' desire to discuss socialism or examine issues of class, race, and money from that perspective; they *are* important issues. But socialism does not have a monopoly on their solution. In fact, the women's movement has begun to confront them both theoretically and practically, and in some instances, more successfully than the Left. The problem is that since socialist feminism lacks a radical feminist perspective, what emerges is primarily another effort, frequently guilt-laden, to contort female reality and feminist concepts into some existing socialist framework. Like all contortions, this process precludes the emergence of a powerful feminist analysis that could lead to new approaches to the questions of oppression and change.

Several of the *Quest* staff went to the National Socialist Feminist Conference in Yellow Springs, Ohio, in July of 1975 eager to see what new directions in feminist thought/action were being developed. We recognized the importance to feminists of many questions raised by a socialist analysis. But to our dismay, the framework of discussion was rarely feminism and instead was the U.S. white male Left. As Nancy Hartsock stated in "Fundamental Feminism: Process and Perspective,"* such an approach does not further our understanding of what socialism can offer to feminist development.

I am also disturbed that many socialist feminists are demanding that independent, nonaligned feminists curtail political explorations by choosing to be pro-Left, by declaring that socialism is THE WAY, just as other feminists are demanding that we renounce socialism or embrace spirituality as THE WAY. For in-

---

*Nancy Hartsock, *Quest: A Feminist Quarterly,* vol. II, no. 2 (Fall 1975): 67–80.

stance, I am often asked *what* I am, in such a tone that I know immediately that my answer will condemn or redeem me, no matter what else I say or what I mean by the terms in question. Although the pressure to align with one or another of these mutually exclusive options is not always stated in these terms, it is there, implicitly if not explicitly, in almost all the big debates in the women's movement. These debates are characterized by an insistence that one choose between two opposing forces and that to align with the other side (not to mention, to consider other factors involved) is as much a moral as a political disaster. The Jane Alpert versus Pat Swinton controversy embodied this mentality most clearly.*

From the beginning there seemed to be only two very hard moral lines on the Alpert-Swinton issue: 1) you were pro-Swinton and according to the other side, a dupe of the male Left; or, 2) you were pro-Alpert and therefore according to your opposition, a dupe of the male government. The self-righteousness on both sides, and the rigid dichotomy it set up, obscured rather than explored important political issues raised by the situation. What should have been discussed was not whom you trusted—Jane or Pat—but what, if any, genuine common interests exist between the Left Weather Underground and feminism—such questions as whether independent feminists have something to gain by helping leftist groups to survive and grow, and if so, what? Which groups, politics, and people on the Left embody it? What are the specific politics of the Weather Underground—which is available in their

*Jane Alpert and Pat Swinton were part of the Left underground, living clandestinely in the U.S. in the early 1970s. In 1975, Alpert wrote a radical feminist article, "Mother Right," in which she denounced the Left underground for its sexism and called on women to give feminism their first loyalty. She also came above ground, turned herself in to the government and served a moderate sentence in jail for her previous activities with the Left.

While Alpert's case was proceeding, Pat Swinton was arrested for her role in the underground. The supporters of Swinton claimed that Alpert had turned Swinton in to the government or at least provided them with sufficient information on how the underground operated for them to locate Swinton. They called on feminists to denounce Alpert and her theoretical article and to give support to the Left underground. Alpert said that while she had criticized the underground, she had never given evidence against Swinton or implicated any other persons. Those who supported her called on feminists to denounce the Left for trying to destroy feminism with this accusation and other similar actions. Without much evidence on either side, many feminists were divided over this case.

publications,* but which I almost never heard discussed—and how do they coincide or conflict with feminist politics? Is it important for all radical groups to protect the existence of an antigovernment underground regardless of its actions or its politics, and if so, why, and how? Instead of discussing such critical political issues, we were urged to condemn or extol Alpert, most often in the form of demanding whether we were prepared *categorically* to support or oppose the Left.

I do not argue that feminists should never ally with other oppressed groups or with a leftist faction; on the contrary, I favor enlightened coalitions with a variety of groups at different times. But alliance—or withdrawal—should grow out of careful political analysis of feminist goals and an assessment of our common interests, not out of generalized moral mandates. The irony here is that socialist organizations or black political groups do not automatically support one another unless they are clear why they want that group to survive and what alliances they want to make with it. (Even the Chinese Communist party, in its thirty years of socialist development prior to taking state power in 1949, sometimes allied with the Chinese Nationalist government—its bitter enemy—against other groups, including other leftists.) Yet the Alpert-Swinton debate, often because it was posed in moral terms, allowed little space for political examination of how different options would affect the future of a radical, but nonaligned, feminism.

Some individual women, acting from their feminist principles, have expressed dismay over this Left/anti-Left polarity and have asserted their right to make distinctions about which politics and which people on the Left they would support. Such efforts to respond case by case have often been sneered at as apolitical or as a refusal to take a stand. I believe, however, that they represent the best sort of active but nonaligned feminism. Further, we must assert ourselves more forcefully in just such a manner, not only in cases involving specific individuals but also in issues posed in terms of these dichotomies.

*In addition to the communiqués written from the underground periodically and published in women's newspapers, see *Prairie Fire: The Politics of Revolutionary Anti-Imperialism,* a political statement of the Weather Underground, printed underground in the United States (May 1974).

Despite the present fragmentation in the women's movement, many feminists are uncomfortable with the growing division between pro- and anti-Left, and between politics and culture or spirituality. We at *Quest* seek a movement that goes beyond those confinements. We are critical of the U.S. political, cultural, economic, and spiritual structures. But as feminists, we are also not satisfied with any existing ideological or strategic model for change. We are prepared to learn from social democratic thought, revolutionary experience, Marxism, and other efforts for change. But our primary task is to develop feminist theory, process, strategy, and direction. Too many issues are not answered by the contemporary left, right, or center stance of the patriarchal world; it is the job of nonaligned feminists to explore those issues.

Our assertion of nonaligned feminism involves keeping the feminist struggle and perspective at the fore as we evaluate all questions, coalitions, and issues. It also recognizes the need to expand what is called "feminist" so that the term responds to the realities of all women, across class, race, sexuality, and national boundaries in order to avoid merely reflecting the interests and needs of only one group.

Nonaligned feminism requires a willingness to explore every possible source for analysis—not only the works of women but also of men like Fanon, Mao, or Freire—regardless of how others have used their insights and without compulsion to declare ourselves a priori for or against any of their theories. It implies an openness to explore coalitions with other forces for change, to evaluate and reassess them constantly, according to how they affect women and our long-range goals. As we engage with others, declare positions on a wide range of issues, and make ourselves available instead of segregated, it is also crucial that we keep our own communities, projects, and organizations intact. We must not lose our independent feminist base; it is the source of our political power. It is the inspiration and touchstone for theory and strategy. And it is the source of our personal and communal sustenance.

This is the mandate for nonaligned feminism. We see *Quest* as one of several vehicles for nonaligned feminist debate and analysis. As our introductory article stated:

We are about open political forums. *Quest* wishes to explore differences and similarities in ideologies and strategies among the various segments of the women's movement. We are a journal of long-term, in-depth political analysis, a searching-ground for answers to unresolved questions.*

Quest's position as a forum can perhaps best be understood in terms of the perspective for nonaligned feminism I have outlined. We do not have a line to push or a final set of conclusions to advocate. But we do have politics, and we have a particular perspective on the crucial theoretical and practical issues facing feminists. We continuously make political choices about what to print. We seek the best elucidation of critical issues from a variety of points of view. In choosing material, we are guided by our nonaligned and radical perspective on feminism. From that perspective, we evaluate what we believe will add most to the development of a strong feminist movement and theory for all women. We are therefore not a liberal forum open to airing all views merely for the sake of equal time. While we do not always agree with each other or with each article that we print, we do agree that each article builds toward an understanding of our past and/or future theories and strategies.

Because we seek articles from different perspectives, within a certain framework, some have been confused about our politics and our printing of "contradictory" views. For example, one woman condemned us for going to the Socialist Feminist Conference, yet when asked if she read what we said about it, she answered, "no"; apparently our presence alone was evidence enough for her conclusions. At the same time, others have called us "antisocialist" for our critique of the conference and of other socialist strategies. I could cite many such stories to illustrate that as a result of exploring various facets of polarized questions, we have experienced the extent of the pressures on feminists to choose THE WAY and label others accordingly.

Our search for different perspectives and contributors to *Quest* has led us to other cities and to as many feminist events as our time and money allow. We have found that the ideas relevant to a

*Karen Kollias, "Spiral of Change: An Introduction to *Quest*," *Quest: A Feminist Quarterly*, vol. 1, no. 1 (Summer 1974): 7.

strong, nonaligned feminist direction are growing in different places and under various labels. We are looking for articles that comment directly on movement developments and debates but also that clarify the long-term goals and problems these involve. Rather than adding to polarization and recrimination, we hope that this process will help to link theory and action. We believe that analyzing current events and controversies can help to provide the groundwork for developing a new synthesis, a new resolution of the old conflicts and problems still plaguing feminism. Ours is an ongoing struggle to help build an independent, nonaligned feminism as a way of providing direction and hope for women seeking to change ourselves and the world around us.

GOING PUBLIC
WITH OUR VISION

I n any discussion of social change and the future of feminism, I
turn immediately to questions of organizing. Organizing is in
my blood. It goes back to my school days when my group would
plot together how to get away with doing something other than
what the teacher said. In every situation where things are not as
people feel would be best my instinct is to organize for change.
This is based on my assumption that people do have the potential
power to change things.

In the United States today, we have a big organizing job because
I do not believe that the majority of the people are represented by
the right wing, the so-called Moral Majority, or the forces that
have seized power in Washington. While many people do still have
racist and sexist ideas that we must work to change, they are head
and shoulders above the elite power-mongers of the right wing.
We should never confuse that elite in Washington with the will of
the majority in this country.

When we identify the majority with those in power, it is more
difficult to organize because we feel alienated from them as femi-

An abridged version of the second pamphlet in the Bunch series "Feminism in the 80's,"
this is an adaptation of a 1982 speech in Montana published by Antelope Publications
(Denver, Co.) in 1983.

61

nists, progressives, or lesbians. It is difficult because we feel different, and yet in a very fundamental way, we are talking about a vision of a way to live that most of the people in the country could also want. Our problem is that we have not yet described that vision clearly enough in concrete ways that show what it would mean in daily life, so that more people could respond to it.

I see feminism in a transition from focusing primarily on consciousness-raising about issues and critique of the existing society to developing structural changes in and alternative policies for the society. In this transition, we are competing with the right wing over the direction that this country will take over the next few decades. At a time like this, there is great need for activism and creativity, not for sitting back and waiting it out. It is not a time, as some suggest, for thinking we have gone too far. Rather, we must realize that *we have not gone far enough* with the implications and development of our ideas. The distance we need to go now lies in being more bold, more imaginative, more assertive, and I dare say, more public with our visions and with our hopes for the future.

Often it is hard to find the women's movement in this country. You can look in the phone book for any church you want; you can probably even look up Moral Majority chapters. But feminist groups are not often listed in the Yellow Pages. One of our failures has been our lack of public visibility as a place that people can come to grow, learn, and develop. The women's movement cannot sell a vision, a perspective, a possibility for the future, if people don't hear and see it and if they don't have entry points into it, where they can come and not be met with criticism for not already being wherever we have arrived politically.

I see feminism as a political perspective, which is one of, if not the most important, political perspectives for the decades ahead. In terms of the questions that we face today, progressives need very badly to develop new approaches to counter the right-wing agenda. I think that feminism has the potential to provide a lot of those insights and approaches. To realize that potential, we must take the movement's successes of the '60s and '70s—in consciousness-raising, in community and culture building, in identifying and raising new issues for the public agenda—and transform those successes into political and economic policy proposals and organized power for structural change.

FEMINIST SUCCESSES

If you don't realize how much has changed in the past fifteen years you should talk to someone who was an adult, especially a lesbian, in the 1950s. Millions of individual lives have been transformed by feminism, and many young people are very different today because the women's movement existed when they were growing up. There are changes in women's expectations and self-images and in the self-affirmation and pride that lesbians and gay men have. There are even changes in many heterosexual men.

While the process of change is hardly perfect or complete from a feminist view, these changes are not ones that can be wiped out with a few acts of legislation. Living a feminist life-style can be made more difficult by such legislation, but the point is that we have an enormous constituency of people who are consciously or unconsciously living lives in opposition to the Far Right. Our job is to mobilize them to conscious political action. The women's movement and the gay movement have the potential to mobilize large numbers of people in this country who can make a difference in defeating the right-wing agenda.

We have also brought important changes through the creation of an environment of support for feminist living. We've created women's spaces and places, words and songs—a women's culture that should help to sustain us and serve as a base for political action. I hope that we will value all of this not as a separate culture that exists simply for its own sake, but as a culture that exists in order to sustain and feed us for a *lifetime* of struggle and change.

Many activists of my generation are presently undergoing what has been called "burn-out" or "midlife crisis." It is important to give time and energy to life sustenance. We must find ways to take six weeks or months to rest and have vacations without feeling guilty, or we will either go on half-depleted or feel we have to drop out totally to get a break. This is not a question of individualistic solutions separate from political struggle. It is an integral part of sustaining a movement of people who are capable of a lifetime of political action—precisely because they do have places to live, and the resources to go on struggling, including money in their pockets for decent health care as well as to give to projects.

Another area of feminist accomplishment is what I call "Putting the Issues on the Agenda." Almost nothing of what feminists have raised was considered political before 1970. In my first consciousness-raising group in 1968, we kept saying, "Well, maybe we've done enough now. We've talked enough. This is just personal stuff." It took us six months to decide that women were a legitimate political constituency, and that the issues of feminism were not secondary.

In that process we began to identify a whole variety of sex-related issues, such as rape, sexual harassment, homophobia, and reproductive rights, as core political issues that are not separate from issues of racism or militarism. At their roots, all of these forms of oppression are based on accepting a fundamental dynamic of domination. Domination that begins in the patriarchal home—the authority and domination of the father which the right wing wants to revive—that helps keep everybody submissive to the dynamic of authority and domination on the basis of race, or class, or nation states. Feminism is not about secondary issues, but lies at the core of the whole question of what kind of society we want.

Where we have not yet succeeded as a movement is in the structural arena. We have not brought this vast, decentralized revolution of consciousness and the small projects characteristic of the women's movement into sufficient engagement with the political structures to create lasting structural changes that would institutionalize some of the new possibilities for life that we seek. This is where the right wing is concentrating on trying to stop us. They are counting on the fact that our ideas are not yet institutionalized and hoping to stop us now while they think they still can.

The Stop ERA movement was a clear picture of the Right's efforts to prevent constitutional, structural equality in spite of majority support for the amendment. The worst thing is that the Stop ERA movement succeeded in thwarting the democratic process by sophisticated organizing and manipulative rhetoric.

The focus on opposition to gay civil rights is also a manipulative tactic with movementwide consequences. In the late '70s gay civil rights was gaining acceptance, with the passage of many local antidiscrimination laws to protect the civil rights of lesbians and gay men. Then suddenly we were forced on the defensive and instead of fighting *for* protection of sexual preference, we had to fight *against* some of the most antigay laws that had ever been introduced in the United States.

The right wing believes that gay men and lesbians are the minority that can be most easily isolated, that the rest of the women's movement and other progressive groups will not stand behind gay rights. Therefore, this is where it thinks it can achieve a clear victory against feminist and progressive changes. This is significant, even if you are not lesbian or gay, because if the Right is successful in isolating the supporters of gay rights, then they will simply go on to the next issue and the next group, one by one. I am haunted by the words of one who lived in Germany during World War II, who observed that when they came for the communists, he was quiet; when they came for the trade unionists, he remained silent; when they came for the Jews, he looked the other way; when they came for him, there was nobody left to speak out.

CONTROL OVER OUR LIVES, BODIES, AND WORK

I connect gay rights to feminism most closely around the question of the individual's right to control one's own body, including the right to control one's sexuality, and therefore to have self-determination at the most basic human level. The right wing has launched an attack on reproductive freedom exemplified by the new Reagan guidelines denying teenagers access to birth control without parental notification. Everywhere we see an erosion of individuals' rights to control over their lives, and this includes control over the way the environment destroys our bodies and health in the workplace. The determination of who has the right to control others is at stake in every issue at the social, political, and economic levels.

The Family Protection Act proposed by the right-wing leaders in Congress is a good example of their agenda in these areas. It seeks to bolster patriarchal authority by such measures as eliminating aid to victims of domestic and sexual violence. The Right doesn't see you as a victim if you are a man's wife or child, because you are the property of the man. This was illustrated by Jeremiah Denton, a U.S. Senator from Alabama, who opposed marital rape laws that would make it illegal for a man to rape his wife, stating: "Dammit! When you get married, you kind of expect that you're going to get a little sex!" The Right also wants to prevent pluralistic images of the family by limiting what is taught in schools and by whom. In reality, the Family Protection Act is the Family Control Act.

Issues of control also tie into economic questions of women's work rights. Reagan recently raised the old shibboleth that "women are taking the jobs of men," thus questioning women's need for and right to paid jobs. Affirmative action is under attack, and women are being pitted against other minorities for jobs. Everywhere women are losing ground economically and corporations are manipulating women as a cheap labor pool globally in order to keep us under control both in the home and the job market.

The right wing has focused its energy on women's issues because those issues *do* touch people's lives. People *do* care about questions feminists have raised about sex roles, about how we're going to work, to love, and to live, about children and about families. All of us have to struggle with these questions in our own lives, so we know that they are not easy matters.

We need to acknowledge that much of what we have raised is hard or threatening, even for women who want those changes. The right wing has become very sophisticated at organizing around such fears and insecurities. When I read their literature, I always dread those "I used to be a feminist but . . ." statements, where someone starts out agreeing with some of what feminism represents, and then moves that idea in a right-wing direction.

Ironically, the right wing has outdone progressive forces in recognizing the potential power of women and the importance of women's issues. Many progressive groups have never taken the women's movement seriously politically; for example, they talk about the '70s, which saw an enormous burst of feminist activity, as personal, introspective, and apolitical. Some haven't yet understood that the issues feminists have raised are not peripheral, that these are central questions of power in society today. Unfortunately, the Right has recognized the power of these issues and has seen women as the newest political constituency—one that is not yet thoroughly committed to any politics, but that is ready to move.

The right wing has therefore set out to organize women by speaking to certain specific concerns and then "educating" them politically in right-wing ideology. Richard Viguerie, the leading direct-mail fundraiser, described this process at "Unity '81," a right-wing conference held in Virginia. As reported in the *Interchange Newsletter,* he described how the abortion issue was used "as the door through which" many people came into conservative politics. But, "they don't stop there," he noted. Their convictions against abortion were like the first of a series of falling dominoes, which led to opposition to "secular humanism, socialism and communism—which led to commitments to free enterprise at home and to aggressive foreign and military policies abroad." This is a capsule version of right-wing political education for women.

Feminists must become more active in this battle for control over who will speak for the constituency of women. It is quite literally a question of control over women's bodies—both the control of our individual right to choose and the control over who is going to determine the direction in which the bodies and minds of women will move politically.

FEMINISM AS A GLOBAL VISION

One of the most potent forces for change in the world today is global feminism, which offers the possibility of women seeking visions and approaches that cross national boundaries. Nationalism is the ultimate expression of patriarchal domination of one group by another, and has frightened people with the threat of nuclear annihilation. Women all over the world are challenging patriarchy and nationalism in various ways. This ranges from the women's peace movement in Europe to women in Southeast Asia who are mobilizing against sex-tourism and forced prostitution (linked with foreign military bases and the economic and sexual exploitation of women). Women in Latin America held their first continentwide feminist conference last year (1981) where they discussed the meaning of feminism in the political struggles of their countries, including a session on lesbianism—a fact that should put to rest once and for all, the myth that lesbians exist only in industrialized countries. In all of these efforts, women understand that one has to work against world problems at the local level where they affect women's daily struggle for survival, not just offer political analysis with abstract internationalist rhetoric.

The global movement of women is not unrelated to the local movement of women in Montana either. Our world and the powers that control it operate globally. If we are to succeed in challenging that power, we must make our struggles for change global in perspective—while still remaining rooted in the grass roots. Whenever we examine a local problem in depth, we see that it is connected to the global patterns of control of multinational corporations, and other transnational brokers of powers. For example, to deal with unemployment in the U.S.A. and to counter Reagan's blaming it on women, we must see that the labor market has become international and is manipulated to provide employers with the cheapest labor possible.

When you look at the "energy crisis," you see similar issues of global interdependence. One aspect of the crisis is quite simply that the superpowers of the world, including the U.S.A., can no longer rape the world's resources without disastrous consequences. There are not enough resources left to permit the pillage that has taken place in the past century. Further, other countries will no longer tolerate it, whether through peaceful or violent resistance. The so-called standard of living in this country, which is based on such squandering, must change. This provides us with the opportunity to redefine the standard in favor of a higher quality of living, with a change in our domestic priorities as well as in our relations with other countries. A feminist vision must address what kind of living and what forms of distributing resources would improve the quality of life for all people, while preserving the world's resources for the survival of future generations. This means creating a model of "development" that means not just industrial progress, as "development" is now defined, but that involves the progress of the human race as a whole.

Only such a vision can prevent the deterioration of our movements into battles among separate interest groups for a larger piece of the dwindling resource pie, with racial minorities, women, gays, and working-class people fighting each other. We must show that there are alternatives, that things do not have to be the way they are now. Indeed, life will change. The only questions are *how* it will change and *who* will determine that. For example, the money that is spent in the world on military budgets in one day would be enough to provide minimal food, clothing, and housing for everyone in the world for one year. There is enough food to go around; it is a question of priorities and of how food is being distributed and controlled. However, there may not be enough food in twenty years if we continue to destroy the world's top soil through short-sighted agribusiness policies aimed at immediate profit and not world survival. These are all matters of priority, and the decisions that are made today will determine the shape of the century ahead. Feminists must create dialogue on such issues from a feminist perspective.

What we are experiencing in this time of transition for feminism can be the coming to fruition of the feminist vision in relation to all issues. This does not mean that we should abandon those "women's issues," such as sexual equality, violence against women, homophobia, and reproductive rights—issues that we have fought so hard to put on the political agenda. Rather, it means taking our experiences and applying what we have learned to other areas as well. What is the question of women controlling our own bodies if not also a question of world nutrition and starvation, which is increasingly destroying more and more women's lives? What is the question of violence against women if not also a question of a violent society—from the home, to the streets, to the military? Feminists are in a good position to try to reach beyond national boundaries, since we did not create them, and to make these wider connections, thus showing that the feminist vision is an integral part of all issues. In so doing, we lay the groundwork for new possibilities in the twenty-first century.

TRANSFORMATIONAL POLITICS AND PRACTICAL VISIONS

To bring the feminist vision to bear on all issues and to counter the right-wing agenda for the future, require that we engage in multiple strategies for action. We must work on many fronts at once. If a movement becomes a single issue or single strategy, it runs the danger of losing its overall vision and diminishing its support, since different classes of people feel most intensely the pressure of different issues. So while we may say at any given moment that one issue is particularly crucial, it is important that work be done on other aspects of the changes we need at the same time. The task is not finding "the right issue," but bringing clear political analysis to each issue showing how it connects to other problems and to a broad-based feminist view of change in society.

Feminist concerns are not isolated, and oppression does not happen one-by-one-by-one in separate categories. I don't experience homophobia as a separate and distinct category from economic discrimination as a woman. I don't view racism as unconnected to militarism and patriarchal domination of the world.

In order to discuss the specific strategies necessary to get through this transition and bring feminism into the public arena more forcefully, we must first be clear that feminism is a transformational politics. As such, feminism brings a perspective to *any* issue and cannot and must not be limited to a separate ghetto called "women's issues." When dealing with any issue, whether it is budgets or biogenetics or wife battering, feminism as a political perspective is about change in structures—about ending domination and resisting oppression. Feminism is not just incorporating women into existing institutions.

As a politics of transformation, feminism is also relevant to more than a constituency of women. Feminism is a vision born of women that we must offer to and demand of men. I'm tired of letting men off the hook by saying that we don't know whether they can be feminists. Of course they can struggle to be feminists, just as I can and must struggle to be antiracist. If feminism is to be a transforming perspective in the world, then men must also be challenged by it.

This does not mean that we do not also need spaces and organizations for women only. Women need and want and have the right to places where we gather strength and celebrate our culture and make plans only with women. But as a political vision, feminism addresses the future for men as well as for women, for boys as well as for girls, and we must be clear that it is a politics for the future of the world, not just for an isolated handful of the converted.

If we are clear about feminism as a transformational politics, we can develop viable public alternatives to Reaganism and all patriarchal policies. These would be policy statements of how we think the world could be organized in various areas if a feminist approach is taken.

We need feminist budgets for every town, state, and nation. For example, you could take the state budget in Montana, whatever it is, take the same amount of money and prepare a budget of how you would reorganize the use of that money if feminists had control of the state government. When you finish that one, you can do a federal budget. And when you finish that, take on the UN budget! Budgets are good indicators of priorities. If we publicized our approaches, people could see that there are alternatives, that we are talking about something different, and they would get a clearer idea of what a feminist perspective means in practical terms.

I would also like to see feminist plans for housing, transportation, criminal justice, child care, education, agriculture, and so on. We need serious discussion as feminists about how we deal with the issues of defense, not only by doing critiques of militarism, but also by deciding how to cope with the competing powers and threats in this world, as they exist right now. We're not going to solve many of the problems immediately, but we have to put forward other policies and practices, so people can see the difference. If we start with how things are now, then we can talk about how to move, step-by-step, toward policies that are based on very different assumptions and values.

To use such feminist policy statements, when we engage in electoral politics for example, would give people a clear and public statement of what it means to elect a feminist. We would also have something concrete to hold a candidate accountable to after election. To work to elect feminists with clear policy content makes a campaign focus on feminism as a transforming politics rather than just on personality or on adding women without clear political statements of what they represent. It can make electoral politics part of a strategy for change rather than isolated from the movement or a substitute for other action.

Developing such policies is particularly important now because the Reagan crowd is also about a "revolution" in social policies. We could call it reactionary, but if revolution means massive change in government policies, that is what Reagan is pulling off right now. We need a creative counter to these policy changes that is not just a return to where we were in the past. We have to put forward approaches that both deal with the problems that we had before Reagan, and reveal the antiwoman, patriarchal, racist, and sexist assumptions of the right wing.

ORGANIZING FOR ACTION

Perhaps the most important thing that we need to do which underlies everything I've said, is organize. Organize. Organize. Organize. All the great ideas in the world, even feminist budgets, will mean little if we don't also organize people to act on them. We have to organize in a variety of ways.

We need to take what has been the decentralized strength of the women's movement—a multitude of separate women's projects and individuals whose lives have been radically affected by feminism—and find lasting forms for bringing that to more political power. The feminist movement has a wonderful array of creative small groups and projects. Nevertheless, when these don't have any voice in something larger, a lot of their potential power is lost simply because what is learned and done is limited to a small circle and has no larger outlet to affect the public. I don't want to abandon the small-group approach to working, but those groups need to band together into larger units that can have a political impact beyond their numbers. This can take the form of citywide or issue-based alliances, which still preserve each group's autonomy. Such feminist alliances then become the basis for coalitions—as a feminist force—with other progressive groups. If we organize ourselves to join coalitions as a community, rather than having women going into other groups one by one, we have a better chance of keeping our feminist values and perspectives in the forefront of that coalition work.

We can utilize the grass-roots decentralized nature of feminism well in organizing around policy changes today, because it is at the state and local level where most of the battles with the right wing are presently focused. But to do that effectively we have to learn how to get our supporters out—to be visible about their politics. If we are trying to influence policy, the policymakers must know that our people are reliable; if we say that a hundred thousand women will be in Washington, D.C., or a thousand in Billings, Montana, they have to know that they will be there.

The agenda for change is often set by the kind of organizing that goes on around specific issues—particularly ones that are very visible and of considerable interest to people, such as reproductive rights or the Family Protection Act. Whatever the issue, as long as it is one that affects people's lives, the task of the organizer is to show how it connects to other issues of oppression, such as racism, and also to illustrate what that issue means in terms of a vision for the future. The Family Protection Act has demonstrated well these connections as its supporters have sought to bring back the patriarchal order through policies against gays, against assistance to battered women and children, against freedom in the schools, and against the organizing of workers into unions, and so on. It provides a clear case for discussing feminist versus antifeminist perspectives on life.

Another task of organizers is to devise strategies to activate people who care, but who aren't politically active. I saw a chain letter circulating among women artists, which instead of having people send a dollar, said: "Write a letter to Senator So and So (participating in the hearings on abortion), and then send this letter to eight of your friends who want reproductive rights but who aren't doing anything about it."

One mistake we often make is to act as if there is nothing that supporters can do politically if they can't be activists twenty-four hours a day, seven days a week. We must provide channels of action for people who have ten minutes a day or an hour a week, because that very action ties them closer to caring and being willing to risk or move toward a feminist vision. We must mobilize the constituency we have of concerned individuals, recognizing that many of them are very busy just trying to survive and care for their children or parents.

One of Jerry Falwell's organizations sends a little cardboard church to its local supporters, who deposit a quarter a day, and at the end of the week, they dump the money out and send it to Falwell. We can learn something from this approach, which provides a daily connection to one's supporters. When I see community resources—health clinics, women's centers, whatever—closing because they're no longer getting outside support, I worry about our connections to our supporters. This movement did not start with government money. This movement started in the streets and it started with the support of women, and it can only survive if it is supported by us.

I have no objections to feminists getting government money or applying for grants as long as we remember that when they don't give us the money, we have to figure out other ways to do what has to be done by ourselves. We have to go back to our own resources if we believe in what we're doing. If the peasants of Latin America have supported the Catholic Church over the centuries, I don't see any reason why the feminists and gay men and lesbians of North America cannot support our movements.

COALITIONS: THE BOTTOM LINE

Coalitions with other progressive groups are important, but we must be clear about what makes them viable. The basis of coalitions is integrity and respect for what each group describes as its bottom line. Now that's not always easy. But with honest struggle over what each group feels is its necessary, critical minimum demand, coalitions can work. If we are to make compromises on where we put our time and energy, it has to be within that framework. Coalitions don't succeed simply for ideological or charitable reasons. They succeed out of a sense that we need each other, and that none of our constituencies can be mobilized effectively if we abandon their bottom-line concerns. Therefore, we have to know where the critical points are for each group in a coalition.

This is a difficult process, but I saw it work in Houston at the National Women's Conference in 1977. As one of the people organizing the lesbian caucus, I can tell you there were moments in that process when I was ready to scream over the homophobia we encountered. But we knew our bottom line and were clear about what compromises we could and could not accept. If it had been an event comprised only of feminists, we would have said more about lesbianism. But as a large, diverse conference, we saw our task as coalescing a critical mass recognition and support of the issue of sexual preference through working as part of the broad-based feminist coalition there.

In order to get this recognition, we had to organize our constituency so that other groups would want our support. We were clear that we would not support a compromise that left us out—that we had to have that mutual respect to make the coalition work. But the success of lesbians was based on the fact that we had organized at the state and local level as well as nationally. Our people were there and others knew we had the numbers. Many women realized that they had a lot more to gain by mobilizing our support for the overall plan by including us, than by alienating us, and creating a very public nuisance. Coalitions are possible, but they are only effective when you have mutual respect; when you have a clearly articulated bottom line; and when you have your own group mobilized for action. If you haven't got your own group organized, your own power base, when the crunch comes, no matter how politically correct or charitable people feel, they are going to align with the groups they feel will make them stronger.

We need more feminist alliances or coalitions that do not coalesce around only one event, but that establish themselves over time as representing a variety of groups and types of action, from electoral and media work to demonstrations or public education. Such ongoing political action groups are usually multi-issue and their strength lies in bringing groups together for concerted action on a city- or statewide basis. These groups then become a reliable basis for coalitions with other progressive organizations.

GOING PUBLIC

I think that it is crucial for the feminist movement to become more public. By going public, I mean we need to move beyond the boundaries of our subculture. This does not mean giving up the women's community, which remains our strength, our base, the roots of our analysis and of our sustenance. But to go more public in actions that are visible beyond our circles, demonstrating to the world that feminists have not rolled over and played dead as the media sometimes implies.

Going public involves statements about our visions for change. This can be through vehicles such as feminist policy statements on housing or the budget, as well as by demonstrating the passion of our visions with militancy, such as the civil disobedience and fasting women did in the struggle for ratification of the ERA. Such actions make our issues dramatically visible, seen as matters of life and death. These also capture the public imagination and re-create some of that spirit of discovery that accompanied the early years of women's liberation. We need more creative community or media-oriented events that bring that instant recognition of what is at stake and inspire people to talk about those issues.

One of the important things that I remember about the early days of the women's movement is that we talked about feminism—incessantly. We talked in the laundromat, we talked on our jobs, we talked to everybody because we were so excited about what we were discovering. And that talk spread—it excited other women, whether they agreed with us or not. The primary method by which women have become feminists is through talk, through consciousness-raising, and through talk with other feminists. It was not through the government or even the media, but through ourselves. And they cannot take that away. They can deny us money, but they cannot take away ourselves, and the way that this movement has grown is through our "beings"—through being active in the world and being visible.

We have to go public by moving out of what may be comfortable places and engage with women who don't necessarily call themselves feminists. You can go public a hundred different ways—whether that is through media-oriented action or by talking to women on the job or at established women's places. In going public, we risk the vulnerability that goes with such interaction, but the rewards are worth it. The challenge to our ideas that comes with it enables us and our ideas to expand and be more inclusive and more powerful. The interaction that comes with seeing feminism in relation to situations that are not familiar to us, or seeing women of different class or race or geographic backgrounds taking feminism in new directions, is a very good tonic for "tired feminists."

The growth of feminism depends precisely on this interaction —of different generations of feminists and of challenges that make our ideas change and go farther than when they started. If we believe that our visions are visions for the world and not just for a cult, then we have to risk them. For if our ideas cannot survive the test of being engaged in the world more broadly, more publicly, then feminism isn't developed enough yet, and that engagement will help us to know how to remold feminism and make it more viable. For if feminism is to be a force for change in the world, it too must grow and change; if we hoard it or try to hang onto it, we will only take it to the grave with us.

Going public with our visions is ultimately the only way that feminism can become a powerful force for change. There is no way that we can get more people wanting to be feminists and supporting and expanding our visions, if they can't even see them, if they never even hear about feminism from feminists rather than the media, and if they don't sense what we care about and believe in. To be seen as an alternative vision for the world, we first have to be seen. It's that simple and it's that important.

Another part of going public is coming out as feminists—in places where we might feel more comfortable not using the word or even discussing the ideas. An academic study has shown what movement activists have said for years—that the most effective counter to homophobia is "knowing one"—that is, people's antigay ideas change most when they realize that they know and care about someone who is gay. But this change would never occur if no one came out, and therefore most people could go on not realizing that they know one of "us" and accepting society's homophobia unchallenged.

"Coming out" as feminists has a similar power. It forces people to get beyond their media stereotypes and deal concretely with a feminist person and with ideas and visions as embodied by that person. Just as coming out for lesbians and gay men has to be decided on a personal basis, so too does coming out as a feminist. Still, it is important to recognize the political power of the personal action and to see that it is useful in advancing feminism and combating the power of the right wing, which includes the effort to intimidate us into going back into closets of fear and adopting apolitical life-styles.

Coming out and going public make it possible for us to communicate our feminist visions to people—the majority of whom I believe would welcome alternatives to the state of the world and have not necessarily accepted the right-wing's visions. They want alternatives to living behind closed doors in fear of violence on the streets and contamination in the air; they want decent work that does not destroy or demean them; they want to be able to affirm freedom and justice, but they may not believe that it is possible. We have to show them that we care about those same things and that our movement is about feminist struggles to create visions of new possibilities in the world, beginning with the struggle for possibilities for women and moving outward from there.

We need to invite people to join us in this struggle, approaching them with something to offer, rather than rejecting them as if they were enemies, or ignoring them as if they were not what we think they should be. If we invite them to join us in trying to become and create something different, we engage in politics as a process of seduction as well as of confrontation. Feminism must be a process of seeing and invoking the best in people as well as in confronting the worst. In this we may discover new ways of moving politically that will enable feminist visions to emerge and to provide the leadership so desperately needed to prevent the patriarchal militaristic destruction of the planet.

This is our challenge in the '80s. It is the particular moment that we have been given in human evolution and in the struggle between the forces of justice and domination. We are the inheritors of a proud and living tradition of creators, dreamers, resisters, and organizers who have engaged in the struggle before us, and we shall pass it on to the next generation. However long each of us lives, that's how much time we have, for this is a lifetime process and a lifetime commitment.

MOVEMENT STRATEGIES AND ORGANIZING

The essays included here are the most diverse, as this section considers a number of issues of strategy and structures that have been debated in the feminist movement over the years. It begins with an article on self-definition, since I see each woman's sense of her own selfhood as providing the basis on which she struggles for political change. The articles following were written as part of my efforts to sort out conflicts and find ways to act more productively around various movement problems or controversies. They deal with reform versus revolution, class and race, leadership and coalitions. This section also addresses the challenge to feminism posed by the growth of the right wing in the United States.

Here we see recurring themes that underlie my work such as the interaction between individuals and social change and the relationship of the personal to the political. There is also a consistent concern for how differences divide people and what can be done to make diversity a source of strength rather than divisiveness. Finally, the essays indicate the crucial importance of having a broad feminist vision that can learn from and respond to a wide variety of concerns and people.

SELF-DEFINITION
AND POLITICAL SURVIVAL

I magine that you are given a large, blank piece of paper, pencils and crayons, and told to depict your self in thirty minutes. You are to demonstrate who you are, what you do and feel, who and what influences you. You can draw a picture, write a list, make an airplane, or whatever you want. In response to this assignment, I draw a multilayered pie with slices and overlapping circles. In the process, I discovered a lot about how I saw myself.

There were some things about myself that were given, out of my control: my sex, race, class background, family patterns, childhood turf, and general physical makeup. All told, these *social givens* constitute a large part of my life. In another layer were those particular characteristics of myself, not determined, yet influenced by external conditions, such as: my talents, skills, temperament, likes and dislikes, emotions, and so on. I called these my *individual traits*. Overlaying the entire drawing were my *attitudes and actions* toward these givens and traits. I discovered that these attitudes and actions were the most important in determining my self-concept.

For example, I am a female—that is a given. But what is most

"Self-Definition and Political Survival" first appeared in *Quest: A Feminist Quarterly,* vol. I, no. 3 (Winter 1975).

crucial is my stance toward that given—I have become a feminist and a lesbian who loves that about myself. I am a white, middle-class American by birth, but most important, I have chosen to use those realities to fight what they stand for: to use privileges to challenge the classist and racist system in the U.S., and to use being a citizen of the U.S. empire to attack its inhumane policies all over the world. Similarly, I looked at my training and individual traits and saw how I had or could direct them, consciously and unconsciously, toward certain activities such as political organizing, or editing.

Our attitudes and actions toward the givens of our lives are the primary means we have of starting to gain control over our own selves and our destinies. We have no control over the social givens of our birth. We have limited control over our individual traits. But we *can* control what we do with those givens and traits. We can use our privileges to change society or to maintain it. We can pity ourselves for our oppression or we can embrace its good effects and struggle to change those that are bad. As we assert this control over our selves, we confront the society that has determined many of these givens. We cannot alter all the ways that these givens control us, but we can begin to change their meaning and impact both now and for the future. As we struggle for such societal change, that very struggle alters how we see ourselves, thus creating a continuous process of change and growth. Two years from now, I will probably find most of the same basic elements in my self-drawing. But there will be new aspects and emphases resulting from the interaction between self-determination and the political struggle to change society, which in turn changes me.

The purpose of talking about self is not to advance abstract knowledge about women, but to understand better our strengths and weaknesses. I am not a psychologist determining motivation patterns, but a feminist seeking to understand how we can improve women's lives and build a more effective movement. My approach to the political and personal question of self is, therefore, to examine the factors that affect us, to uncover the elements that hinder us, and to discover those things that make us stronger both individually and as a movement.

We are those biological, social, political, and economic givens that determine the objective conditions of our lives; we are the various individual traits and skills that make us distinct; and we are what we do with and think about our givens and traits. These factors change somewhat over time. Still, it is useful to be clear about the basics of our self-concept in order to direct further change that makes us stronger women who live fuller lives and are capable of creating a better society. If, however, the search to understand self-concept becomes self-indulgent, consuming all our energies, then we have defeated ourselves. We understand and change ourselves not in isolation but within the everyday context of our female existence—in our work, play, love, dreams, actions, and interactions with others.

The question of self-concept has not been a conscious issue for Western women until recently. For many centuries, women's identity was absolutely determined and circumscribed by her functions: preoccupation with childbirth and motherhood; continual service to her husband, home, and church; and political and sexual passivity. The exceptions to this were few and far between. These functions were rooted in the assumption of male superiority and heterosexuality. Society held little esteem for women and women held little esteem for self.

The Western philosophical tradition of "man's search for identity" was just that—man's search the prerogative of males only. Even among men, it was the luxury of the privileged. Of course, the natural development of selfhood—of the strengths of survival, pride, and self-respect—took place for all peoples, rich and poor, male and female. But history and literature have obscured how this self-concept developed in the ongoing struggles of everyday people.

We can learn from the ways that women developed strengths for survival under patriarchy, and before that, of women's selfhood where matriarchies existed. But we should not romanticize these as the answers for us today. In the USA, the functions that women traditionally performed, their context, and the accompanying self-concepts have been breaking down over the past century. While women still perform most of the family and menial work, the context and importance of the family is being altered radically and women's work has become even more marginal to the centers of economic and political power. Our society is still based on male superiority, heterosexuality, and woman-hatred, but the forms are changing. The new roles assigned to women with the rise of the middle class—sex object, isolated mother/wife in a nuclear family, and active consumer—are not taking root. In less than a century, they are being exposed and rejected. More and more women find themselves caught between old roles that no longer function and new ones that are inadequate. As women caught in this historical process, *we face both crisis and opportunity.* The old patriarchal conditions that determined women's identity are changing; the twentieth-century middle-class replacements are also failing. The resulting confusion leads to crisis, to inner turmoil and insecurity, but it also provides opportunity for fundamental changes in the images and self-concepts of women. Feminists must seize this time to change ourselves, to change the position of women, and to change the society.

Another source of identity for women, both traditionally and today, has been through identification with the place of "our men" in the hierarchies of class, race, and so on. Many a woman has gained her self-worth not from herself as a woman, but from her "superiority" on these male scales. Accepting such supposed superiority keeps a woman tied to the man who gives it to her (husband, father, brother), and divides her against other women, and maintains her dependence on a false consciousness about her position as a woman. Feminists must use the givens of our birth into these male hierarchies to challenge them rather than depend on them for our self-esteem.

We can and must define female reality for ourselves and develop what we as women want to be. But we cannot forget that a male-supremacist society is threatened by independent females. We will not be allowed self-determination without a struggle. We must develop our individual selves in a political context, recognizing that our struggle to become stronger is part of a larger political fight to end all female oppression. If isolated from the political context, our self-development will become diluted, individualistic, and ultimately, futile. Our survival depends on our identification with other women; hence a group identity and politics, as well as a personal one, must develop. Too often, feminists have used the concept "the personal is political" to define all of our personal desires and problems as political. But the personal and political circles overlap only as we incorporate a political analysis and identity into our personal lives and actions.

84

To incorporate a political understanding into our view of self, we must analyze the effects of oppression on self-concept. While race, nationality, and perhaps other social conditions are equally important, I will focus on aspects of class and lesbian oppression since I am most familiar with these areas. In my experience, many of the women with the strongest self-concepts and whose identity is closely tied to the political interests of a group are lower-class (used here to include lower- and working-class women of all races) and lesbians. I have tried to understand why this is so.

Selfhood is strongly affected by necessity. What we must do in order to survive, both materially and emotionally, influences us deeply. This creates a paradox within oppression. On the one hand, oppression is destructive to our self-worth; we are taught to hate ourselves, to see ourselves as personal failures, to look outside for approval, and to accept that much of our life is outside our control, determined by others. On the other hand, oppression also brings out the strengths necessary to survive as oppressed peoples; endurance and ability to cope with changing and difficult situations, less obsession with individual ego, and more focus on group survival.*

All women are oppressed, but there is tremendous variety in the forms oppression takes and consequently in the strengths and weaknesses of our self-concepts. Conventional liberal wisdom argues that lower-class and black women are the most oppressed and need the "freedoms" of middle-class women in order to pursue self-development. True, but not true. Lower-class women of all races are the most materially oppressed and consequently do not have the time, money, or space to pursue many individual interests and talents that can be important to selfhood. For example, a lower-class artist rarely has the resources or opportunity

*There are numerous studies on the effects of oppression on self-concept and behavior, but most focus only on the negative aspects. The paradox created by oppression has emerged in women's liberation primarily in the recognition of positive characteristics of women that may result from our oppressed status. The debate has been over whether we want to develop characteristics labeled masculine (e.g., aggressiveness) or retain those labeled feminine (e.g., sensitivity). Still, we have not sufficiently analyzed what is behind these differences or looked at the parallel questions about differences among women that result from other social and economic oppressions.

to devote as much energy to her art as a middle- or upper-class woman.

Yet, the very demands of everyday survival often create a strength of self and clarity of vision often unknown to the middle and upper classes. Karen Kollias describes these as: strong self-concept, group identity, and accountable leadership.* Without glorifying oppression, we can examine the so-called advances of bourgeois women and ask whether these are really advances or setbacks. Have the legal reforms and economic and social changes in women's status that accompanied the rise of the middle class made women stronger and more self-loving? Or have they further weakened us, made us more passive and woman-hating, made us sex objects and desperate consumers? Is the mother in a male-dominated peasant society or a poor black family any further away from power and control over her life than the middle-class housewife in suburbia? Is her route to liberation through bourgeois reforms or can she draw on other strengths to create new possibilities for women? These are some of the questions we must ask about women's selfhood, feminism, race, and class. The point is not which group is the most liberated, but what elements can be drawn out of each experience and transformed into personal and political strengths.

A similar paradox exists among lesbians, whose self-concept is affected by oppression. Our strengths are partially based on the awareness that we are solely responsible for our survival *all* of our lives. Like lower-class women, most lesbians must depend on our selves and others of our kind, both economically and emotionally. Except for a few from rich families, we rarely can fall back on male privilege. The economic reality of lesbianism has pushed middle-class, previously heterosexual women, to develop strengths and skills seldom encouraged in the middle class. This process has created greater clarity concerning self-concept and direction. Single women, even if they are not lesbians, share some of this experience if they remain unmarried and do not depend on men to rescue or support them.

Some have argued that because we do not have male support, all single and lesbian women are working class. This is not accurate. While we are usually closer to the working-class reality, there

*See Karen Kollias, "Class Realities: Create a New Power Base," in *Quest,* vol. I, no. 3 (Winter 1975): 28–43, for a fuller discussion of these strengths.

are still class differences among us. Supporting oneself with a professional degree is very different from working at jobs available without a high-school diploma. It is true, however, that the economic differences are usually narrower when women are separated from men and this fact affects our self-concepts. Our reality is closer to what lower-class women, lesbian or heterosexual, have always known: we must depend on ourselves for survival; weakness and passivity are luxuries we cannot afford.

Our survival is not only economic but emotional and political as well. The lesbian's self-concept is shaped by the necessity of creating our own ways of living—systems of support and relationships that perform the functions of the traditional family. Since out-of-the-closet lesbians face active hostility and oppression from society, we *must* develop group identity and depend on each other for survival. We cannot fit passively into society's institutions (unless our whole life is a lie), because these were not made to accommodate us: home, school, church, nightclub, and sex itself. The process of creating one's own structures and ways of relating, constantly sorting out old and new forms, demands an *active attitude* toward one's self. This is a vital part of self-determination and the experience of shaping one's own environment. The more we *must* create the structures of our lives, the more we learn what we want and the more we confront the ways society denies that to us. Thus, the process of self-definition can lead to greater political awareness, to rebellion, and can move women toward the creation of a different society.

We must learn more about how race, class, heterosexuality, and other experiences affect us differently. The goal is not to prove who is best or to wallow in comparisons, guilt, or navel-gazing. The purpose is to understand how these conditions lead to different needs and strengths among women so that we can better use our strengths, learn how to develop more strengths in all of us, and meet one another's needs more fully. The women's movement has made some steps in this direction, and in the process, created other problems.

SUBSTITUTES FOR SELF

The women's movement has provided some ways for women to explore the questions of self. Through consciousness-raising, individuals see how sexism affects each woman's self-concept. We

87

have developed analyses of how society's attitudes and institutions cripple us, thus freeing women somewhat from seeing ourselves as personal failures, from blaming ourselves for self-hate, insecurity, or lack of skills. Similarly, particular groups have examined the effects on women of class, age, race, and heterosexual oppression. Increased consciousness has helped us understand our oppression and develop pride in our womanhood, lesbianism, and other identities.

After developing initial consciousness, the movement has floundered in its efforts to create self-determination among women. Often we have confused feminist consciousness and politics with the ability to verbalize about one's self, overlooking women's nonverbal strengths. Consciousness-raising helped us to verbalize our oppression, but often has not led to control over our lives and change in the conditions causing our oppression.

What are the steps toward self-development that have come out of the women's movement and what has gone wrong with these? I have seen four sources of partial identity that have become substitutes for self: 1) oppression, 2) the movement, 3) ideal models, and 4) relationships.*

Building Identity Around Oppression

Starting with the valid assertion that society oppresses us because we are women, lesbians, lower class, and so on, we become proud of our oppression and can get stuck there. We concentrate too much on discovering the intricacies of these oppressions instead of working to get out of them. We may wear them as a chip on the shoulder, a cross to bear, or a badge of honor. In so doing, some women become "professional victims" of societal givens. We create politically legitimate reasons for untogetherness or lack of self-direction, which, as victims, we use to excuse us from responsibility for changing ourselves or society.

Both oppressed and oppressor can use oppression as an excuse. The oppressed says, "I'm just a victim of society and can't fight it." Or the oppressor claims, "No matter what I try, somebody says I'm being oppressive, so why bother?" Our consciousness of oppression thus becomes an excuse for not moving forward, crip-

*I first defined and described these substitutes in an earlier article, "Perseverance Furthers: Woman's Sense of Self," *The Furies* (February 1973): 2–4. Some of that previous description is included here.

pling our self-development instead of freeing us to assert our lives in new ways.

In developing self-respect out of our oppression, we may also fall into false pride and arrogance. Consciousness-raising leads us to assert pride in our oppressions but it is necessary to have a self-concept that is more than that. For example, I am proud to be a lesbian rather than ashamed as society would have me be, but that is not my only source of self-identity. If we fail to develop other traits as well, we become dependent on oppression for self-respect and use it to demand power and respect from others. We do not ask for respect for our particular abilities but simply for our self as a category of oppression—a token—woman, lesbian, working class. If our identity remains dependent on these categories alone and not on other interests as well, we have not achieved liberation but remain limited and defined by the categories of our oppressors. We stagnate. Stagnation leads to false pride and arrogance toward those supposedly less conscious than us. Such arrogance is self-defeating because it cuts us off from other women, preventing a real examination of differences that could lead to change and growth all around.

Building Identity Around the Movement

Some women solve the crisis of self by turning our beings over to the movement, lock, stock, and barrel. While making us aware of our oppression and giving a name to our problems, the movement can substitute itself for our identity. Hours of endless meetings, offices to be run, conversations to be had, articles to be written, good deeds to be done become not only what we do but who we are. When something goes wrong in the movement—someone disappoints us, a project fails, an office closes down, a new split occurs—we are crushed personally because our self-validation is totally dependent on the movement.

This is *not* to suggest that women cannot do movement work and have a clear sense of self-definition. We can and must. The danger is that too often we allow movement life to overpower us, especially when we first become involved. Movement work often can help us identify and develop interests and abilities better. But when the movement becomes a substitute for what a woman doesn't find in herself, eventually there will be a breakdown or a dead end and her work will no longer be useful even to that movement. For all its political and personal importance to each of us, the movement cannot suffice as our only source of identity, pride, and self-respect.

Building Identity Around Ideal Models

Sometimes we escape self-knowledge and development by trying to become different ideal types. We are controlled by these models or by thinking that we have to become the models in order to be accepted. Most feminist ideals embody good things that women can do or be, but they are destructive when they operate as the only acceptable standard. Then they function like the traditional ideals of beauty or motherhood, keeping women dissatisfied with ourselves and forcing us to look outside ourselves for standards of what to be.

Each discovery of oppression brings new ideals: as we learn about the suppression of women's intellect we want to be writers; as we learn about class we try to act like the "workers"; as we hear about matriarchies we must be spiritualists or artists. Each discovery has value and we learn about ourselves by trying new things. But if we do not know our own center, we can float from one newly discovered ideal to another every six months, depending on what is premium in our group.

Ideals or models can inspire and challenge us but often we do not know how to use them without being controlled by them. We create ideals because society has conditioned us to identify with external models rather than to develop our own selves. When we do think of "self-identity," we tend to romanticize it. We think that to have an identity, one must be something that sounds exotic (an artist), or well defined (a professional), or desired (a knockout at the bar). Because of the power of these ideals, women are often unable to see that a sense of self-worth grows out of what we do well and like, and not in trying to copy models.

Feminist ideals are determined by what's accepted in the movement instead of the male media. This is an improvement. But often we are still controlled by external images and group approval instead of by our own sense of self-worth and knowledge of what we can do well.

Building Identity Around Relationships

Traditionally, women have derived self-identity from relationships to others—family, husband, children, the women in our social or work circles. With women's liberation, this tendency has continued. Relationships, whether heterosexual or lesbian, non-sexual or sexual, are often the primary preoccupation of women's time and energy, at the expense of self-development and other political work.

Relationships are important. Relationships do affect us deeply. But a woman cannot find her own self solely through the creation of a lesbian affair or a communal family, just as she cannot through the traditional heterosexual marriage. Each woman must find her center alone as well as in relation to others. We must stop avoiding the reality of our aloneness.

Overconcentration on feelings and relationships often shields and diverts us from our self and the hard but crucial struggle to develop what we can do. Each woman needs a sense of self-worth based on what she knows that she can do and be. Relationships among self-defined women then can be the gaining and giving of positive energy, strength, and love. When relationships do not substitute for self and our strengths are used to build, not control, each other, then they can be positive ways of sharing, pushing, and expanding our lives, personally and politically.

Substitutes for self reflect part of the process of self-development if they are seen as parts, not the whole. We are significantly affected by the givens of our oppressions and privileges—by where we fall in the hierarchies of sex, class, race, and so on. So, too, we are partially determined by the movements that we build, by the ideal models that inspire us, and by the relations with others that we experience. But we are more than the total of all these. We are the particular things that we do and like and feel, our individual traits. We are the consciousness and attitudes that we develop toward these things and the ways that we change ourselves and the world because of that consciousness. And we are still more.

Each of us is a variety of selves that come together to form a center that is solid, yet ever changing. It is expressed in the way we live our lives—in what we do, say, think, dream, plan, love, and feel. In the end, women must explore and live this question daily. Our self-concept becomes stronger and clearer through our life activities—in the struggle for survival, in work for the movement, in efforts to express our own talents and love, and in actions that change the world as it affects us.

The question of self should not be approached as the archetypal romantic individual search, but as a question that moves to the heart of the problem of liberation for women. Confidence and strength in our own selves give us the ability to fight for change and to cope with the problems and instability that go with that struggle. Only those who are taking responsibility for their own selves can create the enormous changes that are necessary in this society. Only a movement that understands the different strengths of women and supports individuals' efforts to grow can succeed in challenging that society. The development of each woman's individual self and the political strengthening of the feminist movement should therefore be mutually reinforcing.

Women in different socioeconomic situations have developed different parts of the strengths that we all need as a movement. We must find ways to learn from each other and move on our collective power. To do this, we must stop being afraid of conflict with each other, stop feeling guilty about the givens of our birth, and stop trying to prove who is best. There will be conflict because women do still oppress one another and must continue to struggle over those oppressions. But as we develop our own strengths, we should be able to struggle more productively, to accept and learn from the strengths of other women.

As we learn from each other's strengths and weaknesses, we can get beyond talk and see how to utilize these in common efforts. We can find ways to provide less-privileged women with time, space, and money to pursue talents and work that is important to feminism. We can and must fight women's tendency to undermine each other's strength and to impose models of correct behavior. We seek an honest diversity, one that encourages individual difference and skills but still pushes for criticism and change. This diversity would not stop our efforts to create a common political vision but provide a broader basis for it.

We have taken important steps toward developing stronger self-concepts as women. Analysis of our mistakes and successes should guide us in what is a long struggle ahead. All of our efforts toward self-clarity and growth must be seen within a political context. We must be strong women who are politically tied to a group but not held down by it—who recognize the effects of oppression on us but do not depend on either oppressed or oppressor identities or behavior. We are moving on an uncharted path to create something new for women. But we can also build on the best of our past. We cannot expect to lose all negative traces of our previous lives. We *can* expect to keep moving forward and to change and examine our selves as we work to challenge and change the society.

CLASS AND FEMINISM

PART I: INTRODUCTION TO CLASS AND FEMINISM

(This section was written as an introduction to *Class and Feminism* [Baltimore: Diana Press, 1974], which I edited with Nancy Myron—a collection of articles drawn from *The Furies,* a lesbian feminist newspaper published in 1972 and '73.)

Understanding class behavior among women is a useful way to begin to understand class as a political mechanism for maintaining not only capitalism but also patriarchy and white supremacy. The development of feminist theory about class structures in society has barely begun. Since we first began this exploration in The Furies collective, we have learned more about class and women. We will mention here some points for further exploration.

Class distinctions are an outgrowth of male domination and as such, not only divide women along economic lines but also serve to destroy vestiges of women's previous matriarchal strength. For example, women in peasant agricultural, and lower-class cultures are often called "dominant" because they retain some of that matriarchal strength. Male-supremacist societies must try to eliminate this female strength. A primary means of doing this in the United States and in other countries is through the domination and promotion of middle-class values, including an image of the female as a passive, weak, frivolous sex object, and eager consumer. Thus, the class system not only puts some women in a position of power over others but also weakens us all. Analyzing how patriarchy, white supremacy, and capitalism reinforce one another is crucial to the future of feminism.

On a more immediate level, it is useful to look at how feminists have responded to the "class issue" in the past few years. At first, it "did not exist." Like most Americans, many feminists believed that we lived in a classless society, with equal opportunity for all hard-working people (or at least for all whites). As working- and lower-class women grew more conscious of being oppressed in the movement and raised the class issue, the myth was shattered. Today many feminists recognize that class exists, but there is still little understanding of its significance or what to do about it. This confusion exists for women of all classes. The following observations describe some of that confusion.

The lack of class understanding in different sectors of the women's movement has caused some lower- and working-class women to separate and form groups and alliances among themselves. Many positive things have come out of this. Working- and lower-class women have discovered that everything about growing up "economically deprived" is not bad because they have, in fact, developed many strengths in order to survive. These strengths went unnoticed by women in a verbal, middle-class movement. From being together, women have developed new approaches to their economic survival and have incorporated that into their survival as feminists. As a result, they have developed a more serious understanding of power—starting with their lives and applying that understanding to the systems that are in control around us.

As with any oppressed group, lower-class feminists have found it often difficult to separate out which parts of oppression are positive and beneficial, and which are negative and self-destructive. Similarly, there are a handful of class opportunists who use real oppression as a stepping stone for personal power or as a club for personal grudges. These women make it difficult for anyone to understand class issues, and they do so at the expense of other lower-class women. But while these are problems, greater class awareness and strength are still developing for many women.

Middle- and upper-class women have tended to respond to the

class issue in several limiting ways: "What, me-oppressive, I'm just a powerless woman"; downward mobility (voluntary poverty) and denial of class privilege; guilt and fear; romanticizing and patronizing the lower-class woman; and all too often retreat into confusion.

Recently, the primary reaction has been to retreat from the issue and label it divisive to the feminist movement. Class is indeed divisive to feminism. So, too, is race. So is lesbianism. Oppression on the basis of these differences does still prevent a real unity among women. However, they are not divisive because those on the short end of the stick begin to scream. They are divisive because more privileged women have not recognized how they and the movement are oppressive and have not taken effective action to eliminate or at least work against these oppressions.

Working-class women cannot be "blamed" for the divisions that are caused by their oppression. This is like radical men who said women who left "their movement" to organize and fight against our own oppression were divisive. In fact, blame is not the issue. No one is to blame for the class position into which she was born. The issue is what do we do with and about that position. The issue is how will we eliminate the cause of these divisions—classist behavior, power, and privilege—not how to shut up those who are bringing the problems out of the closet.

Some middle-class women object that certain feminists are class opportunists, using the issue for personal advantage. A few lower- and working-class women do this just as some feminists have been female opportunists. But so what? This in no way gets anyone off the hook. The issues of class are real and must be confronted no matter how someone else is using them. Class opportunists, as with all opportunists, will be stopped only when we concretely work out class divisions among women and have a base of experience from which to stop such opportunism. Nothing short of this hard work will mitigate class conflict within the women's movement.

Another middle-class cop-out on class issues has been to claim that as women we are powerless. We did not create the class system. True, women did not create class society, which is patriarchal to its core. However, upper- and middle-class women do get privileges from that system and do behave in ways that oppress other women. As long as women support and perpetuate class

96

divisions and privileges, we are responsible for that system, even though we did not start it. The only way women stop being responsible for class oppression is by fighting it.

The question for each upper- and middle-class woman is how to change class oppression in her life, in the movement, and in the society. Behavior and privileges can be examined to see which are destructive to other women and how to change those. Skills and privileges that are gained from class connections can be used to advance all women, not just oneself or women of your class. Each woman can teach what she has gained from her class position and in turn learn from other women those strengths that she has been denied by her class socialization. Finally, we must all work to break down the barriers of classism as well as racism and sexism. These barriers are symbols of the destructive hierarchy that male culture has created to make itself feel superior.

PART II: REVOLUTION BEGINS AT HOME

(This section is taken from an article by the same name written with Coletta Reid for *The Furies,* vol. 1, no. 4 [April 1972].)

Early in the women's liberation movement, I saw class as an issue that men in the Left used to put down feminism. Later it became an issue that many women said we had to discuss, but these discussions never went beyond wondering why welfare mothers weren't beating down our doors. Hours were spent feeling guilty. The verdict: women's liberation was middle class and that's bad, but we never understood why. We never examined how our behavior created and perpetuated that kind of movement. We never looked at how working-class women within our movement were oppressed.

When class became an issue in the development of a lesbian feminist movement in D.C., I was apprehensive. Theoretically, I knew that class divisions existed and ought to be abolished, but I did not connect that to my behavior or to what was happening to women in the movement. Of course, I did not imagine that I was a class supremacist. Only after months of struggle (or should I say, fights, hostility, withdrawal, trauma) did I begin to understand that much of my behavior stemmed from being middle class and was oppressive to working-class women.

I finally recognized that class in our society is not only an economic system that determines everyone's place, but also patterns of behavior that go with and reflect one's status. When middle-class women carry these attitudes and ways of behaving into the movement, it oppresses working-class women. Class divisions and behavior come from male-dominated society, and it is absurd for us to perpetuate them. If middle-class women remain tied to male class values and behavior, we cripple our growth and hinder the development of a movement that can free all women. Class struggle is not a question of guilt; it is a question of change, for our movement's survival.

Classist behavior is rooted in one basic idea: class supremacy—that individuals of the upper and middle classes are superior to those of the lower classes. Middle-class people are taught to think that we are better, and we act out that "superiority" and self-righteousness daily in a thousand ways. Class supremacy, male supremacy, white supremacy—it's all the same game. If you're on top of someone, the society tells you that you are better. It gives you access to its privileges and security, and it works both to keep you on top and to keep you thinking that you deserve to be there. It tells you over and over that the middle-class way is the right way and teaches you how to keep that way on top—to control people and situations for your benefit. No one in our movement would say that she believes that she is better than her working-class sisters, yet her behavior says it over and over again.

Class supremacy shows itself in the attitude that working-class women are less together, personally and politically, because they do not act and talk the way we do. Their politics may not be expressed in the same manner, their vocabulary may not be as "developed," and so they are seen as "less articulate" and treated as less important. Or they may be hostile and emotional so one can hardly trust their political judgment; after all, we've learned to keep ourselves in check, to be reasonable, to keep things in perspective. Looking down with scorn or pity at those whose emotions are not repressed or who can't rap out abstract theories in thirty seconds flat reeks of class arrogance and self-righteousness.

Other middle-class women pull the opposite number: emotionalism, hysteria, and tears when you're feeling bad and things don't go your way, or begging sympathy because it's just too hard to change. To a working-class woman this constant preoccupation with one's feelings and the difficulty of changing is a luxury she could never afford. She is tired of hearing how it's really hard for you to change because your mother was neurotic, while you go on oppressing her. She had to do many unpleasant things that middle-class women complain about, like working at exploitative jobs, just to survive. Endlessly analyzing and discussing your feelings is a way to keep control, which involves outtalking people and using feelings as excuses.

Sometimes a middle-class woman feels superior because she believes that she worked for what she has—that her skills, education, possessions, and position—come, not from her class privilege, but from hard work. I used to feel this way because I compared myself to the rich, not the poor; so, I thought that I did not have a lot to start with and had earned what I did have. By downplaying the role that privilege played in getting each of us to where we are now, we can keep on thinking that anyone can make it if they "try as hard as we did."

For example, I used to think that I had savings because of my good planning and frugality. Although I had saved a lot at a low salary, I did not recognize that my ability to save came from my privilege—that I had inherited economic security and actual possessions so I could afford to live cheaply. If you think that you are where you are just because you worked hard, it is easy to become self-righteous and make classist moral judgments about others.

Often, middle- and especially upper-middle-class women for whom things have come easily develop a privileged passivity. Someone with privilege can conveniently think that it's not necessary to fight or discipline herself to get anything. Everything will work out. Because she has made it by following nice middle-class rules of life, she doesn't like for people to be pushy, dogmatic, hostile, or intolerant. Material oppression doesn't bombard her daily, so she has the time to move slowly and may resist taking a hard political stand or alienating "anyone." She can afford to assume that most people are good and that it is unnecessary to fight or prove oneself to anyone.

Advocating downward mobility and putting down those who don't groove on it is another form of middle-class arrogance. Someone who has never had to worry about eating or being acceptable may leave a job easily without knowing where money will come from, embrace patched pants and brown rice and antimaterialism as good for the soul, and treat with disdain those who are hung up on material needs. She can usually also go back to her parents, college, or a good job when she tires of poverty. Once more, middle-class women set the standards of what is good (and even the proper style of downward mobility that often takes money to achieve) and act "more revolutionary than thou" toward those who are concerned about money and the future. Often these middle-class revolutionaries then live off of working-class women, who haven't discarded all their property (which some middle-class women carelessly destroy) or who keep their jobs because of the fear of real poverty. This sharing is done as "revolutionary communism," but since it ignores the different class realities of those involved, it is oppressive.

The "more revolutionary than thou" attitude is matched in arrogance by the paternalistic social-worker type who understands the "problems" of the working-class woman and wants to "help" her. Psychological paternalism occurs when one middle-class woman explains to another that "you have to understand Mary's background and why she is so hostile." What Mary needs is for other women to stand up and fight classist behavior with her, not to explain away why she is angry. Paternalism can take the form of benevolence prompting the middle-class woman to give out of personal graciousness, rather than from the recognition that she has class privileges that it is her responsibility to share. She usually retains control over the access to privilege and withdraws it when she disapproves or is threatened. Whatever form the behavior takes, it is condescending because it assumes class superiority instead of recognizing that as women raised in the middle class we have received some useful benefits (such as money, education, skills) that we can share. It is arrogant because it accepts society's idea that privilege makes you better when, in fact, being raised middle class has messed us up in ways that working-class women can help us understand and change.

There are a lot of small, indirect, and dishonest ways of behaving that are part of being raised in "polite society" where "being nice" is at a premium. One is being indirect about anger and disapproval in destructive ways: we bitch, harp, withdraw, make snide comments, gossip, pout, and so on. We make people feel our disapproval or anger but we do not say what is really on our minds.

Some of us try to smooth things over and prevent open conflict, which we fear. I did this because I took conflict and anger personally and assumed that if the other person liked me, she wouldn't get angry. It was hard for me to get over an angry scene, so I tried to avoid hostility. This behavior gives the illusion that things are okay, that you're still under control, but it is dishonest and destructive because it does not resolve problems and harms the person who is direct about her opinions and feelings.

These are only some of the forms of classist behavior that we have come to understand in our group. No one woman has all of these traits. On the surface many of these forms seem opposite or contradictory, but what is important is that they are all ways of maintaining the power of the middle class and perpetuating the feelings of inadequacy of the working class. We are not saying that all middle-class values and traits are inherently bad; many are helpful, and when disassociated from supremacist use can help us all. But if we are to use these and to develop nonclassist ways of behaving, we must examine the effects of our present behavior and how we resist changing.

The anger of working-class women toward middle-class women is justified by lifelong class oppression, and the class system will not be changed until *both* middle-class and working-class women see how oppressive it is and unite to change it. Working-class women want middle-class women to take up the struggle against classist behavior as their own, to stop resting on secure class positions. Middle-class women haven't had to make the fight against classism important because we got benefits from it. We were in the superior position. Working-class women want us to stop supporting the class system by accepting its values unquestioningly, to stop resting on our privileges and to start confronting and challenging class-oppressive behavior in ourselves and others. They do not want to be the only ones who fight against classist behavior. If they are, they might as well separate into their own movement.

Working-class women also want us to use and share middle-class privileges with them—the things and skills we have because we were born into the middle class. They want us to share money, property, access to jobs, education, and skills. Many middle-class women think that downward mobility makes them less classist. In fact, all it makes us is poorer and unable to share potentially large salaries with those who don't have the choice of voluntary poverty. Bringing down the male-supremacist system in this country will not be a possibility until we stop acting out our class-supremacist attitudes on the women with whom we're building a movement.

THE REFORM TOOL KIT

I n political discussions among feminists, the question of reform continually comes up. One "revolutionary veteran" states flatly: "What is there to do today that isn't reformist?" Another woman, who has worked on women's reforms for four years, declares that they are a dead-end and that she has to get out, to go beyond. There is a lot of concern, confusion, and rhetoric about reform and revolution, about our survival as women, and about our fears of cooptation. Often, however, it is hard to discern in these discussions what is really at stake, what is essential for feminists. Some women want to abandon the old terms of "reform" or "revolution." I welcome language that clarifies those questions. Until we create the new language, however, we must sort out the old language, see what the basic issues in the debate are, and determine how we can resolve them.

In this essay I begin with a discussion of terms, explore the history of both reform and radical wings of the women's movement, examine the relationship between reform and our long-term goals/strategies, present some criteria for evaluating which reforms are most useful, and discuss conditions necessary for feminists to work on reforms.

"The Reform Tool Kit" first appeared in *Quest: A Feminist Quarterly*, vol. I, no. 1 (Summer, 1974).

What is reform? What is reformism? What is revolutionary? Stereotypes for these words abound. Common stereotypes of what is reformist are white middle-class professionals and politicians working to get a bigger piece of the pie for themselves, organizations lobbying for new legislation, or university women creating a comfortable niche called "women's studies." Stereotypes of what is revolutionary tend toward one of two extremes: either bombing and violent takeover of the government or complete withdrawal from the system in order to create a totally separate feminist community.

When we probe these stereotypes, we find that they primarily reflect *style* (how one lives or the comparative virtues of lobbying vs. shooting) and *surface content* (how far out or different it sounds from the way things are now) rather than *substantive content* (how the activity affects different classes of women and what happens to the women working on it) or *ultimate goals* (where the action leads in the long run and how it will get us there). Style is not irrelevant to the processes of change, but it has become too important a factor in our attitudes toward reform. To get beyond these initial stereotypes, we must define reform and examine it in terms of substantive content and goals.

A reform is any proposed change that alters the conditions of life in a particular area, such as within the schools or throughout the legal system. It *re-forms,* or forms anew, the ways things are. It can alter them in a way that is helpful or destructive. A reform, simply put, is a change or a program for change. It can be a change that alters existing male-dominated institutions directly, such as Equal Rights Amendment legislation, or a change through the creation of women's alternative institutions, such as a record company or a health clinic. Reforms or proposed changes can be part of any group's program, whether conservative or revolutionary in ideology.

Reform*ism,* on the other hand, has come to mean a particular ideological position. That position is that women's liberation can be achieved by a series of changes that bring us equality within the existing social, economic, and political order of the United States. Reformism assumes that the interests of women are not in fundamental conflict with the American system and that therefore, through a progression of changes (reforms), it will grant us freedom through equality. By contrast, a radical analysis sees American society rooted in patriarchy, capitalism, and white supremacy and therefore in fundamental conflict with the interests of women; freedom for oppressed groups ultimately does not come through reforms or equality in those systems, but through a total restructuring of the ideology and institutions of the society. I will use this definition of reformism as an ideological position within the women's movement. It is crucial to separate the word "reform" —a change or strategy that might be used by women of varying politics, from "reformism"—a particular politics. The failure to make this separation has been a problem in the women's movement.

RADICALS AND REFORMS

"I thought getting a good job was immoral until I ran out of money," remarked one middle-class feminist as we discussed reforms, class, and feminist revolution.

Generalizations about the history of the women's movement are always controversial but the following observations are based on my experiences in the movements of the past ten years. In the middle and late 1960s, women's liberation grew from two different directions. The National Organization for Women (NOW) and similar groups were explicitly reformist; NOW stated that its purpose was "to bring women into full participation in the mainstream of American society."* Such organizations developed programs to bring about this equality.

Meanwhile, other small groups began meeting to discuss female oppression and define goals quite different from equality in the American mainstream. These groups, first called "women's liberation," sought a politics that questioned the whole structure of society. The groups were generally composed of socialists who focused on capitalism, or radical feminists who focused on patriarchy, and sometimes those who tried to combine these two approaches.

Over the past seven years, both the reformist and radical trends have developed and changed in many ways, altering and some-

*National Organization for Women, Statement of Purpose, Washington, D.C., 1966.

times confusing both their ideologies and their programs. NOW and some reformist groups were forced by the radicals' analysis, by women joining their groups, and by women leaving their groups to deal with more than just "equality." They were challenged to take up issues that originally had been avoided as too controversial, such as abortion and lesbianism.* They adopted some radical rhetoric (including the term women's liberation) and a broader program of reforms. But, generally, they continued to operate with an ideology of reformism, not challenging the premises of the society and only occasionally moving away from their initial goal of equality within the American mainstream. More conservative women's groups, such as the Business and Professional Women's Club, have worked for reforms that would explicitly bring privilege within existing systems to *some* women, usually white heterosexual middle-class professionals. Such reformist groups aim to get a few women integrated into higher echelons of society; groups such as NOW, because they are more diverse and sometimes responsive to radical ideas, are more ambivalent.

Meanwhile, those feminists who challenged the whole system, with visions of a very different society, splintered in many directions in search of an elusive political clarity. (I am using the term "radicals" for all those who have rejected a reformist ideology and who share a belief that more basic changes in society are necessary. Obviously, such groups as socialist feminists, radical feminists, lesbian feminists, or cultural feminists differ from each other and have divergent strategies, but they usually share the desire to go beyond reformism. Most of the following observations apply to all these groups in varying degrees.)

Radicals found ourselves caught up in an effort to develop a new kind of politics that could not be coopted by the system. This involved numerous struggles over ideological, organizational, and internal issues fundamental to the future of feminism: collectivity, leadership, lesbianism, class, power relationships, and so on. With few exceptions, however, these struggles did not lead to organizational or ideological coherence or to programs that involved large numbers of women.

One reason radicals have difficulty developing programs is our

---

*These issues were considered illegal or outlawed in 1968; NOW was primarily involved with job equality and legal issues at that time.

fear that reforms will coopt us or pacify too many women without overthrowing male supremacy. The American system coopts our visions by incorporating radical rhetoric while distorting the original meaning of the words and ideas; it coopts our leaders by offering token prestige, power, or money if we cooperate, and by isolating and destroying those who won't be bought. It coopts our people by adopting some reforms that improve our lives but leave intact, and often even improve, the structures of patriarchy, capitalism, and white supremacy. Some women also fear reform because it means involvement with power (seen as male) within the slimy institutions we want to destroy. They ask whether we can keep our souls and not be corrupted by such involvement.

Such fears of cooptation are justified, but sometimes they have resulted in the attempt by many to remain pure, to be uncorrupted by association with *any* reforms. For example, radicals who consider working on the ERA, in women's studies, or in women's trade unions can become immobilized by uncertainty about whether we can keep our politics and souls alive. As a result, we often neglect the creation of conditions that could make these actions more progressive, as well as keep us honest. Purism taken to its extreme leaves us immobilized and cynical; if we cannot achieve the final good now, then we feel we cannot do anything at all because it might be cooptable.

Radicals of various ideologies push the hard political questions and project visions of what we could do and what we could be. This process is a source of vital ideas and changes. But we have failed to create the tangible programs or organizations that could show women our potential for power or that could provide concrete steps for involvement in change. For example, some have accurately challenged the white middle-class bias of most women's reforms, but too often the alternative has not been a better program but no program at all. Our strength has been the willingness to raise basic questions, but it has also led to our weakness. Our questions often are so basic, such as those examining power relations in all parts of our lives, that we are unable to move far on them. Not knowing what to do with the immensity of what we question, we often become isolated, discouraged, and immobilized.

Enter Reformism. Where radicals have failed, reformists have flourished. Reformist groups and activities attract many women primarily because such groups are well organized and provide involvement in programs of action that can produce immediate results and tangible—though limited—successes. Women working on reformist programs often have a radical analysis of society but find few places to work concretely on that analysis. For example, a lesbian may be, ideologically, a lesbian feminist, but if she wants job security in order to "come out," she may well put her energy into the organization working on the reform that will guarantee that security, no matter what its overall ideology. Most radical groups fail to develop concrete reforms as a part of their program and direction, because they have not realized that such reforms need not be tied to a reformist ideology.

Other problems have grown out of our focus on internal change—the effort to make our lives and groups reflect the same changes that we advocate outside, such as collectivity, equality, and so forth. Again, this is important, but it cannot be achieved quickly or be separated from the struggle to change the structures of the whole society. The failure to transform ourselves and others more completely has left some women feeling defeated and cynical, or consumed by efforts to achieve that change. Similarly, many service and cultural activities, while providing concrete activity, have come to a dead end because they do not confront society directly and are not integrated into an overall ideology or program for liberating women.

Many women who call themselves radicals are asking, "What is the role of reform in our movement?" Simultaneously, women who work on reforms or in service projects are asking, "What is the political framework for the future that goes beyond reformism and can be used to evaluate our work?" From our different places, we can look anew at women's reforms and political ideology.

REFORM AND LONG-TERM GOALS

> Between social reforms and revolution there exists for the social democracy an indissoluble tie. The struggle for reforms is its means; the social revolution, its aim. . . . Formerly, the activity of the Social Democratic Party consisted of trade-union work, of agitation for social reforms and the democratization of existing political institutions. The difference is not in the what but in the how. At present, the trade-union struggle and parliamen-

tary practice are considered to be the means of guiding and educating the proletariat in preparation for the task of taking over power.

—Rosa Luxemburg

Those interested in fundamental social change or in revolution have long debated the role of reforms. As Rosa Luxemburg put it, the point is not the opposition of one to the other but the relationship between them. The primary issues are: What is our long-range goal? How does a specific reform aid or detract from that goal? How should the reform be carried out to advance our goal best? To state it another way, reform is not a solution but a strategy toward a larger goal.

In using these points to evaluate reforms in the women's movement, we must first ask, what is our goal? We want an end to the oppression of all women. What does that mean? What is our analysis of why and how women are oppressed? Women's oppression is rooted both in the structures of our society, which are patriarchal, and in the sons of patriarchy: capitalism and white supremacy. Patriarchy includes not only male rule but also heterosexual imperialism and sexism; patriarchy led to the development of white supremacy and capitalism. For me, the term patriarchy refers to all these forms of oppression and domination, all of which must be ended before all women will be free.

Stated positively, we need a new social order based on equitable distribution of resources and access to them in the future; upon equal justice and rights for all; and upon maximum freedom for each person to determine her own life. How will we bring about these changes? What is our long-term strategy? What kind of process does this involve? What types of power must women have to make these changes? *These* must be our questions.

The socialist tenet that the first phase of revolution required the taking of state power by the proletariat and the destruction of capitalism guided Luxemburg's discussion of reform. Following her framework, I will sketch initial goals and strategies for our discussion of reforms. In order to end patriarchy and create a new society, women must have power. We must have power in all spheres—political, economic, and cultural—as well as power over our own beings. Since we seek power as a means of transforming society, we must also transform power or find new ways of exercising power that do not duplicate the oppressions of today. We must discover how women can build our own strengths, create these new forms, prepare for, and gain such power. Since all this cannot be accomplished within American society as it now exists, my long-term goal is not the achievement of piecemeal reforms but a feminist revolutionary process that alters the entire social order. Reforms, therefore, are not an end in themselves but an important *means* toward reaching this larger goal. They must be evaluated in terms of it.

Some argue that a revolutionary women's goal is the end of power—to create a world not based on any power dynamics—and that association with male power will necessarily corrupt us. Perhaps, ultimately, we can dream of an end to power. But before we can accomplish that, women must first gain enough control over society today to end patriarchal domination and destruction of the world. In that process, we hope, we can change the nature of power, but we cannot avoid or ignore it.

Radicals often debate when people can be expected to act: when the situation is most unbearable (intense repression or economic depression) or when reforms are making things better and raising expectations. I would pose the question differently. Most people are willing to risk basic change when a movement (or party) has done three things: 1) raised their hopes by pointing to concrete visions of ways in which life could be better; 2) provided organization and strategy for how to achieve those visions; and 3) demonstrated that the existing system is not going to make those changes willingly. As we gain more power both through our visions and our institutions, we will encounter more opposition from the system. We can mobilize more people to fight with us at that time if they can see and believe in what we have done. I would never favor making the conditions of people's lives more difficult just to "raise consciousness." But if repression comes, then we must adapt our strategies to use it.

The crucial point here is not whether the government is liberal or repressive. What *is* crucial is that we are able to demonstrate that we can organize society anew in a way that is better for people and that we have a chance of winning in a battle with traditional forces. If women are to achieve political power, we must convince large numbers of people that we can do this.

Programs of reform, including the institutions that we build, are part of the means, the strategy, by which we demonstrate what we can do. The effect of those reforms depends not only on what is done but also upon how it is accomplished. The "how" includes questions about the ideology, structure, approach, and type of group carrying out a reform. This leads us to a discussion of the criteria to be used in evaluating specific reforms.

CRITERIA FOR EVALUATING REFORMS

We oppose the utopian position which argues against any change until the perfect solution is possible. On the other hand, we also are not for working on any and every reform action that presents itself. Our strategy allows us to define priorities and timetables to lend structure to issues in terms of particular situations.

—"Socialist Feminism:
A Strategy for the Women's Movement"

To say that radicals should reevaluate the importance of reforms does not mean that we should rush out and accept every women's reform as progressive. Criteria depend on goals and strategy. To say that we must evaluate reform in terms of goals and strategy does not mean that our analysis is complete and our direction is set. We begin with what we have. Those who differ with my questions and goals outlined above will differ some on criteria, but the following framework should still be useful.

The primary goal is women gaining power in order to eliminate patriarchy and create a more humane society. We must determine what is necessary in order for women to obtain power and use it for these purposes. We must also look at the class, race, and sexual preference base of that power, if we are to create real change and not just acquire power for a few privileged women. I have outlined five criteria for evaluating reform that correspond to these goals. The criteria often overlap and are ordered somewhat arbitrarily, according to process more than priority: 1) Does this reform materially improve the lives of women, and if so, which women, and how many? 2) Does it build an individual woman's self-respect, strength, and confidence? 3) Does it give women a sense of power, strength, and imagination as a group and help build structures for further change? 4) Does it educate women politically, enhancing their ability to criticize and challenge the system in the future? 5) Does it weaken patriarchal control of society's institutions and help women gain power over them?

1. *Does it materially improve the lives of women and if so, which women, and how many?* Reforms that alleviate immediate pain and economically improve our lives are important because they give us space to breathe, work, and plan; they make it possible for more women to act politically. This is particularly true where reforms center on daily problems like child care, job and housing discrimination, or sexual abuse. Many working-class women of all races have not supported women's actions because these did not directly improve their lives, or even appeared to worsen their situation. When we can show that our programs meet women's survival needs, not just advance the position of a few, then more women will join us.

All women are oppressed, but some have more privilege than others. Reforms that focus on enhancing the status of white heterosexual middle-class women with the most privilege often divide us further. To give an example, working to move women into oppressive executive positions supports the structures of patriarchy and exacerbates class differences among women. Reforms that aid the least privileged, that is, force distribution of resources to women at the "bottom," such as a decent income for welfare mothers, begin to close some of those gaps. Reforms that benefit a wide spectrum of women, such as the Equal Rights Amendment, also have potential for bringing women together. Women are all vulnerable, and each of us is only as secure as those women that society puts on the "bottom," not as powerful as the token top. Material reforms should aid as many women as possible and should particularly seek to redistribute income and status so that the class, race, and heterosexual privileges that divide women are eliminated.

2. *Does the reform build an individual woman's self-respect, strength, and confidence?* A movement is only as strong as the women in it. Self-respect is basic to the success of our own work, to respecting other women, and to believing in the power of women. Reform activities that help women find a sense of themselves apart from their oppressed functions and which are not

based on the false sense of race, class, or heterosexual superiority are important. This is not to encourage individualism or tokens who are personally liberated. It is to encourage women to see their strength and future tied to the liberation of all women.

Consciousness-raising, feminist counseling, and women's skills programs can help build self-respect; so too, successful work on reform activities can build self-confidence. But it is vital that these activities not be done in isolation from a political perspective. By helping women understand why we lack respect in this society and how the society will continue to destroy our confidence until we gain power as a group, these activities can build women's political as well as personal motivation.

3. *Does working for the reform give women a sense of power, strength, and imagination as a group and help build structures for further change?* Women need to win. We need to struggle for reforms that are attainable. We need to act where it is clear that the changes achieved are the results of our efforts—not a gift from the system—but victories won by our pressure, our organization, and our strength. The greater variety and larger numbers of women who benefit from this victory—and who participate in its accomplishment—the better.

To take one example, we need to make clear to people that changes in abortion laws were won by the combined efforts of many women, not given to us by the government. Still, we can't stop with any one reform. Changes in abortion laws, while important, did not bring us control over our bodies. That victory should be used to spur us on to fighting for more changes, such as an end to forced sterilization, and better health care for all. These specific reforms should also help us build structures and organizations that can work for more changes and use each separate reform to gain power. Victories and programs, especially when linked to specific organizations, give us a clearer sense of what we can win and illustrate the plans, imagination, and changes that women will bring as they gain power.

4. *Does the struggle for reform educate women politically, enhancing their ability to criticize and challenge the system in the future?* Working on reforms can teach us about our enemies and about the systems we oppose. Winning a reform, such as the right to enter "men only" accommodations, shows women that ending superficial signs of our oppression changes little. Even reforms

that fail, such as the efforts to ordain women in the Episcopal church, can reveal the limits of the system and raise the consciousness of those who once believed in reformism. I do not propose working on unattainable demands or superficial issues just to educate. Rather, when many women are interested in any issue, we can enhance its educational possibilities through political discussion. Since winning one reform is not our final goal, we should ask if working on that issue will teach us new and important things about ourselves and society. Particularly when a reform fails, political education is important to motivate women to continue, rather than to become cynical about change.

5. *Does the reform weaken patriarchal control of society's institutions and help women gain power over them?* As women, we want to improve the conditions of our daily lives. In order to do this, we must have power over the institutions—the family, schools, factories, and laws—that determine those conditions. One way to build power is through creating our own alternatives, such as health clinics that give us more control over our bodies or women's media that control our communication with the public. Alternative institutions should not be havens of retreat, but challenges that weaken male power over our lives.

Some reforms directly challenge the power of existing institutions, such as hospitals, welfare systems, and schools. In confrontations with such established powers, we seek to change what they do; but above all, we should demand that those most affected by each institution determine its nature and direction. Initially, these challenges and reforms help to undermine the power of patriarchy, capitalism, and white supremacy. Ultimately, these actions must lead to people's control of institutions so that we can determine how our society will function.

CONDITIONS FOR REFORM ACTIONS

Every reform will not necessarily advance all five criteria, but no reform that we undertake should be in opposition to these points. If we seek power for a feminist revolution, we must develop an overall program and organization that links these reforms together, that goes beyond them, and that builds women's power more coherently. Until that coherence is developed, the initial criteria help us evaluate our present activities and potential reforms. Once we are working on a reform, however, we need not only criteria but also conditions that will prevent its cooptation or dilution, that keep the reform consistent with our long-term goals, and that help us know when to move on. Otherwise any reform activity can become an end in itself.

In discussing conditions for working on reforms, it is helpful to summarize some of the problems and pitfalls of reforms. Unless we are determined to prevent it, reforms most often enhance the privilege of a few at the expense of the many. Unless good political education accompanies work on a reform, success can lead to the conclusion that the system works or failure can lead to cynicism about women's ability to bring about change. Reforms should be judged by how they actually affect women; some sound good in theory but work against women's material needs. For example, "no-fault divorce laws" sound like equality, but since male and female incomes are not equal and many women have worked for husbands for years, these laws cut off some women's badly needed and justified rights to alimony. If too much is staked on any one reform, as happened with getting the vote, we are cut off from other vital areas for change. Finally, if we do not make it clear that women made a reform happen, it can look like the result of a benevolent establishment. Therefore, we should maximize women's direct participation in bringing change, emphasize the power of our combined efforts, and avoid backroom styles that tend to obscure where ideas came from and who forced them into reality. Otherwise, devious politicians can take over our reforms in ways that disperse our momentum and pacify rather than politicize masses of women.

There are many types of reforms and ways to work on them— through women's reformist groups, inside male-dominated institutions, by building alternate institutions, through mass actions or coalitions. The conditions required to keep a perspective on the reform will vary in each. Let us take one situation as an example.

Sally Gearhart once described how a feminist might evaluate whether or not to work for reforms in the church. First, she outlined reasons to leave the church: it is totally patriarchal in attitude and structure; remaining may falsely inspire others to believe that it can be changed within itself and within the existing system; it can separate you from your sisters, especially if you move into a higher position that makes you more a part of the system; you and your support group waste lots of energy. She then outlined reasons why one might stay there: it is a job providing some economic stability for a woman; it can be a place to focus on the spiritual questions and needs of women; you can gain certain skills, contacts, and experiences and make similar resources available to other women; you can make room for and help politicize large numbers of women who are at present in the church, giving them a sense of their power and outlining possibilities for women to make change. Finally, she emphasized the minimum conditions that would be essential if you chose to stay: 1) a feminist community outside the church to whom you are accountable and which helps you to stay in touch with why you are working in the institution; 2) a feminist group for support and strategy inside the church with whom you work regularly to build something there; and 3) a clear personal sense of how necessary it is to risk and what the strategies and motives are and must be behind each risk.* Similar conditions could be described for women working in women's studies/universities, business, politics, law, trade unions, or any other established institution.

A radical who works on reforms within a women's reformist group faces similar questions. She must also work out the relationship between her own ideology and the dominant reformism of the group. She must define clear objectives for what she does and does not expect to change about the group and what she hopes to accomplish by working there. She would also need feminists who share her politics outside the group to provide ongoing support and criticism of her work.

Feminists in groups who share a common radical analysis may also work on reforms, either on their own or in coalition with other groups. In determining what to do, the group should consider the five criteria, the particular skills and interests of their group, and the needs and interests of their community. Ongoing criticism must be built into the group so that the reforms can be kept moving in a progressive direction and so that improvements can be made or a project ended if it is not serving its purpose. Feedback from feminists who share their goals but are not working on the same activities would also be useful.

*Sally Gearhart, "The Miracle of Lesbianism," in *Loving Women/Loving Men*, ed. by Sally Gearhart and William R. Johnson (San Francisco: Glide Publications, 1974).

Most feminists are, or will be, involved in various reform activities, no matter what their ideology. The questions we face are "Which ones?" "How?" and "With whom?" Since I believe that women must work toward gaining power to end patriarchy, capitalism, and white supremacy, and to create a new society, I have outlined criteria and conditions for determining which reforms to work on and how to approach them that correspond to that goal. The next evaluations of reform will come out of our ongoing experiences as feminists.

ERA DEBATE:
A TENDENCY TO BLAME THE VICTIMS

N ote: *This essay was written in response to a column by Mary Russell in the opinion section of the* Washington Post *("Outlook") that suggested that the women's movement was losing the ERA because of its support for abortion and gay rights. This debate took place in 1978 while supporters of the ERA were campaigning for a congressional extension of the deadline for state ratification of the Equal Rights Amendment. Following an intense lobbying campaign and an ERA March on Washington in July 1978 attended by over a hundred thousand people, a three-year extension of the deadline was approved by Congress. However, by the end of the extension on June 30, 1982, the ERA was still three states short of the three-quarters needed for ratification and hence was defeated.*

Mary Russell ("Losing ERA Extension Might Help Feminists," the *Washington Post,* "Outlook," July 16, 1978) would have us believe that, to win, women must first fail. She suggests that feminists fighting at this critical moment to gain the ERA through an extension of the deadline should instead be turning

"ERA Debate: A Tendency to Blame the Victims" was published in the *Washington Post,* "Outlook," August 5, 1978.

inward to assess "what went wrong" with the women's movement.

That attitude would not be given credence if she were analyzing any group other than women. It is hard to imagine a serious suggestion that labor needed to abandon its struggle for labor-law reform, before it was defeated, to make "a new beginning." Yet, that is precisely what Russell suggests that women do. Her approach reflects a dangerous trend in the ERA debate: the tendency to blame the victims, women, for their predicament. It is rather like blaming the woman who is raped, rather than the rapist.

What is going wrong with the ERA is not the women's movement. What is wrong is that a very small number of state legislators are blocking a reform that the majority of Americans favor: a reform that was approved by Congress overwhelmingly; a reform that has passed in thirty-five states representing 72 percent of the population; a reform that has been endorsed by both the Republican and the Democratic parties; a reform that has been supported by a majority of women and men in polls since 1972. What is going wrong is not the women's movement but the democratic workings of our political system.

What we need now is a reassessment of our nation's political system and why the will of the majority is being thwarted on the ERA. In doing that reassessment, the women's movement has lea¬ned a lot. We have learned, as Ellie Smeal, president of the National Organization for Women, reported to Russell, that the ERA is "a political issue, not an undeniable human right"; that because the ERA is just and favored by a majority does not mean that it will happen. We have learned, as Elinor Langer detailed in *Ms.* magazine in 1976, why Big Business is putting money into efforts to defeat the ERA. We have learned, as illustrated by the boycott of unratified states and the extension—both of which Russell belittles—how to use tough economic and political tactics to keep the issue alive nationally.

Finally, we have learned that the battle to stop ERA is part of an overall conservative effort to gain more power in society; that those forces who oppose the ERA are by and large the same ones who oppose affirmative action for minorities and women, gay rights, labor-law reform, reproductive freedom, the Panama Canal treaties, and so on.

It is not, as Russell asserts, the taint of gay rights or reproductive freedom that is preventing the ratification of the ERA. It is the organized opposition of a right-wing minority that would still combat the ERA if lesbians disappeared and all women agreed never to have an abortion. While distortions of those issues (along with a host of other diversions) are being used by the opposition, they are just that—diversions—because the ERA does not, in fact, affect those issues. Rather than play into this tactic, the women's movement should expose the politicians who have used these issues as excuses for not supporting the ERA, when, in fact they are not willing to stand up to right-wing, business, and other special-interest groups or they are not in favor of women's equality in the first place. Either way, they are not our allies and should be defeated.

Every group sets priorities of what will get the most attention and money at a given time. However, a distinction must be drawn between setting priorities and repudiating other matters of concern. No movement based on the principles of equality, justice, and freedom gains by discarding those principles internally or in its public stance. Human rights are indivisible. For feminists to divide them out—asking for some while disavowing others—would be a contradiction so great that the very basis of the movement would be destroyed.

Feminist support of gay rights is a human-rights ideal as well as a defense of an allied movement under attack from the same forces that beset the ERA. But gay rights is also crucial to the philosophy and success of feminism because of the role that homophobia has played in keeping women in their place. All women, no matter what their sexual preference, are restrained in many areas of life by the threat of being called "lesbian" and of facing the economic and social consequences that go with that label. When women can give unflinching support to gay rights, that form of control over women's behavior will dissipate. Lesbian-baiting will never end just because feminists deny a connection between the issues; it will only end when women deny it the power to threaten them.

Reproductive freedom is also central to the philosophy and success of feminism because it is based on the fundamental assertion of woman's right to control her body. Russell apparently fails to realize that this does not mean that the movement is pro- or anti-abortion, but rather it is pro-choice—a position that is also supported by a majority of Americans. Many feminists do not personally favor abortion; this does not make them "second-class members of the movement" because that is not the issue.

The issue is one of choice. Feminists do not demand that every woman prefer abortion, or be a mother, or be a lesbian, or put her children in day care, or keep them at home, or go outside the home to work. Feminists demand only—simply and profoundly—that every woman have the right to choose whether or not to do those things. That all women and men should have the greatest number of options possible, not the imposition of any one standard, is the heart of the feminist vision and gives the movement its strength.

Russell reveals her limited perception of the movement when she implies that those working for gay rights and reproductive freedom are ignoring the issues of "better birth-control alternatives, better day care, and economic protection and justice." Nothing could be further from the truth. Across the nation, the women who are fighting for ERA, reproductive freedom, and gay rights are the same ones who have been agitating for birth control, day care, and economic justice for years. It is not the women's movement that is leaving these issues unanswered. It is the institutions in our society that are still resistant to women's equality that are leaving women's needs unanswered.

The women's movement today is leading the challenge to society to meet human needs and to live up to its democratic ideals. In that challenge, priorities are established and a variety of political strategies devised. But if we abandon the breadth of the feminist vision with its concrete concern for all women's needs and rights—indeed, for all human rights—then we abandon the source of our strength and the hope of our leadership for a better future.

WOMAN POWER AND THE LEADERSHIP CRISIS

There is great ambivalence in the United States toward leadership. On the one hand, we have the constitutional notion of checks and balances—of limiting the power of leaders; yet our society thrives on personalities, cultivates and fawns over leaders, and chronicles our disillusionment with current ones, while still yearning for the next "charismatic" leader.

The women's movement in this country, for all its criticism of the dominant culture, reflects a similar desire to have it both ways. No issue has caused more pain and confusion among feminists than leadership. Our experience is complicated by society's inability to honor or even acknowledge leadership from women, as well as by our own desire to create new styles of leadership that are not male-defined or hierarchical. But despite our ambivalence and confusion, thousands of women have performed leadership functions over the past fifteen years, both within the movement and in society, whether consciously or not. Feminist theory and experience of leadership has varied in different sectors of the movement. The current wave of the U.S. women's movement grew out of two

This essay was originally published as "Woman Power" in *Ms.* magazine, July 1980. Background research was done by *Ms.* contributing editor Lindsy Van Gelder, who interviewed sixteen feminist leaders in various parts of the movement.

developments in the 1960s. The first was the reawakening of a women's rights struggle centered around the demand for full integration of women into the mainstream, and symbolized by the formation of commissions on the status of women and the founding of the National Organization for Women (NOW) in the mid-'60s. By contrast, the women's liberation movement strand emerged from the radical political movements of the '60s and was oriented toward revolution in both the form and content of the mainstream and focused on exposing the patriarchal basis of society primarily through small group actions, demonstrations, and consciousness-raising. What distinguished these sectors as much as their politics was their style and attitude toward leadership.

Reacting to the power concentrations and star systems of male-dominated groups, the women's liberation sector was opposed to hierarchy and in favor of collectives, which were seen as a means of eliminating "stars," sharing power, and fostering in every woman the responsibility to develop her own capabilities. In practice, this usually meant being anti-leadership. However, as the movement grew, this anti-leadership bias often hampered the growth of women by burying female talents within group anonymity, and reinforcing stereotypes of women's weakness.

The women's rights sector of the movement objected to society's disregard for female leadership, but generally accepted mainstream institutions, including traditional hierarchies and organizational models based on elected leaders. These groups had visible leaders who could be recognized as such by the society and they had a defined procedure for determining who their leaders would be. But many women in leadership roles within the organization's ranks suffered oblivion, and credit for their work often went to the most public figure. This common feature of traditional organizations was among the things that the women's liberation sector sought to avoid and its critique spread to women's rights organizations as well. Hence leaders there were often caught in the double bind of operating in hierarchical organizations, yet being judged by feminist views of process whose forms were only appropriate to small nontraditional groups.

The media's portrayal of feminism and its leaders caused some resentment and confusion. Initially, most of the establishment press viewed all feminists as crazies. But as the movement grew, the media began to single out certain women as acceptable spokespersons for causes that received legislative legitimacy and widespread public attention. Though still frequently caricatured, these "safe" leaders were most often white, middle-class, straight women who were portrayed as only wanting to learn how to play like the boys in order to get their share of the existing pie. Those "women's libbers" who didn't fit this image continued to be ridiculed as bra-burners, irrational bitches, Communist dupes, and so on. In response to such distortion and ridicule, some women adopted policies of not talking to the media at all or excluding men from their press conferences, which in turn reinforced the media's tendency to disregard the women's liberation sector as serious. Ironically, as the movement grew in complexity, many of the initially acceptable "front" women developed a more radical analysis of patriarchy. Reporters and editors were at a loss when leaders portrayed as "safe" went "crazy"; and even worse, when feminist activism began to emerge among women within their own domain.

Women's liberationists who believed in the anti-leadership policy and avoided individual media coverage felt their efforts were undermined by those who attracted media notice. They in turn often attacked media stars for "selling out." But this was only the most visible form of "trashing" (a type of verbal attack that includes both personal and political criticism) of women who were highly visible or who exerted movement leadership. Often, trashing was a result of personal grudges, suppressed power struggles, or competition, and stemmed more from group frustration than from political differences. It was damaging to the group as well as to the individual trashed. It aimed at bringing an individual down rather than changing her behavior, or developing a means of constructive criticism, or finding solutions to problems.

Trashing of local leaders, especially when it was extended to those who were not particularly visible in the media, highlighted one of the major contradictions in the anti-leadership approach: collectivity had *not* meant that there were no leaders, but rather that leadership had to be hidden. Women continued to perform various leadership functions necessary to get things done or written, to organize demonstrations or recruit movement workers. But when leaders could not function openly, the movement could neither support them nor hold them accountable. Hidden or informal leadership frequently required hidden manipulation that other group members resented; and the leaders whose capacity to lead was hampered and even condemned, often grew frustrated or dropped out.

Jo Freeman analyzed the dangers of informal elites in an early influential article, "The Tyranny of Structurelessness" (first printed in 1972 in *Ain't I a Woman?* and excerpted in *Ms.,* July 1973). She analyzed the contradictions:

> When informal elites are combined with a myth of "structurelessness," there can be no attempt to put limits on the use of power. It becomes capricious. This has two potentially negative consequences. . . . The first is that the informal structure of decision making will be much like a sorority—one in which people listen to others because they like them and not because they say significant things. . . . The second is that informal structures have no obligation to be responsible to the group at large. Their power was not given to them; it cannot be taken away.

The original goal of leaderless groups was to increase everyone's participation. But since there was often little structure to make this happen, a certain homogeneity was required in order to reach consensus, so groups often depended on informal friendship networks to make decisions. This tended to lessen the active involvement of women who did not fit the norms of a group—whether because of race, class, sexual preference, age, motherhood status, or job. Even policies such as rotating project responsibilities or drawing lots to speak, which might encourage some women to participate, could become means of excluding women or stopping those who sought to develop skills that would distinguish them from the group. For example, a newspaper collective's decision to rotate responsibility for designing the graphics might intimidate some women with no confidence or interests in this area; it might prevent others from expanding these skills by forcing them to rotate off that job just as they were beginning to excel in it.

As Caroline Sparks, a founder of the Women's Action Collective in Columbus, Ohio, noted: "The movement doesn't know what to do with its veterans. We've spent a lot of time learning how to pass skills on to new people. But the problem is letting women get even more skilled and allowing them to fly with their capabilities. Sometimes we still can't handle strong, skilled women."

Perhaps the greatest contradiction resulting from the anti-leadership ideology was this: since women's liberation had not acknowledged its own leaders, the media could choose whomever they wanted to empower as movement spokeswomen. These media portrayals of feminist leaders were part of an effort to contain and control the movement. Television and press interviews focused on women in the most publicized areas, so that politicians, writers, and performers became better known than most organizational leaders, and much better known than grass-roots activists. Yet whether organizing a lesbian mothers' group, a women's caucus in the Modern Language Association, or a clerical workers' union, such activists have been the backbone of the movement.

Unfortunately, even feminists have often been more supportive of female public officials or cultural figures who did not come primarily out of the movement—such as politician Carol Bellamy or comedian Lily Tomlin—than of organizational leaders in their own midst. Thus the general public and many feminists remain unaware of women such as Jean Crosby, who founded and sustained San Francisco women's centers, or Joanne Parrent, who organized the first feminist credit union in the nation, or Linda Fowler, in Denver, who helped organize the largest state conference of lesbians in the country, and hundreds more like them.

POWER, FAME, AND LEADERSHIP

Though it sometimes worked to the disadvantage of deserving women, the anti-leadership attitude in the movement was reacting understandably to the traditional definition of leadership as power or domination over others, often based on class, race, and sex privilege. However, while women generally have a stronger sense of the potential oppressiveness of power because we are so often its victims, this does not mean that when in positions of power, we automatically lead in nonoppressive ways. To do so, we must develop models that redefine power and its relationship to leading.

James MacGregor Burns, author of the Pulitzer prize–winning study, *Leadership* (New York: Harper & Row, 1978), makes this distinction:

Leadership has a moral dimension that power does not have. Power is manipulative. It is the exploitation of other people's motives in order to realize the power holder's objectives. . . . The leader engages with or relates to the genuine wants, needs, and aspirations of his [sic] followers rather than manipulating them for his own ends.

Feminists need to go even further. As we develop new modes of leading, we must also confront and change the world of traditional power defined as domination over others. Moreover, writes Nancy Hartsock, a political theorist, in a *Quest* article:

We must constantly ask: To what extent must we build organizations which mirror the institutions that we are trying to destroy? Can organizations based on power [defined] as energy and initiative be effective tools for changing sexist, heterosexist, racist, and classist institutions such as the media, the health industry, etc.? To what extent will both we and our organizations be transformed by the struggle for power (domination)?

The challenge is further complicated by our society's obsession with famous personalities, which generates the feeling that to be publicly recognized is to be superior. If we understand leadership as only one of many skills necessary to a movement, then it need not imply superiority, and we can value and encourage it as we would other skills. Nevertheless, since women have been undervalued and feminists have not developed adequate means of acknowledging each other's contributions, we are vulnerable to these notions of superiority and to the effects of fame, and sometimes money.

Public recognition in the United States is both attractive and onerous. Though Karen De Crow, former president of the National Organization for Women, thinks public life does expand one's horizons, she also notes certain constraints: "I feel self-censoring. I am a spokeswoman for the movement whether I want to be or not." But fame does bring public recognition and concrete rewards that can divide women.

Distinctions must also be made between stardom and leadership. Feminists may become famous for any number of reasons that might make them role models—in sports, literature, or thea-

127

ter, for instance—but this does not necessarily make them leaders. Similarly, fame can accompany leadership, but is not integral to it: what makes someone a leader is the functions she performs and her ability to move others to action, not her public visibility.

But women often have difficulties with success, our own or that of other women. Since leaders are often perceived to be successful or strong, they can seem threatening to women who do not have a sense of their own strength and who already have their hands full coping with the male power and success in their environment. The movement's anti-leadership impulse can reinforce the traditional female experience of being rewarded for failure and penalized for success.

Some of the resentment felt toward famous feminists is based on the money they are believed to be making from feminism. In fact, the overwhelming majority of feminists—famous or otherwise—have not only made little from their lectures, organizing, writing, or art, but have plowed their own resources into the movement. This raises another difficult issue: as long as the movement is primarily dependent on the voluntary giving of time and energy from its participants, its leadership will be limited primarily to those with outside income (distinctions usually based on class or heterosexual privilege) who can afford to work for women's issues without pay, or to those who have the few paying jobs that are movement-related, such as women's studies teachers, staff of women's organizations, feminist editors, filmmakers, and entrepreneurs.

To prevent the fame issue from being destructive, we need to create better ways of acknowledging and encouraging the contributions of all movement participants. We may not be able entirely to eliminate media manipulation of who's a famous feminist, but we can counter its effectiveness by naming our own leaders, and by strengthening every woman's sense of her own value.

Though it has sometimes seemed that feminist alternatives are limited to trying to eliminate all power or advocating that women should have the dominant power to control society, a third possibility exists: a number of feminists have begun to develop a new understanding of power—seen as the ability to act, to get something done—and to see power associated with energy, strength, and effective interaction, rather than with manipulation, domination, and control. This feminist model for leadership can focus on empowering others to act rather than on controlling them, and power thus becomes a vital force rather than something to fear. Operating out of such an understanding of power and leadership, and inspired as a child by a local black YWCA director, Sara-Alyce Wright, executive director of the YWCA, says, "A leader is someone who doesn't throw you in the water and tell you to sink or swim, but who has her hands underneath you in the water if you need it."

THE FUNCTIONS OF LEADERSHIP

In order for feminists to succeed in our goals, it's important for us to focus on the functions of leadership separate from the individual leaders. There are three primary areas in which these functions are exercised: movement-building, which involves maintaining and enlarging movement organizations and projects; extending feminist insights and perspectives to individuals who are not yet movement-identified; and working within traditional, existing institutions in order to transform their structures and priorities from within. Because the three areas overlap, feminist efforts in each are most successful when coordinated. Realistically, however, we know that the specific demands and functions required of leaders in each area vary.

Take, for example, feminist performers. For someone like singer and songwriter Holly Near, who sees herself primarily as a leader in the creation of women's culture as part of movement-building, her politics affect her decisions not only about *what* she sings, but also about *where* and *how* she sings. Near tries to get simultaneous translation for the deaf, sliding-scale ticket prices, songs in Spanish, child care, all-women production crews, and holds concerts for women-only, as well as mixed, audiences. Her audience is consequently limited: "I'll probably sing to a million people in my lifetime," she says. "I could do that in one night on 'The Mike Douglas Show,' but I'd have to sacrifice other things that are important to me."

Another feminist performer who seeks to reach as many people as possible as soon as possible might make different decisions. She should not be criticized for that choice, but she should be expected to share her access to the public and to promote those less visible performers who have opted for movement-building. A performer whose priority is women's culture is less likely to receive recognition from the popular culture. If feminists do not give particular support to those whose priority is movement-building, that task will be neglected and its leaders will necessarily turn to other areas in order to survive.

Edie Van Horn, speaking of her position in the Community Action Program of the United Auto Workers, illustrates one aspect of leadership within institutions: "It's limiting to work in such a huge organization because you have to struggle so hard to move two inches. But when you're moving 1.5 million people even two inches, it has a huge national impact."

Feminist leadership in existing institutions is crucial, but it is not the same as leadership within the movement; and its effectiveness often depends on the strength of feminist pressure and leadership outside. For example, Arlie Scott, former NOW Action vice-president and executive director of the Women's Action Alliance, observes the relationship between the roles of feminist leaders and congresswomen: "The Women's Movement is a political force that creates the conditions and pressures necessary for social change to occur. Its leaders must therefore be movement advocates who make women's issues their total priority. The congresswoman's role is responding to that outside pressure and implementing changes legislatively."

When a feminist in government initiates women's programs, she is usually responsible to other constituencies as well. Therefore, constant pressure on government from groups and leaders on the outside is necessary to push the institutions toward feminist goals, as well as to strengthen the hand of women in that arena.

Feminists working in different areas may have conflicts, but the more each of their particular functions is understood by the others, the more they can cooperate. Catharine Stimpson, women's studies professor and founder of *Signs,* talks about the isolation from the rest of the movement felt by many academic feminists: "I'd really like feminists to draw up an agenda and say, 'Here is what we need to learn from women's studies.' For example, on abortion rights, it could be very productive if the activist people connected up with the academic people who have a more systematic knowledge of group psychology."

Within all three areas, leaders perform political, spiritual, and intellectual functions as well as managerial and group-maintenance tasks. These range from providing vision and strategies for change, to mobilizing a constituency, to facilitating group decisions or creating coalitions. But in all areas, when feminists understand the functions and role that a leader can and cannot perform, we can support her more effectively, evaluate and influence what she does, and realistically hold her accountable to those tasks.

LEADERSHIP STYLES

The most intangible factors of leadership are style and timing. While style is difficult to define, it is affected by racial, ethnic, religious, geographic, and class factors; age and experience; female and family socialization; sexual orientation and self-concept; physical characteristics; and personality. Diversity of style brings richness to feminist leadership. Style may become a problem when it interferes with a woman's ability to function or her willingness to appreciate someone else's contribution. For example, a white, urban group used to operating on middle-class modes of restraint may reject the leadership skills of a rural Chicana worker because its members fear the directness of her style. Or a group of fast-talking activists may never hear the insights of the quieter, more reflective leaders in their midst.

Timing is a very capricious aspect of leadership. One can never "plan" or "manage" every opportunity, and simply being in the "right place at the right time" may be decisive in determining who assumes which leadership functions. One woman becomes famous overnight because she happens to be where a major event occurs and she has the skills to fill the leadership vacuum. A certain image or occupation may be right at one moment and not another. For example, Sonia Johnson, a Mormon who was excommunicated for her support of the ERA, emerged as an ERA spokesperson at a time when religious leadership was especially important in that struggle.

Feminists have found that when we recognize and appreciate our leaders, it is easier for them to teach their skills and extend their power to others. Whether formalized through movement training sessions or taught on the job, sharing leadership skills is necessary to expand the power base of all women, to spread the burdens, and to promote and proliferate new constellations of women activists.

131

When the leadership base is broadened, we are more likely to overcome resistance to leadership, to keep it organically connected to the rank and file, and to prevent its abuse. Developing methods whereby women receive credit for their work is vital to such expansion. For example, some feminist writers mention editors and other individuals who have contributed significantly to their work, even giving credit to ideas gleaned in conversation. Or the president of an organization, recognizing that she is in the public limelight, can acknowledge at public events the women who have worked with her. Gloria Steinem suggests a policy of speaking together with a lesser-known feminist whenever possible so that the public becomes aware of new voices and ideas. Leaders can also share access to money, jobs, training, the media, and other resources crucial to developing each woman's skills.

Feminists have experimented with a variety of leadership approaches in an effort to find ways to share power and responsibility—to empower others rather than to control them, and to spread recognition and public access to the many instead of the few. As Jackie St. Joan, an activist, mother, and lawyer, wrote in the "Leadership" issue of *Quest:*

> A feminist leader, like a mother, must empower her constituents by listening to them and by teaching them what she knows about getting things done. . . . Good leaders do not break our spirits or leave us feeling like losers. Leaders, like mothers, should provide the conditions by which women can be free to make choices—disclosures of facts, goals, process.

Shared leadership and horizontal rather than vertical leadership structures are common forms of feminist experimentation. The founders of *Quest* devised a practical model of horizontal leadership in which each person took responsibility for work within a given area of producing the journal. One woman did bookstore distribution, for example, and she made most of the decisions within that area and performed both its creative and mundane tasks. The entire staff gave overall direction and maintained final decision-making power. Some individuals performed more leadership functions than others, especially those responsible for coordinating the various tasks, but ultimate responsibility was never on one person alone, but on each member of the group.

Shared leadership does *not* mean structurelessness, a misconception on which many early women's liberation groups foundered. On the contrary, it requires a clear delineation of tasks, with a broad set of responsibilities for each participant and a willingness to spread the decision-making power by making it more visible. Structures and clarity about tasks allow individuals to demonstrate their trustworthiness and reliability—two critical traits for sustained leadership. Such clarity also enables feminists to determine which leadership functions each individual can assume, and to see that leaders receive constructive criticism and do not "burn out" from lack of support.

Aileen Hernandez, former president of NOW and founder of Black Women Organized for Action, after years of parliamentary jockeying in various organizations, came to the simple conclusion that "power should go to those who are willing to do the most *work.*" The idea that recognition and "power" should correspond to work done has led some groups to develop formulas for decision making that are based on the work hours put in and responsibilities assumed.

There is no set formula for leadership in the women's movement. But we do have an emerging perspective on new approaches that are effective and that move away from oppressive forms. And we do have many leaders, like those quoted here, who have continued struggling with feminist approaches despite residues of female resistance and growing male hostility to strong able women. The final testament to the importance of feminist experience with leadership lies not in our theories, but in the lives and actions of the women who have effectively led the movement.

As Sally Gearheart, a feminist spirituality teacher and writer, recalled, "For me, the moment of truth came when my morale was so hurt that I decided to resign from the movement. Then it occurred to me that I didn't know whom to resign to. . . . We are a community. What we are articulating isn't just our 'politics'— it's our lives."

FACING DOWN THE RIGHT

I n the future, I think that people will look back on 1980 as a turning point in the United States. But I hope that it will be seen not only as a turning point for the New Right, but also as a turning point for how feminists got organized and made the transition from consciousness-raising and public statements of our oppression to more organized political struggle. Every movement has cycles. The first years of feminism in this wave were centered on consciousness-raising, on identifying who we were and what were women's concerns, and on political actions that brought attention to these. In the next decade we must focus more on political power struggles with the patriarchy. Consciousness-raising was necessary to get us to this point; now we must organize for the rest of the century.

As a movement, we are moving into a period of different kinds of political activity. I never want repression such as that represented by the victory of the right wing in the 1980 election to happen. But when it does, political organizers should use it to help educate people about the nature of power in this country. That's

This is an abridged version of the first pamphlet in the Bunch series on "Feminism in the 80's," which was based on a speech given in Colorado in November 1980 and published by Antelope Publications (Denver, Co.) in 1981.

134

the opportunity we have now. For example, if anybody thought women had gained significant power in Washington, they now know we haven't yet.

There has been a lot of bad news in 1980. Most of it is pretty obvious: Reagan and the new Congress. Their latest suggestion is to repeal the 1965 Voting Rights Act, which enabled many blacks to vote for the first time. Another proposal from Reagan advisers is that no city that has rent control should receive federal funds. One of the antiwoman proposals is for a constitutional amendment removing women's constitutional right to an abortion. Several events illustrated this reactionary mood: The Ku Klux Klansmen who murdered civil rights demonstrators in Greensboro, N.C., were acquitted. Two gay men were killed in Greenwich Village and six more were injured by a "lone gunman" who said that he hated homosexuals because they mess everything up. The trend is also global. Last month, policemen in India were released even though they raped a sixteen-year-old woman when she was in jail. The Indian Supreme Court ruled that sexual assault while in police custody did not constitute rape.

Many in this country have not recognized that the reactionary trend has been developing for some years. In some countries it's been coming a lot faster than it has here. For instance, the victory of a U.S.-backed antisocialist party in Jamaica demonstrated that the International Monetary Fund can strongly affect who will govern in many Third World countries because of the ways in which it can manipulate the economies of those countries. Reagan's victory was one more step in a process that's seen many countries get more reactionary governments over the past decade, such as Britain, Sweden, Argentina, Chile, and Australia. If you look at the governments in the world in 1980 compared with those in the early '70s, you see that a rightward political shift has taken place.

In the midst of the global bad news, there is also good news—for what's going on underneath the surface is a global feminist movement. Don't let anybody tell you that feminism doesn't mean anything in the Third World. Don't let anybody tell you that the women's movement has died. Let me give examples of things I know about because of attending the NGO (Nongovernmental) Forum in Copenhagen in 1980, which was held in conjunction with the UN Mid-Decade Conference on Women. For example, women in Latin America organized their first continentwide women's conference to be held in 1981. Women in Africa introduced into the United Nations a resolution against genital mutilation, and organized a network around the issue. Feminists in the Soviet Union risked their lives to speak out against patriarchy-as-patriarchy whether under socialism or capitalism.

In Mexico City, over 1,500 gays marched last spring, and there's an open Lambda organization with a woman as the staffperson. In Copenhagen, she helped to dispel the myth that there are no Third World lesbians. Three years ago, the International Gay Association had something like eighty-five men and three women at its organizing conference, while last year a caucus of eighty-five women demanded their own secretariat within the association and are now organizing a worldwide lesbian conference.

There is good news in this country as well. Women at the Democratic party convention stood up to the party bosses and demanded strong prochoice and ERA statements in the platform, and we got a gay rights plank at that convention. It is good news that eight hundred lesbians are here in Colorado taking your power and forming a state organization. Feminists all over the country are forming groups and statewide agenda coalitions. This is the year that women must get the movement back in motion. We are expanding our consciousness as a global force and getting onto the streets as well as into the statehouses, and understanding that we have to be in all of these places at once.

One of my concerns about what is happening in 1980 is the fear generated in many places. Perhaps our first task in combating the Right is to fight the fear that is developing among our own people. Fear can make victories happen for them that they will not be able to achieve otherwise. If we become afraid to act, then that fear itself becomes reality, and right-wing successes are possible in part because of our inaction. They are very skillful at manipulating fear. There is already an increase in right-wing terrorism in this country—in terrorism against women, blacks, lesbians, gay men, and against anyone who is speaking out in opposition to them. The purpose of such terrorism is to inculcate fear—to prevent us from acting by making us afraid for our lives, our children, our jobs. Terrorism operates on many different levels—physical assault in the form of lynching or rape, economic assault like losing your job or sexual harassment at work, and verbal assault through insults or jokes. Terrorism is a whole spectrum of ways by which people are convinced they cannot afford to act on what they know they need to do about their own lives and about what is going on in the world.

The only answer to terrorism is to organize. The response is not to be stopped by fear and at the same time not to be stupid about the dangers. If you are not going to be afraid, then you have to do something to provide yourself with some protection, because the danger is real. The New Right is hoping to convince us that we should be quiet—go back to our kitchens and our closets. They want to create an atmosphere like that of the McCarthy period in the 1950s when many people became afraid and quiet politically. Of course, even then some people remained active, but part of the mythology is to make us think that in previous times, everyone gave up. Sometimes when I get discouraged, I think about the Daughters of Bilitis, a lesbian organization that was formed during the 1950s. If you think it's hard to organize what we have to do tomorrow or next month, just imagine starting the Daughters of Bilitis then. It doesn't take away the reality of our own danger, but it puts it in perspective and reminds us that others have gone before us.

HOW THE RIGHT HAS ORGANIZED

If the efforts to make us afraid to act politically, to deny us reproductive rights, and to send us back to the home are not going to succeed in the 1980s, we must learn some lessons from the New Right. Let's examine some of the tactics that gave them the power that they have over our lives now. Feminists should get on the mailing lists of right-wing groups in order to understand what they are trying to do and how. A friend who once worked for a right-wing organization pointed out that while progressives tend to ignore the Right, their groups read and study what is published by their opposition. In the '60s, that was the New Left and civil rights movements, and in the '70s, feminism and the gay movement became primary targets. If you read their propaganda, it's clear that they have built their strength by developing opposition to abortion, ERA, and gay rights. They manipulate the fears that people have about those issues in order to gain power for a right-wing agenda on a whole range of domestic and foreign-policy matters.

Looking at what they achieved, three immediate lessons come to mind: 1) unity, 2) organization, and 3) the ideological offensive. We need to understand how they united Catholics and Southern Baptists, who when I was growing up were quite clear that the other was going to hell. If they could unite those two, along with other very secular constituencies, then we ought to be able to do a better job of uniting feminists. One of our problems is that we act like unity means that we all have to be the same. Rather, unity requires respect for each other and the establishment of some bottom lines for working together so that we can continue to be different, continue to argue over strategies and issues, but not be defeated by our differences.

The key to unity is related to the second lesson from the Right, which is organization. Organization is necessary to create unity, and structures are necessary to express that unity with power. There is a certain feminist reluctance to be organized; it includes a distrust of power and a spontaneity that I like. But politically, we must be organized better. I think we have the creativity and capacity to create organizations that are not stifling, to create structures that aren't bureaucratic. To me, that's the challenge. If we want our society to organize people in this country in a better way, then we have to organize ourselves for that vision. We must express our vision for the world in the ways we organize ourselves.

There are two specific aspects of the organization of the right wing that especially interest me. One is their use of sophisticated technology and the other is their use of women. One of their basic communication techniques is through direct mail. By amassing mailing lists into a computer, they can tap millions of people around the country on any given issue. They have the information in the computer about who is likely to respond to what. Richard Viguerie, master of the lists, went on TV the day after the Reagan victory and said that they were ten years ahead of liberals in how to use this technology. While technology itself can't do everything, we have to learn to make better use of it.

A second aspect of their organization ironically is based on the effects of the women's movement. A lot of their success comes from manipulating fears generated by our success over the past twelve years. We have publicly raised questions about women's roles and about sexuality and created the changes that have allowed them to mobilize. And they are mobilizing women. The irony is that the right wing is male power with a big P, but its base of ongoing daily work is woman power with a small p. It is women volunteers at the grass roots who have done most of the local organizing necessary to give those men at the top the power they now have.

Right-wing organizing is providing some women with a clear channel for their energies, which makes them feel that their lives matter. Feminists first said women have a right to feel that our lives matter, and we began our movement around that assertion. But we haven't reached enough women with specific ways that they can feel they are achieving this. We have to make our visions clearer, more practical, and more accessible in order to reach more women.

If you listen carefully to women in the anti-abortion movement, for instance, you see that this has become a way for them to feel that they can make a difference. We cannot stereotype that as "false consciousness"; we have to deal with the reality of it. It says something about where we have to move. I don't mean that we should step back from any positions, but rather, that we have to make ourselves more available and reach out to more women. We do not need to organize by pretending that we are other than who we are, but we can broaden our understanding of other people's lives and improve our ways of communicating who we are and what it is we are saying.

This brings me to the third lesson from the right wing—the offensive. They stole it from us. They have sold themselves as the "pros"—the positive force—prolife, profamily, and protectors of human values. They have portrayed us as the "anti's." We have to show that we are the forces that are trying to create a better life for women, for everyone, for society. We are the ones who represent hope for a more just and humane future.

The time is ripe to assert our visions more forthrightly. Since most of the Democrats that the right wing ousted from Congress and the White House were not feminists, and some were bankrupt politically, this is the moment to assert new visions, instead of just replacing the old male liberals with new men in power. It is time for women to build coalitions in which we put forward feminist individuals and feminist strategies for the next political stages.

A movement has to be in motion, and it must remember the basic vision and analysis from which it was born. We must remember that feminism is a radical transformational politics that began with the recognition that patriarchy has to be altered fundamentally for women's lives to change. Of course, we have to take hundreds of incremental steps along the way, but we see each one of those as part of the process of achieving a larger change.

Our future depends on the expansion and clarification of feminism as a politics—as a world view, a perspective on life that can transform the next century. Feminism can be one of the most powerful forces in the next fifty years for the transformation of society. But feminism is not understood adequately as a politics. It has been misunderstood as morality; it has been misunderstood as a correct line. It has been diminished to a "laundry list" of women's issues—ERA, abortion rights, gay rights, child care, and maybe health care or a couple of other matters. But feminism is not a list of discrete items—it is a perspective on life, a perspective on everything from budgets to butterflies. For example, feminist work in genetics is important because without a feminist perspective, there may not be many women left to worry about.

Another view of feminism that has limited us is what Mary Hunt and I labeled the "add women and stir" approach to change. I do believe in adding women and stirring, in many situations, but the women added have to be willing to stir up the mix so that it no longer looks the same, so that we are reorienting whatever we've been stirred into. Feminism must be more than adding women into structures as they are; it must also be about transforming those institutions, making them more humane.

Finally, as a politics, feminism is not simply a constituency of women. It is a perspective on the world that grows out of women's oppression, and it is a perspective that I hope most women will develop. But as was clear at the conferences in Copenhagen and again around the New Right's activities, we cannot equate feminism with women. Women can be right wing and antifeminist. All the governments in the world demonstrated in Copenhagen that they are quite prepared to use women for their own political purposes. Feminism has succeeded in letting the world know that women are an important base of power, and many political forces are going to use us more, which does not necessarily advance feminism. The right wing in this country is a clear example of how women are used against feminism. Women are used as a power base for other-than-feminist politics all the time. But it is not very useful to argue with other women over who represents women. It is more productive to argue over which politics—feminist or right wing—are best for women.

Feminism is a political view that grows out of our struggles over women's oppression, out of our lives as women, out of our identification with each other and our love for women. But as a politics, it is a world view anyone can have. I don't expect very many nonwomen to hold it yet; however, if they do adopt a feminist perspective, that's good. The point is not how many men can be feminists; the point is that feminism is a politics with the potential to bring a new approach to the problems of the world. As such, it is a framework for thinking about everything—about structures for living, about the so-called unnaturalness of certain forms of sexuality or the "naturalness" of domination by sex, race, class, or nation. Patriarchy and male supremacy are built on the notion that one group has to be better than another, but feminism questions everything we have been told is natural, and is redefining the social order.

The idea of just adding women to things as they are is not nearly as likely to excite people as the idea that society as a whole could be different. To believe that the degradation of sexism and racism, the violence in our lives that we have today is not inevitable moves people to action. The more radical (by which I mean going to the root of society's problems, and not a description of a set of tactics) we are about what we're saying, the more chance we have to communicate our vision. Most people are interested in developing a better way to live. What initially excited me about feminism was that it suggested a new way of living. I think that excites many women around the world who are exploring feminism today.

The mass media in this country, which controls much of the media around the world, seems to be engaged in a conspiracy to make sure that feminism is not seen as a sensible, viable, positive alternative for the future. It is no accident that feminism is portrayed through stereotypes: either as a few elite women getting to the top of IBM (and why should most women in Latin America identify with that?) or as a group of crazies who don't really have any political ideas and are self-indulgent. The lesbian stereotype is usually part of the crazies, which raises fears used to divide women.

In international workshops with women from all parts of the world, I have found that incredible discussions are possible as soon as we break through such media stereotypes. Only then can we discuss the core ideas of feminism as a transformational politics concerned with individual dignity for women, with control of our bodies and with social, economic, and political change. When feminism is seen as a politics that connects individual dignity for women with changing economic and political structures, it is of enormous interest to many. Women have a wealth of ideas about what a feminist view could be in the world. We have little access to these ideas because we have had too little dialogue with women from other countries, and they have rarely been exposed to the grass-roots movement in this country.

Much of what I've described about international situations applies within this country also. We have a multitude of cultures in our own midst, and many of the techniques that the media and various male political interests use to divide us are used domestically as well as internationally. In order to get beyond these, we have to become clearer about what it means to be a feminist and what that politics means to the world. We must do more communicating and reaching out. The worst thing that could happen to feminists in the '80s as a result of the right-wing advances is retrenchment—pulling back into ourselves. At this point in time what feminism needs is contact with a broader range of people, not a narrower focus.

COMMUNICATION AND CONNECTIONS

What feminists have to say about visions for the future will become clearer and richer if we get out, talk, and listen to people. We must drop some of our stereotypes of others and some of our self-imposed limitations on what that conversation will be. At the same time, we must begin such organizing quite clearly from the basis of our radical ideas and around the specific issues that occur in women's lives. I don't find it as important what issue you organize around or even whether you organize only women— those are decisions made in response to the specifics of the circumstances. The critical question for me is: What kind of vision do you have of where you're going?

My vision, my goal is not that of becoming a small "religious" cult. I do not seek a lesbian island that would be allowed to exist while the rest of the world blows itself up, through patriarchal attitudes. First, I don't think it would work. Even when I have moments of thinking that it would be a lovely retreat, I cannot imagine that they would leave our island alone. Further, I know that I joined this movement because I believe that feminism has the potential to lead to new ways of structuring the world.

When I get discouraged, I try to imagine going back and I realize that we have gone too far to return. We have gone too far in discovering ourselves positively. Lesbians have also discovered our ancestors, not only the Eleanor Roosevelts, but also the medieval nuns. (If you have read the *Lives of the Saints,* you know that many women were sainted for refusing to be heterosexual.) The question for lesbians is not "Did we exist?" but "How did we exist?" What can we learn from the women who existed in harems in the Middle East? What can we learn from the women who existed in Japan as geishas? What can we learn from all the ways we as a lesbian people have devised to survive, and what can we learn that will help us understand the moment in struggle that women now have before us?

Another reason why we cannot go back into the closets of fear and isolation is simply that we know too much. And I am fully committed to making sure that more women know too much faster and faster. One of the best ways for women to know too much is to get them involved in struggle around a particular issue. I know many stories of women who became feminists, who had no expectation of doing so, but there was one issue where they just could not stand what was happening. A woman starts with one thing. As she begins to question that, if she doesn't stop herself, and if she has a community of women who will help her keep moving, feminism often follows.

This is what is happening today with global feminism, and it is going to help us get through the '80s. I suspect that the most important next ideas about what it means to be a feminist are going to come from outside the United States. They will come from places like India, where women started a radical feminist publication recently, and where village women are standing outside the homes of men who beat their wives and shaming them.

Global feminism, however, is not just what is happening in some faraway place: it is the connection between women's activities there and here. Global feminism is what we do about the drug companies who are dumping contraceptives that were banned in the United States onto women in Third World countries. The next time we organize around something that is destructive to women in North America, we have to organize to have it destroyed, not simply banned. It is not that our lives aren't connected to women elsewhere, it is that our consciousness has been kept separate and therefore our ability to fight back together has been kept separate. We have to develop a consciousness of those connections.

The real power of feminism as a global analysis will expand and emerge as women in various situations develop it from their own lives and produce new perspectives. We can learn about global feminism right here at home from female workers and students who come to this country. Many of these women live in places like foreign students' housing where they often feel isolated. We have the resources within this country (within the various cultures here as well as among the women from other countries who live here) to understand more about women globally. You do not have to leave Denver to understand feminism globally. What we do have to do is to think and listen in new ways to what other women's lives are about. If we do that, we will learn and we will gain strength for getting through the '80s and for countering the advances of the right wing.

I want to end with a quote from Mother Jones who said after one labor setback, "Don't agonize, organize." We can take that as a slogan for us in the '80s. For while times are difficult, they are also challenging because we know that this country is going to have to change in the next twenty-five years. Whether you have been a critic of U.S. foreign policy or not doesn't matter. It's going to have to change because American imperialism and destruction of world resources will not be able to continue. The question at stake is whether the response to that change in this country is going to be a new way of dealing in the world and a new way of living at home, or whether it's going to be opposition to progressive forces, as the right wing is proposing.

Feminists can play a vital role in redefining what life in this country can be about, and we can do that in connection with struggles of women in other parts of the world. This struggle can provide the basis for a new society. This should be enough to make women feel that what we do will make a difference. I believe that the world will be different in some way because we dared to live as who we were and we dared to say that the world could be a better place for all.

THE FERRARO FACTOR:
SYMBOL OR SUBSTANCE?

There has been much talk about Geraldine Ferraro's nomination as a symbol of women's new political power and about the role that "gender gap politics" played in making it possible. There also has been extensive coverage of Ferraro's life and positions. But will her candidacy, and the increase in women's power, bring substantive changes in the political process?

Above all, Ferraro symbolizes a commitment to equality for women. This in itself is substantial. The resources devoted to stopping ERA made it clear that this still is a basic issue—and true equity, across sex, race, and class lines, would substantially alter the allocation of power and privilege in America.

Yet, as profound as equity is, Ferraro's nomination symbolizes more. Unlike powerful female politicians in other countries—such as India's Indira Gandhi or Great Britain's Margaret Thatcher—Ferraro is identified with feminism. She is not just a woman who has made it, but a woman who has embraced the women's movement and benefited from it. Thus, she also symbolizes the ideas and approaches feminism brings to the political process.

This is not to say that Ferraro will endorse every feminist proposal. But her nomination should lead to wider public discus-

This article was written for Pacific News Service (August 20, 1984).

146

sion of feminist perspectives on a whole range of issues. For feminism is more than a laundry list of isolated concerns. Feminism is an approach to life that challenges the right of any group to control others on the basis of sex, race, class, sexual orientation, religion, or nationality.

In their search for new ideas, then, the Democrats should look more closely at their new candidate and at the substance of the feminist movement. For example:

Law and order: Women have been working for more than a decade on how to balance the need to end violence, of which women are frequently the victims, while still protecting the rights of all citizens.

Peace and disarmament: A large percentage of activists in this area are women, and they have found new approaches to this issue ranging from the nuclear freeze to peace encampments.

Economics: Feminists, facing the fact that poverty affects women most heavily, have begun to chart new territory with concepts like comparable worth that would redefine the social value of work.

Saving communities and families: Women have often pioneered in solving the problems of sustaining community in deteriorating neighborhoods, of maintaining a sense of family amid a diversity of life-styles—as much out of necessity as out of choice.

Feminism, in short, articulates new needs and demands new policies that take into account women's lives. Whether innately or due to our assigned roles and outsider status, women see the dilemmas of the human family from new angles. This does not make women morally superior, but it can lead to creative approaches to anything from housing to education to the world economy.

The Jesse Jackson and Gary Hart campaigns revealed people's hunger for new ideas. Mondale's choice of Ferraro indicates he wants to be linked, at least symbolically, with those forces. But it still is not clear whether the Democratic party will give space to new ideas or whether they want only to benefit from the good will generated by the symbol.

Geraldine Ferraro has the intelligence, the heart, and the contacts to be a bridge from the old to the new, but this will not be easy. Indeed, the fact that she was chosen partly because she can be "one of the boys" makes many nervous. Will she play their game so well that she becomes a token woman at the top, or will she help break down the doors for others? Can she show not only that women can play ball, but also that America needs women and other disenfranchised groups to help redefine the political game?

Ferraro's candidacy also can be a watershed for the women's movement. Now that a woman is running for the nation's second-highest office, it is no longer necessary to prove we can run. Rather, feminists must produce concrete policies that reflect their vision of the future—while continuing to press Ferraro and other politicians to bring these ideas into mainstream debate.

For the nation, the challenge, as Ferraro has said, is not really what America can do for women but what women can do for America. I would add that while women can do a lot to help this country change at a time of great need, it still is an open question what those who control our national institutions are ready to allow women as political leaders to do.

MAKING COMMON CAUSE:
DIVERSITY AND COALITIONS

I want to begin by questioning the title of this panel, "Common Causes: Uncommon Coalitions—Sex, Race, Class, and Age." In my twenty years of political organizing, I have been part of numerous coalitions. Some were successful, others disastrous, and most fell somewhere in between. I am not sure that any were really uncommon. For coalitions are one of the most common strategies for creating social change, and the problems that accompany them are recurring themes in all movements. Discourse about when, where, and how to build coalitions is particularly important when we seek to make change that is inclusive of diverse perspectives. For feminists, the ability to create a movement that includes and responds to the diversity of women's lives is crucial.

What feminists need to explore is why coalition efforts have not been more common in our movement, and what is required to build effective coalitions? We must ask why, instead of coalescing more, women have to continually separate into distinct groups in order to be heard? Whether on the basis of race, class, age, ethnic identity, sexual preference, or physical abilities, each group has

This speech at the National Women's Studies Association Annual Convention in Seattle, Washington, in June 1985, was published in *Ikon*, no. 7 (Fall 1986).

had to find a separate space and identity in order to create conditions where their perspectives would be seen by others. Why do we have such difficulty responding to diversity, and how can we move beyond the necessity of separatism to building inclusive coalitions? In short, I want to talk about how to make coalitions more common, less frightening, more comprehensive, and more successful.

I assume that if coalitions are to work, there must be a common cause. The reason to go through the process, which is often painful and difficult, is because we have some shared goal, broadly or narrowly defined, that motivates us to work across diverse lines. As diverse groups unite around some common goal, there is greater possibility of learning about and incorporating diversity at a deeper level. The particulars of each coalition vary, of course. But assuming that one goal of feminism is struggling against domination in all its forms, then a critical issue for all our coalitions is how to approach diversity and domination.

DIVERSITY AND DOMINATION

Patriarchy has systematically utilized diversity as a tool of domination in which groups are taught that certain powers and privileges are the natural prerogatives of some people. We learn in childhood that such things as sex and race bring differences in power and privilege, and that these are acceptable. This idea that difference justifies domination is deeply embedded in society and defended as natural. Take, for example, the refrain: "there will always be poor people" used to perpetuate class privileges. But as women who have challenged the so-called naturalness of male supremacy, feminists must also question it in other areas of domination.

When power hierarchies are accepted as inevitable, people can be manipulated to fear that those who are different are a threat to their position and perhaps even to their survival. We are taught to be afraid that "they" will hurt us—either because they are more powerful or because they want our privileges. While that fear takes multiple forms depending on where we fit in the various scales of domination, all of us are taught to distrust those who are different. Some aspects of this fear may be necessary to survival— whites *do* lynch blacks, men *will* rape women—and we must watch out for such dangers. But fear and distrust of differences are most often used to keep us in line. When we challenge the idea that differences must be threatening, we are also challenging the patriarchal assignment of power and privilege as birthrights.

Opposing the ways that differences are used to dominate does not mean that we seek to end diversity. Feminist visions are not about creating homogenized people who all look like a bland middle-class television ad. Many aspects of diversity can be celebrated as variety, creativity, and options in life-styles and world views. We must distinguish between creative differences that are not intrinsically tied to domination and the assignment of power and privilege based on the distinctive characteristics of some. Diversity, when separated from power to control others, provides valuable opportunities for learning and living that can be missed if one is embedded in an ethnocentric way of seeing reality.

Diversity among feminists today can be a resource for gaining a broader understanding of the world. We see more clearly and our ability to create effective strategies is enhanced if we move beyond the boundaries of our assigned patriarchal slot. Quite specifically, in 1985, white women can look to the growing women of color movement in the West and to feminism in the Third World as sources of both insight and information. But too often, we fail to respond to each other's potential for enriching our lives and the movement because of unconscious fears of race, class, or national differences. It is not just a matter of learning about race and class—although that is important—but also of understanding women's lives and the world as viewed by others.

Learning from a wider diversity of women and making coalitions does not mean watering down feminist politics as some fear. Rather, it requires engaging in a wider debate about those politics and shaping their expressions to respond to more women's realities. I see this process as reclaiming the radical spirit of feminism that calls for going to the roots of oppression. In the United States, for example, this wave of feminism began in the 1960s in close connection to the black civil rights movement and its demand for recognition of the rights of racially diverse groups. Yet, racism is all too often reflected in the lack of acknowledgment of those origins and the invisibility of women of color who were a part of feminism's resurgence. As Gloria T. Hull and Barbara Smith note in *But Some of Us Are Brave* (Old Westbury, N.Y.: The Feminist

151

Press, 1982, p. xx), "Black women were a part of that early women's movement as were working-class women of all races." This included famous speakers such as Florence Kennedy as well as women like the welfare rights mothers that worked in the late '60s in coalition with Washington, D.C., Women's Liberation to achieve improvements in the city's health services for women. In the 1970s, efforts to develop diverse coalitions and a broader-based agenda were often eclipsed by many factors including intense movement controversies and the media's emphasis on the pursuit of equality within the system. By focusing again on the diversity and depth of women's perspectives and needs in the 1980s, I see feminists reasserting the radical impulse for justice for all and thus strengthening the movement as a force for fundamental change.

There is commonality in the fact that all women are subordinated, but when we examine our diversity, we see that the forms that takes are shaped by many factors. Female oppression is not one universal block experienced the same way by all women, to which other forms of exploitation are then added as separate pieces. Rather, various oppressions interact to shape the particulars of each woman's life. For example, an aging black lesbian who is poor does not experience oppression as separate packages—one sexism, one poverty, one homophobia, one racism, and one ageism. She experiences these as interacting and shaping each other. Seeing this interaction is vital for coalitions around issues.

Too often analysis of women's oppression isolates single factors such as class or sexual preference in a simplistic manner, trying to show the effects of each separately. But this fails to take account of their interrelatedness. Further, it often winds up in battles over a hierarchy of seriousness of forms of oppression or over how one really is the cause of the other. But a feminist method suggests the necessity of looking at their interaction—at how race, class, sex, and age oppression shape each other. For example, race and class affect an older woman's problems—whether it means being abandoned in her house, trapped in an abusive nursing home, or entirely homeless. Or in looking at the exploitation of women's work, we can see the effect of factors such as race, homophobia, or physical disability, as well as class.

Strategies that fail to examine how female exploitation is shaped in different forms often set some women up against others. The interactive approach—taking into account female diversity —is thus essential for effective coalitions. However, it is often

152

difficult to look at all the features of oppression because they are complex and demand continuous reevaluation of our assumptions. Further, attitudes and emotions around diversity are deeply rooted and often volatile. Systems such as racism, anti-Semitism, classism, nationalism, and homophobia are so much a part of the culture that surrounds us from birth that we often have biases and blind spots that affect our attitudes, behavior, strategies, and values in ways that we do not perceive until challenged by others.

Many problems that arise in coalitions stem from resistance to being challenged about oppressive attitudes and reactions. These need to be approached matter-of-factly, not as moral judgments on one's personhood, but as negative results of growing up in patriarchal culture. We must change such attitudes and behavior because they oppress others and interfere with our own humanity as well as impede the process of creating feminist strategies and coalitions. For example, white middle-class North Americans are often unaware that the perspectives of that culture—which usually coincide with the media's portrayal of reality—are not the only way of seeing the world. Since these ethnocentric biases are reinforced constantly, we must make an extra effort to see other points of view. This does not mean that nothing of this culture is of value. It simply means that we must go beyond its limits to see what can be taken as useful and not oppressive, and what must be challenged.

In looking at diversity among women, we see one of the weaknesses of the feminist concept that the personal is political. It is valid that each woman begins from her personal experiences, and it is important to see how these are political. But we must also recognize that our personal experiences are shaped by the culture with its prejudices—against people of color, lesbians and gay men, the aged, and so on. We cannot, therefore, depend on our perceptions alone as the basis for political analysis and action—much less for coalition. Feminists must stretch beyond, challenging the limits of our own personal experiences by learning from the diversity of women's lives.

DIVISIVE REACTIONS TO DIVERSITY

In the 1980s, various groups, such as the women of color movement, are expanding the definitions of, and possibilities for, feminism. But many women's reactions to diversity interfere with learning from others and making successful cross-cultural, multi-racial coalitions. I call these divisive reactions because, bringing up racism or class or homophobia is not itself divisive to the movement. Rather, what is divisive is ignoring such issues or being unable to respond to them constructively. I want to outline some reactions that I have seen interfere with efforts at coalition-building and suggest ways of getting beyond them.

The most obviously divisive reaction is *becoming defensive* when challenged around an issue of diversity. If one is busy making explanations about how some action or comment was not really what you meant, it is hard to listen and understand criticism and why it is being made. This does not mean passively accepting every critical comment—for in dealing with such emotional topics, there will be exaggerations, inaccuracies, or injustices that must be worked out. But these problems do not excuse anyone from struggling with the issues. If one remains open, while retaining a sense of your own authenticity, it is usually possible to deal with these by listening and responding constructively. If a critique does not make sense to you, ask about it, or try to figure out what led to it—even if it seems unfair. It is not always easy to listen to criticism first and then sort through what it means, but it is the job of feminists to do just that. To listen carefully, to consider what other views mean for our work, and to respond through incorporating new understandings where appropriate—this is a feminist necessity if we are to make coalitions among diverse women.

Often defensiveness is related to another unhelpful reaction—*guilt.* It may be appropriate to experience shame over the actions of one's ancestors or at how one has participated in another's oppression. But personal guilt is usually immobilizing, particularly if one sits with it for long. Successful coalitions are not built on feeling sorry for others or being apologetic about one's existence. Coalitions are built around shared outrage over injustice and common visions of how society can be changed. Few of us had control over our origins, and the point is not to feel guilt about the attitudes or privileges that we inherited. The question is what are we going to do about them now—how are we going to change ourselves and work to end domination in the world? For example, white women feeling sorry about something like racism is not as useful to women of color as working to eliminate it in society as well as in one's personal life.

Often women are sidetracked by *overpersonalization* when dealing with diversity. The issues raised are personal and do require individual change, but it is important not to get stuck there. Sometimes feminists become so involved in trying to be pure and personally free of any oppressive behavior that they become paralyzed and fear taking any political action because it might not be correct. Yet, it is through concrete efforts to challenge domination—no matter how small—that we learn and can become more effective and more inclusive in our political work. For example, if a man tells me that he is becoming totally antisexist but is not in some way challenging the structures of patriarchal power that continue to oppress women, then his personal changes—if I believe him at all—are of minimal value to me. The same is true for women of color who see some whites talking about racism but not taking action against it in the world.

Another aspect of overpersonalization is *withdrawal.* Sometimes feminists have become so personally hurt by criticism or feel so left out when a group is creating its own space, that they withdraw from political engagement. For example, some heterosexuals during the height of lesbian feminist challenges in the 1970s withdrew into their feelings of being attacked or left out rather than working on how they could fight homophobia while still being with men personally. This only reinforced the separation between us. I see similar behavior among some white women today. The hurt is often understandable because there is pain in confrontations around difficult issues, and feminists sometimes spend more energy criticizing women's oppressive behavior than taking on the systems of oppression. Still, reacting to this by withdrawing prevents learning from what has happened. This is sometimes like children who want to be center stage and pout when not in the forefront. Instead, we need to see that at any given moment one group may be the creative edge of the movement, but that will enrich all of us in the long run.

One of the more infuriating reactions is *acting weary and resentful* when someone brings up "that issue" again. No one is more tired of homophobia and having to bring it up again than a lesbian like myself. Probably women of color feel the same way about racism, Jewish women about anti-Semitism, the elderly about ageism, and so on. But the problems still exist and someone must address them. Until feminists learn to include the concerns and perspectives of those women whose oppression we do not directly

155

experience, then the "others" will have to keep bringing up those issues. We must strive to become "one-woman coalitions"—capable of understanding and raising all issues of oppression and seeing our relationship to them—whites speaking about racism, heterosexuals about homophobia, the able-bodied about disabilities, and so on. Only as we do this will we be able to build lasting coalitions.

The last divisive reaction that I want to include here is *limiting outspoken "minority women" to "their issues."* When someone speaks out strongly about her group's specific oppression, she often becomes a token whose leadership in other areas is restricted. For example, I have felt pressure either to work only on lesbian issues, or to downplay them if I am involved in other areas of feminist activity. Yet, while I am out of the closet and concerned about homophobia, there are many other topics that I want to address besides lesbianism, just as women of color have much to say about many issues in addition to racism. To counter this tendency, I decided in the late '70s that I would not write any more only about lesbianism, but instead I would address other subjects and incorporate my lesbian feminist analysis within them. Women of all races, classes, ages, and nations have much to say on a whole variety of topics from their particular perspectives. If we limit each to one identity and approach feminism as a string of separate unrelated issues, we narrow the possibilities for insight, growth, and leadership throughout the movement.

Our chances of building successful coalitions are greater if we can avoid divisive reactions such as these and see diversity as a strength. As we struggle to learn from our differences rather than to fear or deny them, we can find our common ground. In this process, we also build the atmosphere of good faith and respect necessary for strong coalitions. For while we do not need to love one another or agree on everything, we do need to be able to challenge each other from the assumption that change is possible. Another requirement when diverse groups coalesce is that each be clear about its bottom line. We must each know what we need in order to survive in a coalition and how to communicate that to others.

Coalitions that are successful must also be aimed at taking meaningful action in the world. Coalition is not abstract. It functions when groups or individuals are working together around something that each cares about and sees as advancing its goals or vision, or at least protecting the space necessary to develop that. When a coalition has some effect, then it is worth going through the trouble and strife of making it work. It is in the process itself that we often discover the common causes that make it possible to create common coalitions of women in all our diversity working toward both common and varied feminist visions.

LESBIAN FEMINISM

T his section traces the evolution of my thinking about lesbian feminism from separatism through my involvement in the gay movement and my efforts to take this issue out of the lesbian and male homosexual ghetto. Perhaps more than any other section of the book, this one demonstrates how my original concept of an issue—lesbian feminism—expanded and modified in response to particular experiences and to stages of the movement. Thus, it illustrates how theory develops in relation to activism.

The essays in this section begin with the theoretical manifesto for The Furies—a lesbian feminist separatist collective founded in 1971—and then proceed to questioning separatism as a long-term strategy and to evaluating the lessons of that period. Several of the articles develop an analysis of heterosexism as a crucial part of all female and gay male oppression. While there is some overlap among these pieces, they illustrate the evolution of my ideas and how I sought to express them to different audiences. This section also deals with lesbians in the women's movement and the gay male movement and it ends with selections from speeches seeking to connect lesbian feminism and an analysis of heterosexism and homophobia to other topics.

159

LESBIANS IN REVOLT

The development of lesbian-feminist politics as the basis for the liberation of women is our top priority; this article outlines our present ideas. In our society, which defines all people and institutions for the benefit of the rich, white male, the lesbian is in revolt. In revolt because she defines herself in terms of women and rejects the male definitions of how she should feel, act, look, and live. To be a lesbian is to love oneself, woman, in a culture that denegrates and despises women. The lesbian rejects male sexual/political domination; she defies his world, his social organization, his ideology, and his definition of her as inferior. Lesbianism puts women first while the society declares the male supreme. Lesbianism threatens male supremacy at its core. When politically conscious and organized, it is central to destroying our sexist, racist, capitalist, imperialist system.

LESBIANISM IS A POLITICAL CHOICE

Male society defines lesbianism as a sexual act, which reflects men's limited view of women: they think of us only in terms of sex. They also say lesbians are not real women, so a real woman

"Lesbians in Revolt," first appeared in *The Furies*, vol. I, no. 1 (January 1972).

is one who gets fucked by men. We say that a lesbian is a woman whose sense of self and energies, including sexual energies, center around women—she is woman-identified. The woman-identified-woman commits herself to other women for political, emotional, physical, and economic support. Women are important to her. She is important to herself. Our society demands that commitment from women be reserved for men.

The lesbian, woman-identified-woman, commits herself to women not only as an alternative to oppressive male/female relationships but primarily because she *loves* women. Whether consciously or not, by her actions, the lesbian has recognized that giving support and love to men over women perpetuates the system that oppresses her. If women do not make a commitment to each other, which includes sexual love, we deny ourselves the love and value traditionally given to men. We accept our second-class status. When women do give primary energies to other women, then it is possible to concentrate fully on building a movement for our liberation.

Woman-identified lesbianism is, then, more than a sexual preference; it is a political choice. It is political because relationships between men and women are essentially political: they involve power and dominance. Since the lesbian actively rejects that relationship and chooses women, she defies the established political system.

LESBIANISM, BY ITSELF, IS NOT ENOUGH

Of course, not all lesbians are consciously woman-identified, nor are all committed to finding common solutions to the oppression they suffer as women and lesbians. Being a lesbian is part of challenging male supremacy, but not the end. For the lesbian or heterosexual woman, there is no individual solution to oppression.

The lesbian may think that she is free since she escapes the personal oppression of the individual male/female relationship. But to the society she is still a woman, or worse, a visible lesbian. On the street, at the job, in the schools, she is treated as an inferior and is at the mercy of men's power and whims. (I've never heard of a rapist who stopped because his victim was a lesbian.) This society hates women who love women, and so, the lesbian, who escapes male dominance in her private home, receives it doubly

162

at the hands of male society; she is harassed, outcast, and shuttled to the bottom. Lesbians must become feminists and fight against woman oppression, just as feminists must become lesbians if they hope to end male supremacy.

U.S. society encourages individual solutions, apolitical attitudes, and reformism to keep us from political revolt and out of power. Men who rule, and male leftists who seek to rule, try to depoliticize sex and the relations between men and women in order to prevent us from acting to end our oppression and challenging their power. As the question of homosexuality has become public, reformists define it as a private question of whom you sleep with in order to sidetrack our understanding of the politics of sex. For the lesbian-feminist, it is not private; it is a political matter of oppression, domination, and power. Reformists offer solutions that make no basic changes in the system that oppresses us, solutions that keep power in the hands of the oppressor. The only way oppressed people end their oppression is by seizing power: people whose rule depends on the subordination of others do not voluntarily stop oppressing others. Our subordination is the basis of male power.

SEXISM IS THE ROOT OF ALL OPPRESSION

The first division of labor, in prehistory, was based on sex: men hunted, women built the villages, took care of children, and farmed. Women collectively controlled the land, language, culture, and the communities. Men were able to conquer women with the weapons that they developed for hunting when it became clear that women were leading a more stable, peaceful, and desirable existence. We do not know exactly how this conquest took place, but it is clear that the original imperialism was male over female: the male claiming the female body and her service as his territory (or property).

Having secured the domination of women, men continued this pattern of suppressing people, now on the basis of tribe, race, and class. Although there have been numerous battles over class, race, and nation during the past three thousand years, none has brought the liberation of women. While these other forms of oppression must be ended, there is no reason to believe that our liberation will come with the smashing of capitalism, racism, or imperialism today. Women will be free only when we concentrate on fighting male supremacy.

Our war against male supremacy does, however, involve attacking the latter-day dominations based on class, race, and nation. As lesbians who are outcasts from every group, it would be suicidal to perpetuate these man-made divisions among ourselves. We have no heterosexual privileges, and when we publicly assert our Lesbianism, those of us who had them lose many of our class and race privileges. Most of our privileges as women are granted to us by our relationships to men (fathers, husbands, boyfriends) whom we now reject. This does not mean that there is no racism or class chauvinism within us, but we must destroy these divisive remnants of privileged behavior among ourselves as the first step toward their destruction in the society. Race, class, and national oppressions come from men, serve ruling-class white male interests, and have no place in a woman-identified revolution.

LESBIANISM IS THE BASIC THREAT TO MALE SUPREMACY

Lesbianism is a threat to the ideological, political, personal, and economic basis of male supremacy. The lesbian threatens the ideology of male supremacy by destroying the lie about female inferiority, weakness, passivity, and by denying women's "innate" need for men. Lesbians literally do not need men, even for procreation.

The lesbian's independence and refusal to support one man undermines the personal power that men exercise over women. Our rejection of heterosexual sex challenges male domination in its most individual and common form. We offer all women something better than submission to personal oppression. We offer the beginning of the end of collective and individual male supremacy. Since men of all races and classes depend on female support and submission for practical tasks and feeling superior, our refusal to submit will force some to examine their sexist behavior, to break down their own destructive privileges over other humans, and to fight against those privileges in other men. They will have to build new selves that do not depend on oppressing women and learn to live in social structures that do not give them power over anyone.

Heterosexuality separates women from each other; it makes women define themselves through men; it forces women to compete against each other for men and the privilege that comes

164

through men and their social standing. Heterosexual society offers women a few privileges as compensation if they give up their freedom: for example, mothers are "honored," wives or lovers are socially accepted and given some economic and emotional security, a woman gets physical protection on the street when she stays with her man, etc. The privileges give heterosexual women a personal and political stake in maintaining the status quo.

The lesbian receives none of these heterosexual privileges or compensations since she does not accept the male demands on her. She has little vested interest in maintaining the present political system since all of its institutions—church, state, media, health, schools—work to keep her down. If she understands her oppression, she has nothing to gain by supporting white rich male America and much to gain from fighting to change it. She is less prone to accept reformist solutions to women's oppression.

Economics is a crucial part of woman oppression, but our analysis of the relationship between capitalism and sexism is not complete. We know that Marxist economic theory does not sufficiently consider the role of women or lesbians, and we are presently working on this area.

However, as a beginning, some of the ways that lesbians threaten the economic system are clear: in this country, women work for men in order to survive, on the job and in the home. The lesbian rejects this division of labor at its roots; she refuses to be a man's property, to submit to the unpaid labor system of housework and child care. She rejects the nuclear family as the basic unit of production and consumption in capitalist society.

The lesbian is also a threat on the job because she is not the passive/part-time woman worker that capitalism counts on to do boring work and be part of a surplus labor pool. Her identity and economic support do not come through men, so her job is crucial and she cares about job conditions, wages, promotion, and status. Capitalism cannot absorb large numbers of women demanding stable employment, decent salaries, and refusing to accept their traditional job exploitation. We do not understand yet the total effect that this increased job dissatisfaction will have. It is, however, clear that as women become more intent upon taking control of their lives, they will seek more control over their jobs, thus increasing the strains on capitalism and enhancing the power of women to change the economic system.

LESBIANS MUST FORM OUR OWN MOVEMENT TO FIGHT MALE SUPREMACY

Feminist-lesbianism, as the most basic threat to male supremacy, picks up part of the women's liberation analysis of sexism and gives it force and direction. Women's liberation lacks direction now because it has failed to understand the importance of heterosexuality in maintaining male supremacy, and because it has failed to face class and race as real differences in women's behavior and political needs. As long as straight women see lesbianism as a bedroom issue, they hold back the development of politics and strategies that would put an end to male supremacy and they give men an excuse for not dealing with their sexism.

Being a lesbian means ending identification with, allegiance to, dependence on, and support of heterosexuality. It means ending your personal stake in the male world so that you join women, individually and collectively, in the struggle to end your oppression. Lesbianism is the key to liberation and only women who cut their ties to male privilege can be trusted to remain serious in the struggle against male dominance. Those who remain tied to men, individually or in political theory, cannot always put women first. It is not that heterosexual women are evil or do not care about women. It is because the very essense, definition, and nature of heterosexuality is men first. Every woman has experienced that desolation when her sister puts her man first in the final crunch: heterosexuality demands that she do so. As long as women still benefit from heterosexuality, receive its privileges and security, they will at some point have to betray their sisters, especially lesbian sisters who do not receive those benefits.

Women in women's liberation have understood the importance of having meetings and other events for women only. It has been clear that dealing with men divides us and saps our energies, and that it is not the job of the oppressed to explain our oppression to the oppressor. Women also have seen that collectively, men will not deal with their sexism until they are forced to do so. Yet, many of these same women continue to have primary relationships with men individually and do not understand why lesbians find this oppressive. Lesbians cannot grow politically or personally in a situation which denies the basis of our politics: that lesbianism is political, that heterosexuality is crucial to maintaining male supremacy.

Lesbians must form our own political movement in order to grow. Changes that will have more than token effects on our lives will be led by woman-identified lesbians who understand the nature of our oppression and are therefore in a position to end it.

DOÑA CATALINA DE ERAUSO:
WOMEN REMEMBERED

D uring most of the past two thousand years, women who
sought to revolt against their sexual oppression found little or
no social space to do so. If they were successful, it was usually
because they came from the upper class and/or because they
denied their sex and passed for men. A handful of women from
the upper class were often allowed to deviate either because they
had so much power that they could not be stopped (e.g., Queen
Christina or Queen Elizabeth), or because they did not threaten
the male power structure but used their class privilege to live
marginal lives. For a lower-class woman, these options did not
exist as her survival depended on accepting her lot.

Every land has its tales of women who masqueraded as men in
their search for a freer life. Female roles and dress were so confin-
ing that women who could not accept these bonds pretended to
be men, not because they believed men to be actually superior but
because this was the only individual escape they could see. These
women took great risks since most of their societies and churches
forbade women to wear men's clothing without special permission
and this sin was often punished by death. (The excuse used for the

"Doña Catalina de Erauso: Women Remembered," first appeared in *The Furies,* vol. I, no.
3 (March 1972).

168

burning of Joan of Arc was her refusal to wear women's clothing.) Such a woman always lived in fear of detection and knew that men and other women opposed her. Occasionally, after a woman had managed to excel in certain fields and to survive in her disguise, she gained a begrudging admiration from society; if she then revealed her true sex, she sometimes acquired acceptance as an exceptional "neuter."

In all times and places, such women existed. They are a testament to woman's continual drive to escape her oppression. Many of these women were lesbians and a proud part of our history. Their lives are often ignored, or if recognized, their lesbianism is denied by male historians. We should know more about them. Yet, we need not romanticize them. Far from ideal, their lives were hard and usually tragic; society so circumscribed them that they had to hide their real identity, deny their womanhood and love of other women, and usually lived lonely lives as the price of their revolt.

Doña Catalina de Erauso was one such woman. A legendary figure, sometimes referred to as a Robin Hood of Latin America, Catalina was born in Spain, at the height of Christendom's oppression of women. She spent most of her adult years in male terrain, as a soldier of fortune in Mexico, Peru, and Chile. Many stories about her exploits have been passed down, although as with all legends, the details vary with the telling over time. But her existence and her general character are always consistent and not to be doubted.

Doña Catalina was born, sixth or seventh child to Captain and Maria Erauso, in Basque in 1592. At that time, noble Spaniards believed that it was the duty of men to serve the King and of women to enter religion. So, her father and brothers were trained for the military and her mother and sisters instructed in religion. Some say that Catalina's father gave her at birth to a nearby convent to be raised by her aunt, because he already had two daughters and had no use for more. Another source puts her in the convent at age four, while others say that she was sent when her parents realized that no male was likely to marry her because of her powerful physique. Regardless of detail, she spent much of her childhood in the convent, where she was expected to take the religious veil.

By her fifteenth birthday, she had had numerous fights with the pious nuns and was fed up with her confinement. She stole her aunt's keys and escaped to a field where she cut her hair, made male clothing out of her habit, and sallied forth as a young boy. One source suggests that she left this letter to her parents:

> By the time you get this letter, I shall either be free or dead. I will no longer endure the unjust imprisonment to which you condemn me. Why did you bring me up like my brothers? Why have made me take part in their work and play? Why have made me manly and strong like them, only to compel me, now that I am fifteen, to do nothing but mumble a lot of interminable prayers? Farewell. Forgive me if you can.
>
> Your daughter, Catalina

She roamed around Spain in her male disguise for a year or so, learning to survive by her wits and physical prowess. Eventually, she sailed to Latin America to try her hand on the new frontier, as did many an adventuresome young Spaniard. She wandered around the continent, taking on odd jobs, serving in the Spanish army, engaging in banditry, gambling, dueling, and earning herself a reputation as the best swords"man" in the Americas. She mastered the frontier arts of survival, robbed the rich, and helped out individuals in trouble. (Once she saved a woman from her avenging husband who sought to kill her because of an affair with one of Catalina's friends, whom the husband had already killed.) She lived by the frontier ethic where each person made his own laws and interpreted his own codes of justice. The book, *Historia de la Monja Alfcrez*, supposedly written by her, tells the stories of her escapades and escapes. She was sentenced to die at least four times and always managed to get away.

As a dashing young Spaniard, she was openly attracted to and sought after by many women. She was engaged on several occasions (usually as a strategy to get out of a jam) but she always disappeared before the wedding day when she would be revealed. In Lima, she was fired from one job because of her intimate relation with a young lady. She said of it:

> At the end of nine months he bade me go and earn my living elsewhere; and the reason of this was that he had at home with

him two unmarried sisters of his wife's, with whom—with one especially whom I preferred—I used to sport and frolic. And one day, when I was in the parlour, combing my hair, lolling my head in her lap, and tickling her ankles, he came by chance to a grating through which he saw us, and he heard her telling me that I ought to go to Potosi and make a fortune, and then we could get married. He withdrew, called me shortly afterwards, asked for and checked my accounts and discharged me, and I departed.

After fifteen lively years, she was wounded near to death and so confessed her sex to a priest, lest she die in sin. (Since she required major surgery on her wounds, she may have confessed out of physical necessity as well!) She lived; she then used the revelation of her female sex to get herself out of some troubles. Soon after this, she entered a convent briefly and then returned to Spain, much to the regret of the nuns she had befriended.

In Europe, news of her legendary exploits and of her newly discovered sexual identity had spread like wildfire. She was greeted everywhere by throngs of excited townsfolk. One person described her entry:

> When she came to go ashore, Catalina had flung her woman's dress to the devil and was once more flaunting it in the gorgeous trappings of a gallant cavalier. Thus attired, she set out for Seville, Madrid, Pampeluna, filling the hearts of the girls with love, of their gallants with terror.

The stories of her life were published; a famous poet, Montalban, wrote about her; and she sat for a portrait by Francesco Crescentio. King Phillip received her and rewarded her with a pension for her service defending the Spanish territory and flag. She went to Rome, where the Italians were captivated by her, and Pope Urban VIII, fascinated by her tales, granted her special permission to wear men's clothing. One man who met her in Rome described her as:

> tall and burly for a woman, artificially flat-chested, not plain in feature and yet not beautiful, showing signs of hardship rather than of age; with black hair, cut like a man's, and hanging in

a mane, as was customary at the time. She was dressed like a man, in the Spanish fashion, and wore a sword, tightly belted; her head inclined forwards, and her shoulders were slightly stooped, more like a fiery soldier than like a courtier given to gallantries.

But Europe was too boring for Catalina. She returned to Mexico in 1630, still as one author put it "untamed." She escorted a young woman to Mexico to meet her husband-to-be and fell madly in love with her. She resented the couple's subsequent marriage. Then the new husband insulted her; he accused her of molesting his wife and forbade her to enter their home or to walk on their street. Catalina responded in a letter challenging him to a duel; the letter ended:

> Now although I am a woman, as this seems a thing insufferable to my valor, in order that you may behold my prowess and achieve your boast, I shall await you at the back of the St. James Church from 1 to 6 o'clock.

(Duels were an honorable Spanish tradition, yet the male author who reports her letter called it, "incomparable arrogance"—had it come from a man, he would have called it, "defending his honor.") The husband chickened out, claiming that his honor as a gentleman forbade him to use arms against a woman. Clearly, he was terrified of Catalina's prowess as an experienced dueler. Catalina's friends persuaded her to leave the town. She continued a life of adventure, dressed as a swords"man," until her death in 1650.

Her story became popular folklore in both Spain and Latin America, where novels and poems were written about her as La Monja Alferez (The Nun Ensign). In the 1800s, European interest in her spread to France and to England, where translations of her stories appeared. None of these sources wrote about her as a lesbian, although it is clear that all her romantic experiences and feelings were with women, both when she was masquerading as a man and after her sexual identity was known.

Male authors enjoyed the titillation of Catalina as a woman in male disguise and made "cute" sexist comments about her. They saw her life as an intriguing individual aberration. In fact, her life is one of revolt against male supremacy. She was forced to disguise herself as a man, not because she thought women were inferior but because women were oppressed. She saw clearly that freedom was only available if she were a man. Her high spirits could not tolerate the bonds that society successfully clamped on most women and she was fortunate that her physical and mental quickness enabled her to revolt. She was not a social reformer in a political sense, but her life did dispel myths of female physical and mental inferiority for those who would listen. But male society was not about to hear her message in the 1600s and so she went down in history as a curious "nun," another exception to the sexist world rule.*

*I want to thank the Women's History Research Center in Berkeley for first bringing this woman to our attention. Major sources for this article included: *Historia De La Monja Alferez* by Catalina de Erauso (translated by James Fitzmaurice Kelly); *La Monja Alferez,* a play by Juan Perez de Montalban; *Women in Men's Disguise* by O. P. Gilbert; and *The Spanish Nun* by Thomas DeQuincey.

NOT FOR LESBIANS ONLY

T he following is an expanded and revised version of a speech given at the Socialist-Feminist Conference, Antioch College, Yellow Springs, Ohio, July 5, 1975. Many of the ideas expressed here about lesbian-feminist politics were first developed several years ago in The Furies. Nevertheless, I am continually discovering that most feminists, including many lesbians, have little idea what lesbian-feminist politics is. This speech takes those basic political ideas and develops them further, particularly as they relate to socialist-feminism.

I am listed in your program as Charlotte Bunch-Weeks—a rather ominous slip-of-the-tongue (or slip in historical timing), which reflects a subject so far avoided at this conference that I, for one, want to talk about.

Five years ago, when I *was* Charlotte Bunch-Weeks, and straight, and married to a man, I was also a socialist-feminist. When I left the man and the marriage, I also left the newly developing socialist-feminist movement—because, for one reason, my politics then, as now, were inextricably joined with the way I

"Not for Lesbians Only" first appeared in Quest: A Feminist Quarterly, vol. II, no. 2 (Fall 1975).

lived my personal, my daily life. With men, with male politics, I was a socialist; with women, engaged in the articulation of women's politics, I became a lesbian-feminist—and, in the gay-straight split, a lesbian-feminist separatist.

It's that gay-straight split that no one here seems to want to remember—and I bring it up now, not because I want to relive a past painful to all concerned, but because it is an essential part of our political history which, if ignored, will eventually force lesbians to withdraw again from other political women. There were important political reasons for that split, reasons explicitly related to the survival of lesbians—and those reasons and the problems causing them are still with us. It is important—especially for political groups who wish to give credence and priority to lesbian issues—to remember why separatism happened, why it is not a historical relic but still vital to the ongoing debate over lesbianism and feminism.

In my own personal experience, I, and the other women of The Furies collective, left the women's movement because it had been made clear to us that there was no space to develop a lesbian-feminist politics and life-style without constant and nonproductive conflict with heterosexual fear, antagonism, and insensitivity. This was essentially the same experience shared by many other lesbian-feminists at about the same time around the country. What the women's movement could not accept then—and still finds it difficult to accept—is that lesbianism is political: which is the essence of lesbian-feminist politics. Sounds simple. Yet most feminists still view lesbianism as a personal decision or, at best, as a civil rights concern or a cultural phenomenon. Lesbianism is more than a question of civil rights and culture, although the daily discrimination against lesbians is real and its alleviation through civil-libertarian reforms is important. Similarly, although lesbianism is a primary force in the emergence of a dynamic women's culture, it is much more. Lesbian-feminist politics is a political critique of the institution and ideology of heterosexuality as a cornerstone of male supremacy. It is an extension of the analysis of sexual politics to an analysis of sexuality itself as an institution. It is a commitment to women as a political group, which is the basis of a political/economic strategy leading to power for women, not just an "alternative community."

There are many lesbians still who feel that there is no place in socialist-feminist organizations in particular, or the women's movement in general, for them to develop that politics or live that life. Because of this, I am still, in part, a separatist; but I don't want to be a total separatist again: few who have experienced that kind of isolation believe it is the ultimate goal of liberation. Since unity and coalition seem necessary, the question for me is unity on what terms? with whom? and around what politics? For instance, to unify the lesbian-feminist politics developed within the past four years with socialist-feminism requires more than token reference to queers. It requires an acknowledgment of lesbian-feminist analysis as central to understanding and ending woman's oppression.

The heart of lesbian-feminist politics, let me repeat, is a recognition that heterosexuality as an institution and an ideology is a cornerstone of male supremacy. Therefore, women interested in destroying male supremacy, patriarchy, and capitalism must, equally with lesbians, fight heterosexual domination—or we will never end female oppression. This is what I call "the heterosexual question"—it is *not* the lesbian question.

Although lesbians have been the quickest to see the challenge to heterosexuality as a necessity for feminists' survival, straight feminists are not precluded from examining and fighting against heterosexuality. The problem is that few have done so. This perpetuates lesbian fears that women remaining tied to men prevents them from seeing the function of heterosexuality and acting to end it. It is not lesbianism (women's ties to women), but heterosexuality (women's ties to men), and thus men themselves, which divides women politically and personally. This is the "divisiveness" of the lesbian issue to the women's movement. We won't get beyond it by demanding that lesbians retreat, politics in hand, back into the closet. We will only get beyond it by struggling over the institutional and ideological analysis of lesbian-feminism. We need to discover what lesbian consciousness means for any woman, just as we struggle to understand what class or race consciousness means for women of any race or class. And we must develop strategies that will destroy the political institutions that oppress us.

It is particularly important for those at this conference to understand that heterosexuality—as an ideology and as an institution—upholds all those aspects of female oppression which have been discussed here. For example, heterosexuality is basic to our oppression in the workplace. When we look at how women are defined and exploited as secondary, marginal workers, we recognize that this definition assumes that all women are tied to men. I mention the workplace because it upset me yesterday at the economics panel that no one made that connection; and further, no one recognized that a high percentage of women workers are lesbian and therefore their relationship to, and attitudes toward, work are fundamentally different from those assumed by straight workers. It is obvious that heterosexuality upholds the home, housework, the family as both a personal and economic unit. It is apparently not so obvious that the whole framework of heterosexuality defines our lives, that it is fundamental to the negative self-image and self-hatred of women in this society. Lesbian-feminism is based on a rejection of male definitions of our lives and is therefore crucial to the development of a positive woman-identified identity, of redefining who we are supposed to be in every situation, including the workplace.

What is that definition? Basically, heterosexuality means men first. That's what it's all about. It assumes that every woman is heterosexual; that every woman is defined by and is the property of men. Her body, her services, her children belong to men. If you don't accept that definition, you're a queer—no matter who you sleep with; if you do not accept that definition in this society, you're queer. The original imperialist assumption of the right of men to the bodies and services of women has been translated into a whole variety of forms of domination throughout this society. And as long as people accept that initial assumption—and question everything *but* that assumption—it is impossible to challenge the other forms of domination.

What makes heterosexuality work is heterosexual privilege—and if you don't have a sense of what that privilege is, I suggest that you go home and announce to everybody that you know—a roommate, your family, the people you work with—everywhere you go—that you're a queer. Try being a queer for a week. Do not walk out on the street with men; walk only with women, especially at night. For a whole week, experience life as if you were a lesbian, and I think you will know what heterosexual privilege is very quickly. And, hopefully, you will also learn that heterosexual privilege is the method by which women are given a stake in male supremacy—and that it is therefore the method by which women are given a stake in their own oppression. Simply stated, a woman who stays in line—by staying straight or by refusing to resist straight privileges—receives some of the benefits of male privilege indirectly and is thus given a stake in continuing those privileges and maintaining their source—male supremacy.

Heterosexual women must realize—no matter what their personal connection to men—that the benefits that they receive from men will always be in diluted form and will ultimately result in their own self-destruction. When a woman's individual survival is tied to men, she is at some intrinsic place separated from other women and from the survival needs of those other women. The question arises not because of rhetorical necessity—whether a woman is personally loyal to other women—but because we must examine what stake each of us has in the continuation of male supremacy. For example, if you are receiving heterosexual benefits through a man (or through his social, cultural, or political systems), are you clear about what those benefits are doing to you, both personally, and in terms of other women? I have known women who are very strong in fighting against female job discrimination, but when the battle closes in on their man's job, they desert that position. In universities, specifically, when a husband's job is threatened by feminist hiring demands, I have seen feminists abandon their political positions in order to keep the privileges they receive from their man's job.

This analysis of the function of heterosexuality in women's oppression is available to any woman, lesbian or straight. Lesbian-feminism is not a political analysis "for lesbians only." It is a political perspective and fight against one of the major institutions of our oppression—a fight which heterosexual women can engage in. The problem is that few do. Since lesbians are materially oppressed by heterosexuality daily, it is not surprising that we have seen and understood its impact first—not because we are more moral, but because our reality is different—and it is a *materially* different reality. We are trying to convey this fact of our oppression to you because, whether you feel it directly or not, it also oppresses you; and because if we are going to change society and survive, we must all attack heterosexual domination.

CLASS AND LESBIANISM

There is another important aspect of lesbian-feminism which should be of interest to a socialist-feminist conference: the connection between lesbianism and class. One of the ways that lesbianism has affected the movement is in changing women's individual lives. Those of us who are out of the closet have, in particular, learned that we must create our own world—we haven't any choice in the matter, because there is no institution in this society that is created for us. Once we are out, there is no place that wholeheartedly accepts us. Coming out is important, partly because it puts us in a materially different reality in terms of what we have to do. And it is the impact of reality that moves anyone to understand and change. I don't believe that idealism is the primary force that moves people; necessity moves people. And lesbians who are out are moved by necessity—not by choice—to create our own world. Frequently (and mistakenly), that task has been characterized as cultural. While the culture gives us strength, the impetus is economic: the expression of necessity is always material. For middle-class women this is especially true—lesbianism means discovering that we have to support ourselves for the rest of our lives, something that lower- and working-class women have always known. This discovery makes us begin to understand what lower- and working-class women have been trying to tell us all along: "What do you know about survival?"

I heard a lot about class analysis when I was in the Left, and some of it was helpful. But it wasn't until I came out as a lesbian and had to face my own survival on that basis—as an outlaw, as a woman alone—that I learned about class in my own life. Then I learned what the Left had never taught me—what my middle-class assumptions were and the way in which my background crippled me as a woman. I began to understand how my own middle-class background was holding me back personally and the ways in which middle-class assumptions were holding back the growth of our movement. Class affects the way we operate every day—as has been obvious in much of what has happened in this conference. And theories of class should help us understand that. The only way to understand the function of class in society, as far as I'm concerned, is to understand how it functions right here, on the spot, day to day, in our lives.

Another way in which class consciousness has occurred in the lesbian community—and I want to acknowledge it because it is frequently one of the things kept locked in the bedroom closet—is the cross-class intimacy that occurs among lesbians. This intimacy usually leads to an on-the-spot analysis of class oppression and conflict based on the experience of being hit over the head with it. Understand that I am not advising every middle-class woman to go out and get herself a lower-class lesbian to teach her about class-in-the-raw; but also understand that I am saying that there's no faster way to learn how class functions in our world.

Cross-class contact occurs all the time in the lesbian community, frequently without any self-conscious politics attached to it. For example, in lesbian bars, a political process that is often misinterpreted as a purely social process is going on in women's lives. Because there are no men in that environment, the conflicts around class and race—those issues basic to women's survival— become crystal clear, if you understand them not in rhetorical or theoretical terms, but in the ways that women's lives are interacting with each other's. This is one reason why a lot of class analysis, particularly the practical kind, has come out of the lesbian-feminist movement—analysis based on our experience of class contact and conflict, our recognition of it, and our integration of its meanings in the way we live our lives. This material experience of class realities produces real commitment to struggle and to the class question not out of idealism but as integral to our survival. Idealism can be abandoned at any time. Survival cannot.

I want to be clear about what it is that I am *not* saying. I am not saying that all lesbians are feminists; all lesbians are not politically conscious. I *am* saying that the particular material reality of lesbian life makes political consciousness more likely; we can build on the fact that it is not in the interests of lesbians to maintain and defend the system as it is.

I am also *not* saying that the only way to have this political analysis is to be a lesbian. But I *am* saying that so far most of the people with lesbian-feminist politics who have challenged heterosexuality are lesbians. But ours is not the only way, and we've got to make it not the only way. We, as lesbians, are a minority. We cannot survive alone. We will not survive alone, but if we do not survive the entire women's movement will be defeated and female oppression will be reenacted in other forms. As we all understand survival more clearly, we see that the politics and analysis of women's oppression coming out of the lesbian's life experience have got to be integrated into the politics of socialist-feminism and the rest of the women's movement.

180

It is not okay to be queer under patriarchy—and the last thing we should be aiming to do is to make it okay. Nothing in capitalist-patriarchal America works to our benefit and I do not want to see us working in any way to integrate ourselves into that order. I'm not saying that we should neglect work on reforms—we must have our jobs, our housing, and so on. But in so doing we must not lose sight of our ultimate goal. Our very strength as lesbians lies in the fact that we are outside of patriarchy; our existence challenges its life. To work for "acceptance" is to work for our own disintegration and an end to the clarity and energy we bring to the women's movement.

It is not okay, and I do not want it ever to be okay, to be queer in patriarchy. The entire system of capitalism and patriarchy must be changed. And essential to that change is an end to heterosexual domination. Lesbians cannot work in movements that do not recognize that heterosexuality is central to all women's oppression: that would be to work for our own self-destruction. But we can coalesce with groups which share the lesbian-feminist analysis and are committed to the changes essential to our survival. This is the basis upon which we can begin to build greater unity and a stronger, more powerful feminist movement.

LEARNING FROM LESBIAN SEPARATISM

t was December when I first slept with a woman: I was married, it was snowing outside, and my days were filled with the unceasing events of women's liberation. Six months later, my four-year-old marriage was finished, my life with women was entire, and the sweltering summer heat of Washington, D.C., had replaced the snow. I sat on a mattress in a back room with eleven other women planning what to do now: we had just declared ourselves *lesbian-feminist separatists* and had disassociated ourselves from all women's-movement activities. It was 1971. We realized, as similar groups did in other cities during that early, fast-moving spread of lesbianism through the women's movement, that we had to figure out what had happened to us, and why. A few members of our group had been lesbians for years, some had previous experience in the gay liberation movement; but the majority of us—for a variety of reasons—had come out within the context of feminism. The movement had been our family—our mother and our child. When we began to proclaim our love for one another in ways that went beyond the boundaries of "familial love," most of us did not realize how savagely we would be disinherited by our "sisters."

"Learning from Lesbian Separatism" was first published in *Ms.* magazine (November 1976).

We had to ask the difficult question: why? Why was a movement devoted to women's freedom of choice so afraid of women who chose to love women—instead of men? We could tell ourselves that such organizations as the National Organization for Women were frightened of losing their acceptance in the male world, but that didn't seem enough of an answer. Furthermore, most of our own experience had not been in reformist structures like NOW, but in the radical feminist movement: that loose network of consciousness-raising, theoretical, and activist groups talking about a deep and revolutionary change in every part of society, not just reforms that left basic patriarchy intact. Yet our experiences as lesbians in radical feminist groups had been no less painful than those of other lesbians in NOW.

Coletta Reid was a feminist who had also recently left her husband, found her identity as a lesbian, and then chosen a lesbian-separatist stance. In an article called "Coming Out in the Women's Movement" (*Lesbianism and the Women's Movement*, Baltimore: Diana Press, 1975, pp. 94–95), she describes an incident that helps to explain why we became separatists:

> The full range of attitudes and prejudices came out in the course of a meeting of a day-care center I had helped found and worked in for nine months. One woman expressed misgivings about me or my friends being around her daughter since I had become a lesbian. She evidently thought I would molest her little precious; she had no similar qualms about my being around her son when I was heterosexual. Nor had she any qualms about the heterosexual men being around her daughter, which is strange since 100 percent of the child molestation cases reported in the District of Columbia last year were committed by men. Another woman said she thought lesbians were too hostile, angry, and man-hating to be around children who needed love and good vibes. . . . Some of the men at the day-care center were outrageously piggy toward the children, but they were never called on the carpet at a meeting or put in the position of having to defend themselves as I was.

The lesbians who had been gay prior to the existence of the feminist movement were less surprised by our rejection than those of us newly gay and full of enthusiasm for our recent self-discoveries. The "older" lesbians knew something that we had just begun to learn: lesbianism is not only a threat to men, but also to many heterosexual women. It suggests that women do not inevitably have to love men, or to love them at any cost.

Of course, challenging heterosexuality in any form is seen as threatening by some women. We are sometimes accused by "straight" feminists of guilt-tripping them about their personal lives; of implying that sexual dependence on men made them somehow less feminist. In fact, we were less concerned about an individual woman's personal choice than about the institution of heterosexuality; less concerned with sex roles than with sex power. Furthermore, challenging almost any issue impacting women— marriage, motherhood, and so on—necessarily raises questions about women's lives. We cannot abandon our insights into these institutions of male supremacy in order to avoid making each other uncomfortable.

As separatists, we stopped trying to justify our lives to straight society and instead concentrated on ourselves. We began to analyze our experiences and our perceptions of the world in the relative isolation of a collective of twelve white lesbians from varying class backgrounds. In January of 1972, we began a newspaper, *The Furies,* dedicated to lesbian-feminist political analysis and ideology.

For the first time, our reality was the dominant one, and we were able to begin to understand how it differed from the heterosexual reality that dominated everywhere else. We had become separatists for many reasons, but one was to learn about ourselves as a people—and learn we did. We discovered the strengths of women who have to live on their own. Heterosexuality, in providing some of us with a buffer zone in a man's world, had stunted our growth. We also encountered acute class and race conflict in our own midst, made all the more clear by the absence of men and male influence. We experienced the pain and the exhilaration of developing relationships where society gave us no models; relationships among equals, not based on preset male and female roles. Most of all we saw that lesbians are indeed a people, similar to other women, but also different: our uniqueness provided us with a perspective on feminism that we began to develop into a politics, called lesbian-feminism.

Separatism was the only way we saw to create lesbian-feminist politics and build a community of our own in the hostile environment of the early seventies. Many lesbians chose a separatist strategy in order to build our own pride, strength, and unity as a people, to develop an analysis of our particular oppression, and to create a political ideology and strategy that would both force the movement's recognition of us and lead to the end of male supremacy.

Thanks in part to this time of separatism by lesbian groups in many cities, lesbian communities can now exist openly and proudly throughout the nation as the backbone of many feminist political, cultural, and economic activities. Most women's groups now recognize the "legitimacy" of lesbians' civil rights in society, as well as our right to exist openly in their midst.

Lesbian-feminism, however, is far more than civil rights for queers or lesbian communities and culture. It is a political perspective on a crucial aspect of male supremacy—heterosexism, the ideological and institutional domination of heterosexuality. The development of this political perspective was one of the most important results of lesbian separatism.

The first public statement of lesbian-feminist politics can be dated, at least symbolically, from a paper called "The Woman-Identified Woman," issued by Radicalesbians in New York City on May 1, 1970. It begins:

> What is a lesbian? A lesbian is the rage of all women condensed to the point of explosion. She is the woman who, often beginning at an extremely early age, acts in accordance with her inner compulsion to be a more complete and freer human being than her society—perhaps then, but certainly later—cares to allow her. . . . On some level she has not been able to accept the limitations and oppressions laid on her by the most basic role of her society—the female role.

The paper went on to analyze the nascent political power and consciousness in the personal act of being a lesbian in a male-supremacist society; of putting women first in defiance of a culture that has structured the female life around the male. It discussed how the word, the label, "lesbian," has been used to keep women divided:

When a woman hears this word tossed her way, she knows she is stepping out of line . . . for a woman to be independent means she *can't* be a woman—she must be a dyke. . . . As long as the label "dyke" can be used to frighten women into a less militant stand, keep her separate from her sisters, keep her from giving primacy to anything other than men and family—then to that extent she is controlled by the male culture.

The statement expanded the definition of lesbianism by developing the idea of women-identification as an act of self-affirmation and love for all women; primary identification with women that gives energy through a positive sense of self, developed with reference to ourselves, and not in relation to men. As Rita Mae Brown, one of the founders of both Radicalesbians and *The Furies,* explained in "The Shape of Things to Come" (*Lesbianism and the Women's Movement,* Baltimore: Diana Press, 1975, pp. 69–77):

Women who love women are lesbians. Men, because they can only think of women in sexual terms, define lesbian as sex between women. However, lesbians know that it is far more than that, it is a different way of life. It is a life determined by a woman for her own benefit and the benefit of other women. It is a life that draws its strength, support, and direction from women. . . . You refuse to limit yourself by the male definitions of women. You free yourself from male concepts of "feminine" behavior.

Since all traditionally defined lesbians are not women-identified in their heads and hearts, this definition might not apply to some of them. Yet potentially, any woman could become woman-identified. The original paper concluded with a call for woman-idenification and suggested that this was the central importance of lesbianism to the women's movement.

The heart of the woman-identified-woman statement and of all lesbian-feminist politics is the recognition that, in a male-supremacist society, heterosexuality is a political institution. Both lesbianism and heterosexuality are therefore political forces as well as personal life-styles. At first, we saw this insight as a natural outgrowth of feminism and expected it to be incorporated into the theory and action of the women's movement. However, as many

186

feminists shied away from the political significance of lesbianism, most of that politics was developed by separatists, outside the formal confines of the movement.

Recognition of the political significance of lesbianism led us to an analysis of how heterosexuality functions to support male supremacy. Every institution that feminists have shown to be oppressive to women—the workplace, schools, the family, the media, organized religion—is also based on heterosexism, on the assumption that every woman either is or wishes to be bonded to a man both economically and emotionally. In order to effectively challenge our oppression in those institutions, we must also challenge the ideology of heterosexism.

Granted, this challenge must seem initially difficult for women whose sexual life is bound up with men; but less difficult as we understand that heterosexuality is more than sex. In our society, heterosexuality goes hand in hand with the sexist assumption that each woman exists for a man—her body, her children, and her services are his property. If a woman does not accept that definition of heterosexuality and of herself, she is queer—no matter whom she sleeps with. Heterosexism depends on the idea that heterosexuality is both the only natural and the superior form of human sexuality, thus providing ideological support to male supremacy. Heterosexism is basic to women's oppression in the family and to discrimination against single or other women who live outside the nuclear family.

Heterosexism also supports male supremacy in the workplace. Women are defined and exploited as secondary and marginal workers on the assumption that work is not our primary vocation; even if we work all our lives, we are assumed to be primarily committed to home and to have a second (major) breadwinner supporting us. No matter how false this is for most women, especially gay, black, and lower-class women, the ideology of heterosexuality continues to justify the mythology, and thus the discrimination against women at work.

One of the things that keeps heterosexual domination going is heterosexual privilege; those actual or promised benefits for a woman who stays in line: legitimacy, economic security, social acceptance, legal and physical protection. Through these privileges, a woman is given a stake in behaving properly and in maintaining her own oppression. She works against her own self-

187

interest by becoming dependent on a man and on male privileges and undermines her self-respect. She also separates herself from her sisters—in particular her lesbian sisters—who have no such privileges. Unless a woman, no matter what her personal connection to men, realizes that her own survival is tied more to that of all women than it is to one man, the "privileges" she receives are not lasting benefits but links in the chain of oppression.

Feminists, whatever their sexual orientation, have to understand that heterosexual privilege is a small and short-term bribe in return for giving up lasting self-discovery and collective power. Straight feminists sometimes ask how they can fight heterosexism if they do not choose to live a lesbian life-style. This is a crucial question in bridging the gay-straight gap. Heterosexual women can, for example, challenge the assumptions and privileges of heterosexuality as they encounter them daily, in every area from the denial of spousal benefits for lesbians in various health, life insurance, and pension policies to social attitudes about correct behavior at a party. (For example, why must people come in pairs, or be seated alternately "boy-girl" no matter what their interests?)

One of the ways to understand better what I am saying—and what anyone can do—is to "think queer," no matter what your sexuality. By "think queer," I mean imagine life as a lesbian for a week. Announce to everyone—family, roommate, on the job, everywhere you go—that you are a lesbian. Walk in the street and go out only with women, especially at night. Imagine your life, economically and emotionally, with women instead of men. For a whole week, experience life as if you were a lesbian, and you will learn quickly what heterosexual privileges and assumptions are, and how they function to keep male supremacy working.

You will also see, as lesbians have learned, that it is *not* okay to be a lesbian in America. And it is not okay for a reason that goes beyond individual attitudes or bigotry. It is not okay because self-loving and independent women are a challenge to the idea that men are superior, an idea that social institutions strengthen and enshrine. The more any woman steps outside of society's assumptions, the more "lesbian" she becomes and the more clearly she sees exactly how those heterosexist assumptions confine her as an individual and women as a group.

One week of pretending will show you why the life of a lesbian is not the same as that of a straight woman. This does not necessarily make lesbians better or worse feminists; but it does make our perspective on male society different. That difference, like differences of race and class, can be the basis of division among women or it can be an opportunity for broader feminist analysis and action. To deny these differences is to deny both our particular oppression and our particular strength. True unity is grounded not on a false notion of sameness, but on understanding and utilizing diversity to gain the greatest possible scope and power.

A lesbian's reality and perspective are also not the same as those of a gay man. This was one of the first and hardest lessons that we learned in the gay liberation movement. Gay men, because they frequently challenge sex-role stereotypes, are punished in this society: to seem like a "woman" when one can be a "man" is to betray male supremacy. But gay men are still men. And they rarely challenge male prerogatives and power directly. In fact, those gay men who want to share equally with straight men in male privileges are no less our oppressors than their heterosexual counterparts. For this reason, many lesbian-feminists have been no more comfortable in the gay movement than in the women's movement.

Nevertheless, our experiences have shown us the close relationship between male supremacy and heterosexual domination: homophobia and gay oppression are based in sexism and the institutional power of male supremacy. While gay men have some male privileges, particularly when they remain closeted, they will be scorned as long as women are scorned. Their long-term interests lie not in attempting to gain straight acceptance as "real" men but in challenging sexism along with heterosexism. Gay men face a choice of either seeking male privilege, or rejecting the patriarchal basis of those privileges and working for a long-term elimination of the entire system of sexual oppression.

In the past couple of years, many lesbian-feminist separatists have begun to work again with straight feminists and with gay men. My own move away from complete separatism began in 1973. I had learned, changed, and grown during those years as a separatist, but I felt that I was becoming too isolated. Since the core of a lesbian-feminist politics and community had been developed, it seemed important that we become involved with other feminist projects and analytical developments. (In reporting my own experiences, I do not mean to imply that separatism is dead.

189

In some places it is still performing that first task of uniting lesbians. Separatism is a dynamic strategy to be moved in and out of whenever a minority feels that its interests are being overlooked by the majority, or that its insights need more space to be developed.)

Lucia Valeska analyzed the separatist situation concisely in an article for *Quest: A Feminist Quarterly* entitled "The Future of Female Separatism," where she wrote: "Whatever your opinion of it, female separatism has just as long and viable a future as male supremacy." So, too, lesbian-feminist separation will no doubt continue in some forms as long as there is heterosexual domination. And, as Valeska concluded: "In the meantime, regardless of the strategical success of feminism, individual women will continue to find a perpetual wellspring of freedom, affirmation, strength, and joy in lesbianism. That is, reduced to its smallest conceivable contribution, lesbianism remains a powerful political force." (Pp. 2–16.)

We must not lose sight of why separatism happened in the first place. It happened because straight feminists were unable to allow lesbians space to grow—to develop our personal lives and our political insights. Unless lesbian-feminist politics is incorporated into feminist analysis and action, we will reexperience the old and destructive gay-straight split. Furthermore, we will ultimately lose the battle against male supremacy, for no woman is truly free to be anything until she is also free to be a lesbian.

Lesbian-feminist separatism has produced not only a political analysis vital to all women, but structural innovations as well. After all, lesbians must create new institutions for survival, particularly once we have come out publicly, because we do not fit anywhere, whether it's the family or church, schools or nightclubs. Of necessity, we must challenge those structures to change or create alternatives.

Lesbians have played a leading role in the creation of women's art, media, and other cultural institutions, as well as in feminist economic ventures such as credit unions, bookstores, and restaurants. Our enforced economic independence has led to a growing class-consciousness and an emphasis on the economic problems of women. When lesbians come out and actively pursue the meaning of woman-identification, survival questions must immediately be faced.

190

If I return to the women whose story started this article—for instance—the women who formed The Furies collective, the life-force of lesbian feminism becomes very clear. Most of the women in that group have continued to be involved in the development of feminist theory, communications, economic and cultural strategies. *The Furies* ceased publication in 1973, and many of us went on to found and sustain a variety of projects, all national in scope. Rita Mae Brown and I became part of the group that started *Quest: A Feminist Quarterly;* Coletta Reid and Nancy Myron helped develop and expand Diana Press into one of the major feminist presses; Joan Biren was one of the founders of Moonforce Media, a national women's film company. Several other Furies members helped to conceive and develop Olivia Records, a women's recording company, and later, Women in Distribution (WIND), a national distribution service for women's media.

Our time as lesbian-feminist separatists, like that of lesbians in other cities, was less a period of being "out" of the women's movement than of being profoundly "in" the heart of its matter. It was a time that allowed us to develop both political insights and concrete projects that now aid women's survival and strength. We learned that change is a process. And in that process, becoming women-identified women may be the only way that women, whatever our sexual identity, can begin to see our potential for change.

ELECTION YEAR:
GAY PERSPECTIVES

W hat is the gay political perspective for the Bicentennial year? Red, white, and blue closets or a red and lavender star? I trust I'm not exposing any national secrets or washing movement laundry in public if I say there *is* no gay political perspective in 1976. This year, more than ever—since gays went public in a big way some six years ago—it has become clear that there are as many divergent politics in the "gay community" as in the straight. And if one also asks how gays relate to straight politics, we wind up with an enormous array of issues, perspectives, and options—a multitude of positions on important questions. Gay people in this country share an exclusion from legitimate channels for expression, not a particular politics.

Most gay political opinion clusters around one of four basic positions: assimilationist; civil rights reformist; socialist; radical feminist. As with any spectrum of political categories, individuals are not necessarily pure types but are often expressions of various combinations. Still, an examination of each of these positions should be useful for understanding gay politics in 1976.

1. The assimilationist position is best characterized by the state-

"Election Year: Gay Perspectives" first appeared in *Christopher Street* magazine, vol. I, no. 1 (July 1976).

ment "gay is just like straight." It attempts to outstraight the heterosexual middle-class American way by proving that gays are not different. Those making this effort are embarrassed by faggot culture and outraged by dyke separatists. While not necessarily in the closet, they certainly do not view gay people as distinct and are often uncomfortable to be identified as gay. In falling all over themselves to deny that there is anything special about being gay, they commit their greatest mistake—they lose that very thing that distinguishes us and saves us from the great American malaise: the sense of difference that comes when one is not just perpetuating what is but is actively involved in the creation of what is to be. They are like travelers scurrying to get on board the *Titanic.*

2. Civil rights reformists go further than the assimilationists. They are comfortable being identified as gay and sometimes admit that there may be differences between gay life and straight. They say, "Gay is just as good as straight." Many people support gay civil rights but this political position as I define it is that of hardcore reformers who are distinguished by their abiding faith that achieving civil rights for gays will end oppression—an astounding notion that flies in the face of all the evidence of the sixties. This hard core works for legislative, electoral, and judicial victories. They seek recognition of particular gay concerns (e.g., a mention in the Democratic party platform); above all they labor to prove that queers are good enough to hold any job or any political responsibility and fulfill the dream of middle-class America. The ideal might be seen as a TV series, "Marcus Welby, Gay M.D."

This position represents the mainstream of gay politics. In addition to the core with faith in the American reform tradition, there are others whose politics go beyond reformism but who work on civil rights for practical reasons. Civil rights reformers have a variety of opinions about their radical counterparts—ranging from a view of them as "gay spoilers" to genuine allies using different methods.

3. The gay socialists are the leftist counterparts of the gay reformists. For them the motto changes to "gay is just as revolutionary as straight." By and large, the gay socialist works for acceptance in the heterosexual counterculture or in a particular leftist sect, seeking to prove that queers are good enough to hold any job or take any political responsibility in the left: "Marcus

Welby, Gay M.D." becomes an underground film about a gay, socialist-activist law commune.

Efforts spent defending gays from being defined as products of "bourgeois decadence" or unnatural side effects of capitalism are not unlike the defense mounted by reformists against claims that we are immoral, un-Christian, and/or sick. Once more, gays are on the defense to establish credentials for political leadership on straight terms. While gay people may be socialists for many reasons, the gay-socialist stance is firmly embedded in the notion that homosexual oppression collapses or can best be ended with the advent of socialism—*if only* gays work hard enough, prove their revolutionary ardor, and don't let the kinky or feminist elements get out of hand.

4. This brings me to the gay radical feminists who say, "Gay, or lesbian, is proud," and insist that we *are* different and that our differences should lead to changes in straight society. Primarily developed by women, the heart of this position is lesbian-feminist politics. Lesbian-feminists assert that homosexual oppression is intricately connected to women's oppression through the patriarchal institutions of male supremacy and heterosexuality, and therefore heterosexism and sexism must be fought together. The lesbian-feminist maintains that gays, particularly lesbians, are not like straights—will not be like straights—since straight society is synonymous with male supremacy, heterosexual roles, and woman-hatred. To deny the difference is to deny our power and potential for change.

Lesbian-feminism founders on the question of what to do with these politics. Most of us are concentrating on building our own institutions and developing strategies for power that can lead to changes in the structure of society. However, views on questions like separatism and how to relate to men, gay or straight, vary. Some totally reject separatism. Some see it as a strategy to be used when necessary. Some proclaim it the goal for lesbians. Attitudes toward reformists vary from cordial working relations to denunciation of all reform as collaboration. The male counterpart to the lesbian-feminist is that small but significant band of gay men who accept the feminist analysis. They try to understand how male supremacy works against their interests and how gay men can participate in the destruction of patriarchy.

While individuals may have a mix of particular views, involvement in any political activity is usually based, consciously or unconsciously, on one or another of these four positions. The particular activity that a person engages in, however, does not always locate them on this spectrum; many issues, such as legislative changes, can be approached from any of these political positions. But the arguments and methods that someone uses in making the case for change and its consequences usually do reveal one or another of these four basic political perspectives as the premise.

While agreeing that lesbians and homosexual men are oppressed, each of these groupings views that oppression, its causes and its remedies, differently. Therefore, individuals within each grouping tend to find allies in the particular sector of straight society—conservative, liberal, socialist, or feminist—that shares their political attitudes and approach, rather than within other gay positions. This minimizes the potential of a gay united front: consequently there is no united gay position in 1976.

As the election year rolls on, with debate over gay planks and the nature of the gay vote, the real gay "politics" nationally is the competition among leaders and activists over who will be the legitimate representatives to define what straights will see as *the* gay political perspective in 1976. This competition can be as exciting, diverse, instructive, and vicious as the Democratic presidential lottery. How much is learned from this struggle depends on how well we understand the underlying political issues. Whatever else happens, one thing should remain clear: gay is not the same as straight but we are also not all the same.

195

LESBIAN-FEMINIST THEORY

esbianism and feminism are both about women loving and
supporting women and women revolting against the so-called
supremacy of men and the patriarchal institutions that control
us. Politically, understanding the connection between lesbianism and feminism is essential to ending the oppression of all
women and of all homosexuals, both female and male. The political theory that embodies and defines that connection is called
lesbian feminism. It is a theory that has grown out of the experiences of lesbians in both the feminist and the gay movements; out
of both our participation in those movements and our separation
from them at various times and places. It is the theory that holds
the key to the relationship between homosexual oppression and
female oppression—a connection linked in the lives of lesbians.
And it is a theory that is unknown or misunderstood by many
feminists, lesbians, and gay men.

In this article, I hope to erase that last sentence by clarifying
the principles of lesbian feminism: to illustrate to the homosexual
that *no queers* will ever be free as long as sexism persists because
male supremacy is at the root of both gay oppression and homo-

"Lesbian-Feminist Theory" was first published in *Our Right to Love,* Virginia Vida, ed.
(Englewood Cliffs, N.J.: Prentice-Hall, Inc., 1978).

196

phobia. To demonstrate to the woman that *no females* will ever be free to choose to be anything until we are also free to choose to be lesbians, because the domination of heterosexuality is a mainstay of male supremacy. And above all, to show the lesbian (the homosexual and woman) that these two parts of our oppression are linked and not only need not but also should not be separated in our struggles for liberation.

The development of lesbian-feminist theory began for most of us with the recognition on some level that in a male-supremacist culture, heterosexuality is a political institution as well as a sexual preference, and, therefore, lesbianism is political as well as personal. "The Woman-Identified Woman" statement, one of the earlier lesbian-feminist documents issued by Radicalesbians in 1970, pointed to the political implications of lesbianism when it stated: "On some level, she [the lesbian] has not been able to accept the limitations and oppressions laid on her by the most basic role of her society—the female role." That paper and subsequent discussion went on to analyze the nascent political power and consciousness in the personal act of being a lesbian in a male-supremacist society; it is the act, whether consciously or not, of putting women first in defiance of a culture that has structured the female life around the male. Based on this recognition, the concept of woman-identification came to describe the life stance of self-affirmation and love for women; of primary identification with women that gives energy through a positive sense of self, developed with reference to ourselves, and not in relation to men.

In this context, lesbian feminism takes on its political significance. It is not just a personal choice about life-style, although it involves one in a highly personal and intimate way. It is not limited to civil rights for queers, although equal rights and job protection are absolutely essential. It is more than the dynamic female culture and community that has emerged recently, although that is crucial to our survival and power as a people. Lesbian feminism as it has developed over the past decade involves all of these, but as a political theory, it is primarily a critique of heterosexism—the institutional and ideological domination of heterosexuality, as a fundamental part of male supremacy. This theory extends the feminist analysis of sexual politics to an analysis of sexuality itself, as it is structured into our society today. Its practical application involves an orientation of one's life around

197

women (woman-identification) and a commitment to women as a political force capable of changing society as well as our life-style.

Before discussing lesbian-feminist analysis further, let me clarify my use of terms that have often caused confusion. *Lesbian-feminist theory,* as a critique of male supremacy and heterosexism, is a perspective, analysis, and commitment that can be embraced by anyone, gay or straight, female or male—just as socialism or Pan-Africanism are theories that can be adopted by anyone regardless of race, sex, or class. A *lesbian* is a woman whose sexual/affectional preference is for women, and who has thereby rejected the female role on some level, but she may or may not embrace a lesbian-feminist political analysis. A *woman-identified woman* is a feminist who adopts a lesbian-feminist ideology and enacts that understanding in her life, whether she is a lesbian sexually or not. All lesbians are not woman-identified; all feminists are not woman-identified; but a clearer understanding of lesbian feminism should enable more of both to unite around this common identification.

As more lesbians recognized the political significance of lesbianism, we began to see that heterosexism functions in every institution that feminists have shown to be oppressive to women: the workplace, schools, the family, the media, organized religion, and so on. All of society's institutions are based on the assumption that every woman either is or wants to be bonded to a man both economically and emotionally and they depend on the idea that heterosexuality is both the only natural and the superior form of human sexuality. These assumptions—the ideology of heterosexism—help to maintain the institutional oppression of all women and of those men who openly deviate from the heterosexist masculine norm.

The family and women's oppression within it are obviously based on heterosexism, as are forms of discrimination against single women or any who live outside the nuclear family. Less obvious, but equally important, discrimination against women in the workplace is also supported by the ideology of heterosexism. Women are defined and exploited as secondary or marginal workers on the assumption that work is not our primary vocation: even if we work outside of the home all of our lives, we are assumed to be primarily committed to family and to have another (major) breadwinner (male) supporting us. This assumption has been

198

proved false repeatedly, not only for lesbians but also for many others, especially Third World and lower-class women. Nevertheless, the myth prevails—the ideology of heterosexism linked with the institution of the nuclear family continues to justify job discrimination and the refusal to regard work as a serious goal for women.

One could similarly describe how heterosexist attitudes permeate all the other institutions of our society. Perhaps most important is how heterosexism has been used to deny women's strength, to tie her self-concept and survival to men. According to society, if you are not with a man, you are not fully a woman; whether celibate or lesbian, you are seen as "queer." If you are independent and aggressive about your life, you are called a "dyke," regardless of sexual preference. Such labels have been used to terrify women—to keep straight women in their place and to keep lesbians in the closet.

Labels are not just name-calling. Behind each label is the implicit threat of social, economic, or physical reprisal—the denial of life-support systems or even life itself if you step too far out of line. Thus, the most pervasive and insidious thing that keeps heterosexual domination going is the control over granting or denying women heterosexual privileges: social and family acceptance, economic security, male legitimacy, legal and physical protection. The degree to which you receive these benefits depends on race, sex, and class, and on how much you play by the patriarchy's rules. Through heterosexual privilege, a woman is given a stake in behaving properly (or, in the case of a lesbian, of pretending to behave properly), and thus, in maintaining the system that perpetuates her own oppression. Women, no matter what their sexual orientation or personal ties to men, must realize that our ultimate survival is more connected to that of all women than to one man. Heterosexual privileges are not lasting benefits or power but small, short-term bribes in return for giving up lasting self-discovery and collective power.

If we examine the labels and the language that have been used against us from another angle, they reveal the potential power of lesbianism and woman-identification. Why does society equate female assertiveness, independence, and wholeness (ability to live without a man) with the terms "lesbian," "man-hating dyke," "butch" (male imitator or potent one), "ball-breaker," and so on?

The language used against us is the language of power and battle. Men sense in the presence of lesbians the power to revolt, to threaten their "supremacy." They perceived this potential power before we ourselves understood it, and they sought to repress our sexuality as one aspect of our potential for independence of them and for changing society.

Lesbian-feminist theory did not spring up in a vacuum; it developed out of our experiences in coming out, from the reaction against us, and particularly from our efforts to understand and analyze that reaction. Most of us who enthusiastically came out and asserted our right to be "lesbian, woman, and proud" in the late sixties and early seventies did not understand fully the threat to patriarchal society of our statements and actions. We had been warned by "older" lesbians about the dangers, but we only learned what a threat lesbianism is by the reactions we experienced both in society and in the movements that we knew—civil rights, feminist, leftist, and even gay male. Then we learned that we are outlaws. We realized that it was not okay to be lesbian in America. And we learned that it is not okay for a reason that goes far beyond individual attitudes and bigotry. It is not okay because self-loving and independent women are a challenge to the idea that men are superior, an idea that patriarchy's institutions strengthen and depend upon.

The lesbian is most clearly the antithesis of patriarchy—an offense to its basic tenets: it is woman-hating; we are woman-loving. It demands female obedience and docility; we seek strength, assertiveness, and dignity for women. It bases power and defined roles on one's gender and other physical attributes; we operate outside gender-defined roles and seek a new basis for defining power and relationships. Our very existence is an attack on what men have defined as "their" territory. The lesbian's future lies not in surrendering our position as outlaws for token acceptance but in seizing and using it to bring change in patriarchal society. It is our very situation as outlaws that gives us much of the strength and imagination to challenge male definitions of us and of the social order. Some of the early lesbian slogans and titles caught the essence of that power: The Lavender Menace; The Furies; Spectre; We Are the Women Your Mother Warned You About.

While working for our civil rights and the space to develop our own life-styles and institutions, we must not think that we can be absorbed into patriarchy as it is. We must be cautious about using the "we are just like you" strategy. We *are* different. And society needs our differences: our ability to love women in a woman-hating world; our strength and self-sufficiency in a society that says you must have a man; our powers of imagining and discovering new possibilities that come from having to create our lives without models or the support of existing institutions. While all lesbians are obviously not the same, we are also not the same as straights. To deny our differences is to deny both our particular oppression and our particular strength. Rather, we must bring our experiences and differences to all who are seeking to develop a new reality for women and thus for men as well. Some of these differences will be shared by others who do not fit society's norms of color, age, physical appearance, marital status, class, and so on. In fact, the more any woman is already or steps outside of society's assumptions of who she should be, the more "queer" she is and the more she can usually see how sexist and heterosexist assumptions confine her individually and women as a group.

Since lesbian-feminist theory is also based on our experiences of female oppression, we have come to see that homophobia and gay oppression, even for men, are based in sexism and the institutional power of male supremacy. Gay men have some male privileges in society, particularly if they remain closeted or out-woman-hate heterosexual men. But they will remain scorned as less than men and more like women, as long as women are scorned and as long as "real" men must have sex with and dominate "real" women in patriarchy. Their long-term interests, therefore, lie not in identifying with and attempting to gain more male privilege but in challenging male supremacy along with heterosexual domination. Gay men face a choice similar to that of straight women: they can accept society's offers of short-term benefits (male privilege for one and heterosexual privilege for the other), or they can challenge the patriarchal basis of those very privileges and work for a long-term elimination of the entire system of sexual oppression.

Lesbians as both homosexuals and women have no real stake in maintaining either aspect of sex-based oppression and should be the quickest to see the importance of lesbian-feminism and to enact it politically and personally. It is, then, the lesbian's ignorance about or indifference toward lesbian-feminism that I find most perplexing. To embrace and transform our status as outlaws and challenge the dual problems of sexism and heterosexism may not always be the most comfortable option; it is, however, the most powerful and fulfilling one. No matter what one's particular sphere of activity, it is a perspective that provides the basis for both individual and group strength in the struggle to gain control over our lives and to bring fundamental change in society. It sometimes appears easier to seek acceptance on patriarchy's turf and terms, but ultimately, our freedom depends less on society's acceptance than on changing its basic tenets.

In discussing lesbian-feminist theory and the lesbian as outlaw to patriarchy, I am not speaking about what specific tactics to use when (e.g., legislation versus demonstrations). Rather, I am referring to the underlying analysis and approach that we bring to any political action and the view that we have of how heterosexism and male supremacy reinforce one another in maintaining our oppression. Tactics will vary widely according to circumstances, but lesbians must ground ourselves in lesbian-feminist theory. From this point, we can decide which issues to pursue in what manner and we can make alliances with other individuals and groups who also understand that patriarchy does not serve their individual interests or the interests of a more just and humane world order.

SPEAKING OUT, REACHING OUT

After 1977, I stopped writing about lesbianism as a separate issue and worked instead to incorporate an understanding of lesbian-feminism into other areas. The following is a medley of excerpts taken from speeches where I discussed lesbian/gay rights in relation to other topics in a variety of contexts between 1977 and 1985.

GAY RIGHTS/HUMAN RIGHTS AND TRADITION IN AMERICA

(This is taken from my presentation at a "Speak Out For Human Rights" in Washington, D.C., on September 23, 1977, sponsored by a coalition of organizations called the Dialog for Human Rights.)

I decided to speak about patriotism tonight after watching a spoof on a TV talk show where the "human rights" expert discussed the solution to the "problem" of gays. He suggested that people in the United States might be willing to grant rights to homosexuals if we formed our own country, outside of North America or in a desert that not too many people were using, with a fence around it. It was meant to be funny, but it sounded all too familiar: Indian reservations for the Native American problem; Japanese detention camps during World War II; sending Negroes "back" to Liberia when their labor was no longer needed here, and so on.

203

One tendency in this country is indeed to deal with "problem populations" by trying to get them out of sight. A territory, a ghetto, a closet, a jail or mental hospital—anywhere, so long as it is not necessary to look at and treat "them" as human beings. Our struggle for gay rights today is one of the present stages of a civil war that has been going on within the U.S. for centuries. That war is the conflict between the tradition of human rights and tolerance for diversity versus the tradition of bigotry and intolerance.

Both sides in this war have seen themselves as battling for what they thought was good versus evil. But recently, we have seen the right wing using more of that language and claiming to be "saving America" through everything from "right to life" and "save our children" slogans to the waving of the flag by Ku Klux Klansmen. But I believe that it is the people represented here from civil rights, feminist, gay rights, and community-activist groups who are upholding the better traditions of our country. We should claim to be saving the possibility of a humane society in America. We must resurrect some of the spiritual conviction that freedom and justice are on our side that sustained the civil rights movement of the '60s.

We have talked a lot about unity among our groups tonight, but we also need to see that unity as part of a long-term tradition of struggle in this country. Radicals often lack a sense of connection to the past, seeing ourselves as breaking away from the old rather than as continuing the best ideals of certain traditions. I think that we can gain strength from recognizing ourselves as carrying on a tradition we inherited from the abolitionists and trade unionists as well as the women's and peace movements of the past century.

In thinking about our claim to traditions in this country, I was reminded of that bumper sticker, "America, love it or leave it." I don't know how many of you have felt uncertainty about responding to this, but I, for one, feel ambiguous about being an American. I feel shame over the injustices perpetrated in my name, but I also have hope that we can move toward the promises for justice and freedom of this country. So, since I do not intend to leave it, I am trying to learn what it means to love a sinner like America.

I have thought about the Vietnamese making a distinction between hating the U.S. government waging a war against them and the people here whom they always tried to reach as human beings. I remember the focus on love in the early civil rights movement as well as among women and gays who have sought to counter the self-hatred taught to us by society with love for ourselves. America is like an unfaithful lover who promised us more than we got. Yet, if we do not choose to leave, we must find ways to love what is best in her traditions and fight against the transgressions. Now I say to "love it or leave it," that we are going to "love it and change it."

In order to realize our hopes for change in this country, we must find more ways to unite and not allow any of our groups to be isolated and defeated. At the moment, the attack on gay rights is like the tip of the iceberg of reactionary efforts. If other progressives allow gays to be persecuted, all of us will suffer. Our society has tried to keep us divided and fighting each other for small privileges. But if we realize how little those privileges mean in terms of power, we can see that we have more in common as those seeking to broaden human rights and tolerance for diversity and choice, than we do in identifying with the status quo.

I have been encouraged by the state and national coalitions that diverse groups of women—including lesbians and women of color—have built around the International Women's Year National Conference to be held later this year. At the California state conference where this coalition passed a progressive feminist plan of action, we also saw the intensity of our opposition. One of the right-wing delegates gave a raving speech about how she was going to appeal the proceedings "all the way to the Supreme Court until they finally rule on what a woman really is." I see her as a symbol of those forces in America who want some authority— church or state—to straighten out the issues of sex and sex roles and enforce their views on all of us. To counter them, we must unite in defending our vision of a diverse America that does not draw lines limiting what a woman or any other person is, and what he or she can be in life.

If those of us fighting against oppression in this country see that human rights are indivisible and that our battles are connected, then we can further all of our concerns and avoid becoming isolated in our struggles. For this, we must work together and understand better what each of us needs to survive and flourish. In so doing, we continue the tradition that has sought justice, tolerance, and the advance of human rights in America. Indeed, we will not leave her, but we will love her and change her. For we are your children, America, we are your sisters and brothers, your teachers and students; we are your future and we are here to stay.

LESBIANISM AND EROTICA IN PORNOGRAPHIC AMERICA

(This is taken from a speech delivered at the first March on Times Square [New York City], organized by Women Against Pornography, on October 20, 1979.)

We are here to demand and organize an end to violence against women in pornography. But we are also here to ask some questions of America: What kind of society is it that calls love and affection between two women perverse, while male brutality to women is made profitable? What kind of society is it that takes a child away from a loving mother simply because she is a lesbian, while another child can be used by her parents to produce child pornography? What kind of society is it where the lifelong partnership of two women has no standing in court, while a husband can batter and rape his wife without interference?

It is a pornographic society; America is a pornographic patriarchy. We are here to say that it is not the kind of society we want and that it is going to change. We are here to demand better of America. Last week at the National Gay Rights Rally in Washington, over a hundred thousand people demanded the right to control our bodies, including our sexuality, and called for an end to social degradation and violence against lesbians and gay men. Today many lesbians are marching again to demand that same right as women—to control our bodies and to protect ourselves from the violence of pornography. Both of these marches are about the right of all people to the dignity of our sexuality, to the control of our own bodies, and to an end to all forms of violence and degradation against us.

Lesbians are tired of having our love labeled "pornographic," while the real pornographers make money off of women's bodies. Lesbians know about love, sex, and eroticism of the female body: we know it and we love it. And we know that it has nothing to do with woman-hating pornography. Indeed, it is only in such pornography where men exploit lesbianism to their own ends, that the portrayal of lesbianism becomes okay to patriarchy. Lesbian love is for women, and it is abused precisely because it is outside of male control.

Lesbians are tired of having our love, our culture, and our publications threatened with censorship by labels of "perversion." We will continue fighting for our right to proclaim and portray our love and our sexuality openly. But we will not be intimidated into silence about woman-hating and violent pornography out of fear that we will then be labeled and censored as "pornographic." We will not be pushed into a closet of blindness toward pornography and the culture it thrives on. Lesbian oppression is perpetrated by the same forces that promote pornographic culture; bringing lesbian love out of the closet goes hand in hand with exposing the woman-hating bias of most pornography.

We have seen the exploitation of lesbian love in pornography. We can tell how phony are the lesbian scenes in which our reality is distorted to fit male fantasies and feed male consumption of female bodies. As lovers of our sex, if we had a small portion of the money that goes into pornography, we could produce genuine erotica about lesbian love, portraying the real beauty of women and of women loving women, for ourselves, not for male consumption. I am sure that our productions would be different from woman-hating pornography.

Finally, I must add that pornography is not just symbolic violence against women. It is part of an international slave traffic in women that operates as a multinational effort, where our bodies are the product, often procured unwillingly and usually abused. Our fight against violence in pornography in its widest implications is therefore a global struggle. It extends from local street actions to the United Nations. It includes exposing the cover-up of reports on slave trade in women that has gone on at all levels for decades.

We begin this international struggle in our own streets and nowhere is that more appropriate than here on Forty-second Street—Times Square—the pornography capital of America. We begin by reclaiming our bodies and our sexuality for ourselves. We begin by demanding that a society that punishes us for loving ourselves and each other, and then demeans our bodies for the profit of others, must change. We begin by no longer tolerating a pornographic and heterosexist patriarchy in any of its aspects. We begin by calling on America to do better—to take violence and degradation out of the category of sexuality in order to discover fully and celebrate the joy and eroticism of female sexuality.

JUNE 12TH DISARMAMENT RALLY

(This speech was given at the National Disarmament and Nuclear Freeze Rally held in Central Park, New York City, June 12, 1982.)

I am especially proud to be here today for all the lesbians and gay men of all races, classes, and nations who have been present in movements for equality, justice, peace, and liberation for many years. We have always been here, but until we began a movement for our own liberation as gay people, we were present in those movements as second-class citizens, hiding ourselves and hiding those whom we loved. And you can be sure that fighting for change from behind closet doors cost us a lot; it cost us in terms of our personal dignity and it diminished the energy that we had to give to those movements.

Today that is changing. Today, we are a proud and open part of this struggle. Some of us are wearing lavender armbands at this rally to make our presence among you more visible. Today, we bring the energies released by our movement of love for ourselves to join in this demand for an end to the nuclear arms race.

We know that the forces of bigotry, fear, and violence that threaten to destroy our lives simply because of who we love are linked to the forces of militarism, prejudice, and greed that threaten to destroy this planet—denying all love, all justice, all freedom, indeed all life on earth.

We understand that the demand by some for control over our intimate lives—denying each person's right to control and express her or his own sexuality and denying women the right to control over the reproductive process in our bodies—creates an atmosphere in which domination over others and militarism are seen as acceptable. For society to continue accepting the idea that certain groups have the right to control and violate others can only end in our day with nuclear holocaust.

Something is amiss in our world.

We know that priorities are amiss in the world when there is enough food to feed the hungry but political and economic policies prevent that and allow food to rot.

208

We know that priorities are amiss in the world when a man gets a military medal of honor for killing another man and a dishonorable discharge for loving one.

We know that priorities are amiss in the world when children are not protected from parents who abuse them sexually while a lesbian mother is denied custody of her child and labeled immoral simply because she loves women.

We know that priorities are amiss when the military budgets of all nations combined for one day equal enough money to feed, clothe, and house all the people in the world for one year.

The list is endless and each of you can add examples. But we are not here to lament. We are here to act. We are here to turn those priorities around—to value love in its many forms and to bring an end to the violence of militarism and the arms race.

As we join together, there is great strength in our diversity. Too many of us have come too far—out of closets, kitchens, ghettos, and out of our isolated fears about the nuclear age—to allow this madness to destroy us now. We cannot go back. We can and must go forward to stop the arms race so that we can address the tasks of meeting human needs and expanding human capabilities for life and love. The possibilities are endless if we stop this nuclear madness in time. Let us go forward and be proud of what we do with the future that is in our hands.

AIDS AND THE GAY/LESBIAN COMMUNITY AS FAMILY

(This is an edited version of a presentation given at the National AIDS Forum held as part of the National Gay Leadership Conference in Dallas, Texas, August 14, 1982.)

Several people have asked "why me?" speaking on this panel, since I am not directly affected by this disease and am not a medical expert. Even I asked this question at first, but then I realized how important it is that we be clear that lesbians are affected by AIDS, and that we not simply treat it as a medical matter. As a community, lesbians and gay men must respond to this crisis together. How we approach issues that affect only some of us most seriously—whether those some are men, women, racial minorities, or another group—reflects the nature and future of our movement.

This crisis challenges us to demonstrate to ourselves and to the world that our community has the capacity to be a caring, intelligent, and effective unit in society. Gay pride rallies have asserted that "we are family." Now we can show the substance behind that slogan. Families are not always about agreeing with each other, but they *are* about uniting in a crisis. Families must respond to matters of sickness, fear, and death as well as to joy, sex, and food. Much of the right wing's "profamily" rhetoric against us has assumed that our sexual activity is antithetical to such family concerns. This is a time to counter that stereotype of us. For while we are not units of Mom, Pop, and two kids, our community is an extended family that can take care of its own in matters of life and death.

Understanding ourselves as family can help in organizing both short- and long-term responses to AIDS. Other speakers have outlined the organizing needed: to give personal assistance to those in immediate need and pressure to get social-service resources for them from government. To educate our community about this problem and to educate the heterosexual world in order to prevent antigay use of this issue. To mobilize support for medical research and demand more government assistance in this effort.

We must also deal with the fears that have been generated within our own community. This requires looking at a whole range of issues brought into focus by this crisis: questions of disease and death; of aging, security, and love; of stress, drugs, and life-style; and of lingering guilt and self-hatred that is exacerbated by hostility from the society toward gays.

These issues are not causes of AIDS nor are they unique to lesbians and gay men. Rather, most of our concerns are the problems of environmental health in industrialized urban society. But since the life-styles of lesbians and gay men in the twentieth century are generally entering into uncharted territory, we face such issues with particular intensity. Our efforts to create new forms of family and community that respond to stress, aging, and death may also be useful to other groups dealing with these concerns in today's world.

In addition, we face the particular problem of homophobia in the society as well as within our own psyches. We tend to react to discussions of health and life-style either moralistically, as issues of right and wrong, or defensively, asserting our right to do what we please. But neither of these attitudes is very helpful in dealing with AIDS. We need to discuss these questions honestly and nonjudgmentally. We must understand them as matters of survival for our people, just as ethnic groups understand survival of the race as the responsibility of all its members. Or, to use another example, if your family has a history of heart attacks, you pay attention to the factors that contribute to that disease—because it is wise to do so, not in order to be morally correct; and you do not conclude that your family is to blame for having "bad blood" because of it.

In looking at our fears about illness and aging, we face questions of who will care for us and will we be desirable as we age. In considering drugs and alcohol, we need to look at how they affect our health and also to remember that they are often used politically to defuse movements. I am haunted, for example, by reports of the FBI promoting heroin in Harlem in the '50s as part of a plan to divert political energy. In relation to life-style, we need to discuss not only sexuality but also stress and how our community can help us to reduce tension in our lives. These are only some of the discussions we need to have, but we must do so without adding to the guilt and self-hatred felt by so many homosexuals. We must reaffirm that gayness is positive and our examination of our health is part of the process of improving, not judging, our lives. It is a way to value ourselves and express love for each other, not to deny or punish us for being gay.

In facing homophobic reactions to AIDS, we can remember that we are not the only oppressed group that has had health problems used against it. The fact that blacks are the only ones to get sickle-cell anemia has kept it a low medical priority and been used to justify prejudice against blacks as "inferior." Women who get toxic shock from tampons or diseases from faulty birth-control devices face the insinuation that this is the price of control over reproduction or of wanting more sex. But has anyone suggested that the American Legion should stop having conventions because of Legionnaire's disease?

We need all the intelligence, care, and cooperation of the lesbian and gay community to respond to this crisis in its broadest implications. We have the opportunity to set a model for how a community can cope with such a difficult and deadly problem as AIDS, and we can demonstrate to the world what we can be as a community. Perhaps most important, we can expand our capacities as a community in crisis and show ourselves that we are indeed a family that cares for its own.

LESBIAN LIVES: A BLUEPRINT FOR ACTION

(These are excerpts from my keynote speech at a National Lesbian Agenda Conference in New York City, sponsored by the National Gay and Lesbian Task Force, November 23, 1985.)

The agenda for this conference, calling for a lesbian blueprint for action, is very ambitious. But I am glad to see that ambition because addressing such a task is long overdue in the lesbian movement. One of the problems that lesbians have is that while we are everywhere—in all kinds of groups making many things happen—we have few lesbian political groups nationally or locally. We seem to organize others well and certainly thrive in our own culture, but a lesbian political action agenda is not always clearly stated. And that agenda should serve as a linkage between our woman-selves as part of the feminist movement, our participation in the gay movement, and our actions around other issues of concern.

Over the past few years, a number of us have sought to expand concern about gay rights and homophobia into other arenas besides the gay movement. This has often been difficult. There is a tendency for others to feel that it is okay for us to be open about sexual preference if we work on gay/lesbian issues; but if we work in other areas, we are asked to be in the closet publicly or at least not to keep bringing up "that issue." Unfortunately, we do have to keep bringing up homophobia because if we do not, no one else will. It is still an issue that most nongay people wish would go away. Yet, many of us do not want to work on lesbian/gay issues in isolation from feminism or from other concerns such as racism or militarism. So each of us devises her own balance of how to keep our various interests and needs alive.

What I miss since I left the women's caucus of the National Gay Task Force is a place where lesbians talk together about that balance and share strategies for personal survival and political work. We need more lesbian spaces—whether caucuses in national organizations or locally based groups—that make plans for how each of us can affect issues and how we can support each other's efforts.

212

In 1971 when I was part of The Furies, a lesbian-feminist collective, I wrote a twenty-five-year plan with a five-year timeline for how we would change the world. I really believed in such planning, but no one would discuss it, so I put it away. I think that it is now time for us to talk in terms of five-year plans. When we state what our goals and strategies are, as is proposed for your working groups in this conference, we gain greater clarity on where to move politically. With such a framework, we can evaluate each opportunity and tactic more productively.

A lesbian agenda or blueprint can serve also as a useful way to show nongay supporters what it means to deal with homophobia concretely. For example, in the women's agenda coalitions that exist in about ten states, we can tell them our specific lesbian demands in relation to such areas as employment and child custody so that inclusion of our perspectives is not just an abstraction to them. The lesbian caucus for the National Women's Conference in Houston in 1977 did this by first deciding on three specific points on lesbian-feminism that we wanted to have included in the Plan of Action; this then enabled us to show concretely how we are oppressed and to establish a way that others could support us.

We have to keep pushing on this issue because it is still unpopular, often even with our friends. While we have made progress, the backlash we see today over the AIDS crisis demonstrates that our work on homophobia has just begun. In fighting that backlash, we can gain strength and insights from the growth of the feminist and gay movements globally. For as feminism has developed, not only in the West but also in Third World countries, there is greater possibility for discussion of lesbianism.

We saw this growth at the NGO Forum held as part of the UN World Conference on Women in Nairobi, Kenya, in July 1985. Every day there was a lesbian caucus with several hundred women on the lawn, and many African women came there eager to talk. There was visible leadership from women of color and Third World women in the lesbian workshops, including one press conference on lesbianism. The topic has also gained greater acceptance among women in Latin America, where at the regional feminist conferences held every two years since 1981, significant lesbian sessions have been held. There are several lesbian-feminist groups in the region, and some have started publications. There is also now a newsletter for South Asian lesbians.

We can draw inspiration from lesbian-organizing around the

world as an indication that we can have a more diverse movement in the future. We can also draw inspiration from the lesbians in our past whose survival against all odds shows that we are a strong and determined people. We are learning more about that past all the time and we have just begun to see the breadth of possibilities for our future. All of this should help to sustain us for we have a lot of work to do today.

MEDIA AND EDUCATION

This section chronicles my experiences as part of the feminist media along with my commitment to feminist education. I have believed in education as a means to empower people to take more control over their lives and to work for social change for many years. In the mid-'60s, I experimented with and wrote about activist-oriented approaches to education and found them quite powerful. The work included here is based on my assumption that people *do* change through exposure to other views and that both media and education are critical tools for furthering this process.

The first essays look at feminist media as crucial to the development of the women's movement. Here, I examine both the promises and problems of feminist publishing primarily from the perspective of my six years as an editor of *Quest: A Feminist Quarterly.* The later articles address feminist education, teaching, and theory. They consider how to combine the demands of a movement for social change with the tasks of educating women. The section closes with a discussion of how the black community's emphasis on education has influenced feminism, and what we can learn in addressing race, class, and sex as topics that require continual education both in and outside of the classroom.

215

READING AND WRITING
FOR A FEMINIST FUTURE

The question that I find nobody in women's publishing wants to talk about—not even at the Women in Print Conference held in Omaha last year (1976)—is do most women in the United States read anymore? And if not, what should we do about it? Should we continue to write and publish? Or if people do read, what do they read, and how does that affect feminist publishing?

I think that reading and writing are vital to feminism. The struggle for access to education was a crucial part of women's efforts for change in centuries past as it has been throughout the last decade. Only in this century, and now only in some countries and among some classes, have significant numbers of women gained access to the tools of writing that Virginia Woolf explored in her essays—literacy, money, space of one's own, and admission to the "public world" with its range of experiences. Women's struggles to write and to gain these and other attributes of freedom are connected. It is small wonder, then, that writing and publish-

This piece is an edited combination of two articles written in 1977 and '78: "Feminist Publishing: An Antiquated Form?" *Heresies: A Feminist Publication on Art and Politics,* no. 3 (Fall 1977), and "Feminist Journals: Writing for a Feminist Future," *Women in Print II,* Joan Hartman and Ellen Messer-Davidow, eds. (New York: The Modern Language Association, 1982).

ing are passionate concerns for many feminists. The first large purchase of Washington, D.C., Women's Liberation in 1968, for example, was a mimeograph machine. Then, as now, women spread the word about feminism and argued its future course in everything from novels to political essays and personal diaries.

In thinking about the challenges facing feminist publishing, it is useful to look at what functions the written word serves. First, it conveys ideas and information about feminism, especially those that are not readily available in the mainstream media. If we had more control over other forms of media, such as radio and TV, these could do some of this. However, given the expense of other media, feminists depend primarily on our own network of periodicals and books for information exchange.

The written word is also still the cheapest, most available form for all women to use, as both writers and readers. Books and magazines can be found for free in a library and read in privacy, allowing women access to ideas that might be censored in their homes. It is therefore vital that feminists get our materials into public and university libraries. For creating her own work, almost any woman can get the materials—pencil and paper—for writing and probably access to a mimeograph (or Xerox) to disseminate her ideas, while larger sums are required to make films, paint, and so on.

Another advantage to the written word is that it allows for complexity as well as creativity and imagination. Since printed material is cheap and can be read whenever the reader chooses, it can devote more space and time to exploring the various angles of an issue than most electronic media, which usually oversimplify issues. Further, reading (like radio) requires the use of visual imagination. As a child I had to picture in my mind what the "Little Women" looked like while reading the book or imagine "The Shadow" as I listened to the radio. Television and movies, however, provide preprogrammed images, and according to many studies, act as a pacifier on children rather than stimulating them to create images of their own.

This creative rather than passive aspect of the written word is important for encouraging people to rebel and make change in society. Lack of access to the printed word has characterized most oppressed groups, and the struggle for control over words, thoughts, and deeds is one. Movements for change usually make literacy for their people a high priority. Literacy is a way to give individuals more information about their oppression and to assist their ability to think about and choose alternative courses of action for their lives. In the U.S., we tend to assume that people are literate. But our society is rapidly becoming postliterate since reading is no longer given much encouragement. If we want women to rebel against patriarchy both individually and as a group, these are essential skills. Literacy should be a feminist issue, and teaching women to read, write, and think a priority in our movement.

In this context, we need to look at the specific role and importance of feminist publishing and writing. If the written word is important, then where, why, and how we do it matters also. I am not speaking now of the individual decision of a particular woman about where she will publish—that is a complex matter that varies from case to case, and debate over what each of us *should* do is already too polarized. Rather, I am speaking of why feminist publishing is vital to feminist writing and to women's power, and why it needs to be supported by feminists as crucial to our future.

The existence and visibility today of feminist and especially of lesbian-feminist writing is largely a result of the establishment of feminist presses and periodicals over the past ten years. This is so not only because feminist publishers have printed much of our own work, but also because we have demonstrated that a market exists for such material. Further, the existence of feminist media has inspired and created new writing; new ways of exploring subjects has been possible because of the atmosphere created by women's publishing. Those who produce feminist material actively stimulate new work by asking questions that may be unpopular and by printing what is still unprintable or unspeakable for many.

Feminist publishers have created new possibilities in writing because they have been closely tied to the evolution of the movement. In the days of the mimeograph machine when our struggle to define our movement involved cranking out five hundred copies of "Why Women's Liberation," we believed with a religious fervor that getting more copies into more women's hands would ensure that change would happen. Those days of early feminist publishing were also times of channeling erotic energy. Even when women could not yet admit sexual feelings for each other, they were there, sparking our work together around the mimeo machine. Feminist presses have always been integral to some of feminism's major tasks: bringing women together and spreading the word.

However, we soon realized that we needed more than the occasional mimeoed tract, although those can still play a role in introducing ideas. Women wrote for male-dominated media and saw our ideas distorted and our material chopped up if it was printed at all. Remembering the old maxim that "freedom of the press belongs to those who own the presses," women started our own periodicals in 1970 with titles like *Off Our Backs, It Ain't Me Babe, Women: A Journal of Liberation,* and *Ain't I a Woman.* The mimeograph machines have largely been replaced by over two hundred women's periodicals and presses in the U.S.—local, regional, and national—covering an array of special interests and general themes in both fiction and nonfiction. All of that material from mimeo to finely published books is what I call the feminist press.

The feminist media exists not only because the boys won't always publish us. In fact, today they will print us more because we have proven our market, and that is something valuable, which we can use to our benefit. But even if they print feminists, we must also keep our own media alive, growing, and expanding, for it is part of women's power base made up of political, economic, and cultural institutions of our own. Having a feminist press is also important to controlling our words and making sure they are disseminated even when not popular. Perhaps most important, we need to keep feminist publishing alive as a method of creating new words/new works.

In my experience, feminist publishers are not passive receptacles for what is already out there but are actively creating new directions for thought and action. In *Quest,* for example, our goal is to create new feminist theory that combines the best of political tracts and academic work. We want to build and reflect analysis based on the experiences of the movement that is at once accessible and informed by research or facts. In this we seek to counter the anti-intellectual trends in the movement, but not to be a journal for the academy only. In order to achieve this, we do not wait for articles to fall from the sky. We solicit and coax women to try to write theory; we will go to any length necessary to get an article.

It is not just publishing or even just editing. It is also a process of teaching activists to write; of encouraging academics to write in a way that more people can read; and of learning how to recognize new possibilities for material and to ask questions that will lead us toward such works.

The relationship of author, editor, and publisher in this endeavor is then one of mutual effort involving debate, turmoil, and conflict as well as creativity and growth. Such interaction naturally has problems and sometimes authors feel feminist publishers interfere in content too much. But generally there is a commonality of purpose and mutual desire to move feminism forward that makes feminist publishing lively and vital.

Of course, there are also particular problems involved in feminist publishing. Perhaps the greatest limitation is the small distribution and circulation of most such works. This is made more difficult by the fact that most feminist publishing enterprises are understaffed and underfinanced. Dedicated but poorly paid women do the work of many without sufficient backing or support, which can cause delays and conflicts with authors. Nevertheless, the audience of feminist periodicals and publishers is usually select and the influence of the ideas goes beyond the numbers published.

We must see the feminist media not just as an "alternative" but as a crucial part of our future. It is not just a training ground to get us into the big-time publishers. In fact some "big-time" publishers lose interest and do not promote feminist work in spite of its proven audience. For example, I published a women's liberation anthology with Bobbs-Merrill in 1970 that had sold sixty thousand copies as a special issue of a magazine before they took it, yet they never promoted it and let it die without beginning to tap its market.

So the feminist media is not just a stopgap for women who cannot publish elsewhere. Supporting it is not so much the question of individual choices about where to publish when, but of support for one of our movement's vital institutions. Feminist publishing is a critical part of our future—it is an institution and a wellspring of our words, thoughts, and action. As a people, it is our looking back and going forward in the written word.

221

WOMEN'S PUBLISHING:
AN INTERVIEW BY FRANCES DOUGHTY

F● Will you talk about why you think reading and writing, which
 some think are becoming obsolete, may be more important than
● television, speeches, tours, and other kinds of media?

C: My interest in print grows out of my sense that being able
to read and write are critical tools for creating change and thinking for oneself. It's not surprising that revolutionary movements
have often seen literacy as useful to revolution because it enables
people to understand their situation, it gives words to experience,
and it helps one figure out what is desirable and how things could
be different. I know stories of women who grew up in oppressive
environments where reading was their only access to any other
reality. Their ability to imagine that life could be different was
based on what they read.

The written word is also important politically for getting our
ideas out to people. Occasionally, feminists might get fifteen minutes on TV, and that is important. But it goes on when they want
it on, and an individual woman cannot see it when she has the
time. But with the print media, once we get our books and magazines out, the women who have them can do whatever they want
with them on their own schedules.

This interview with the author was published in *Sinister Wisdom*, no. 13 (Spring 1980).

222

We can usually have more control in producing print, in part because there is less equipment and expense involved compared to other media. This also makes producing print possible for a wider range of women from different backgrounds. Something like television also tends to be more controlling of others, and our goal requires the ability of people to think differently from the mass culture. Print is important to creating new space for women as well as to creating theory, which requires the process of thinking through and disseminating new ideas. Many things can be done with films and art—different media do not have to be seen as competitive. I simply want to emphasize that we still need the basic process of reading and writing.

F: So you would say that print is our primary vehicle for the development of an educated feminist movement—educated in the sense of being able to reach conclusions for oneself, being able to digest different messages, interpret them, and see what they lead to, in both action and theory?

C: Other vehicles like TV may be the first to reach someone with an idea. But print is still the primary vehicle for the development and expansion of those ideas.

F: For those of us who weren't directly involved, the first Women in Print Conference is legendary as an event where many important things happened, but I'm not sure exactly what.

C: The first Women in Print Conference was held in Omaha, Nebraska, at a Campfire Girls' campsite in August 1976. It was June Arnold's vision that women involved in publishing—including presses, journals, newspapers, bookstores, and distributors—all come together and discuss what we had learned and how we could cooperate more. It was a landmark—slightly over a hundred women came from around the country. We spent a week together with the grasshoppers and the dust storms. There wasn't any one result to point to because the emphasis of the conference was on what is now called "networking" and developing resources for improving cooperation.

The conference helped end the isolation a lot of people felt in their own particular work; it enabled us to see how large the women-in-print movement was. There was a magnificent feeling in that early women's liberation sense of finding each other—finding those who had the same problems and were working on the same issues you were. Most of the women who came were involved in projects that survived because a small number of people stuck together over time and worked long hours in underpaid conditions. It was easy to become so involved in the survival of your project that you began to feel that it was you against the world. We would lose track of the fact that we were part of a larger movement, and that our problems were not ours alone and were *not* because of any lack of effort on our part. As feminists, we knew that patriarchal society oppressed us, that big business had control, and that small businesses had trouble making it in the world. Nonetheless, we still felt that our project's destiny was a personal matter—if we just worked harder, if we just did it better, our projects would survive. Some of those myths were disspelled at the conference as we talked about the problems of publishing. We looked at the facts: for example, no matter how high you priced a journal, even though you thought it cost too much, you still couldn't make it financially. We learned that publications do not survive solely on sales—they are either financed through advertising or subsidized by interested universities or organizations. We had a lot to learn about publishing.

F: Did you find that discovery liberating, energizing, depressing? What effect did it have on you?

C: It liberated us from individual guilt. I don't know whether it was energizing. It energized us to look for other solutions. In another way it was reality crashing down on us. Things were not going to get better just by working hard for a couple more years. The mythical break-even point where this bad period would be over was not going to come. It meant that each of us had to make more realistic decisions about what we were going to do. Some decided to end their groups or publications. Others began to develop different structures to survive. Or they accepted different standards. For example, if you didn't come out four times a year, but still produced interesting issues, it was okay—we didn't have to meet the culture's standards of publishing to still be a valuable enterprise.

A turning point for me was facing the limitations of the small press world much more squarely than I had been willing to before. I realized that we were not going to become *the* press instead of being alternative media. Some of the exciting, idealistic theory we had put forward was simply not working. If I was going to continue to work in that press, I would have to do so because it was still satisfying and without any illusion that it would reach the masses or become the popular culture. If I wanted to reach the popular culture in that way, I would have to be more willing to deal with some of the mainstream presses and publications—not necessarily to the exclusion of women's presses but in addition to them. That was a choice I began to see, and I think other people did, too.

F: When you're talking about popular culture, you mean mainstream American culture. I've been wondering whether within the lesbian-feminist world we're also developing some kind of split between popular lesbian-feminist culture and a smaller culture of people who are interested in theory. Did you experience that kind of split when you were working with *Quest?*

C: Definitely. *Quest* started at the same time as Olivia Records, for example. We both began in Washington, D.C. A few of us were ex-Furies members. It was interesting to observe the difference in the development of those two projects, which came out of relatively similar politics and yet took two very different media to develop. It was sometimes hard to watch Olivia Records—which I liked and was glad to see succeed—take off in the popular culture of the lesbian movement in the way that theory did not. Yes, there are those divisions. I think that we at *Quest* have had to keep reaffirming that the ideas developed in a small place do begin to spread out in other ways and in other forms. That was one division. The other division is with the mainstream culture. For me, joining the mainstream was to write for *Ms.* magazine, yet *Ms.* is still not the mainstream for most people.

I decided that I would write for more of the mainstream women's movement, for *Ms.* and for *National NOW Times,* which reaches over a hundred thousand NOW members. I wanted to take what we were developing in the women-in-print subculture into the broader sphere of organized established women's groups. The next step is taking that into the popular culture beyond just women's publications. I think we need more of that because otherwise what we end up having is a set of professional women's writers who haven't had the experience of the feminist press movement. If no one from the feminist press does that, then the division will become greater and greater.

F: How have you seen the women's presses go on since the Women in Print conference?

C: I don't think any of us that week realized the effect that being there was going to have on us. At the end of the Women in Print Conference we were on a high, but the seeds had been sown for a more realistic assessment, which came later. For example, Women in Distribution (WIND) was a distribution company that had been started by a couple of women from Olivia Records. They found themselves a year and a half after the Women in Print Conference further in debt than they had been when they started. They did a careful financial analysis whereby they were able to project that in the next couple of years they would not break even. Furthermore, if they went out of existence at that moment, they would owe a certain amount of money, but if they kept on they would owe more money, and therefore would have taken more money away from women's presses. There were two central issues. One was that they had not chosen to involve more people in the project, so they didn't really have new blood to revitalize and inspire them. The other was that they couldn't see any way of becoming financially viable without major contributions of energy and money from a significant number of women. So they went out of existence.

The other thing that a lot of us did after Women in Print was to recognize that we couldn't go on with the high publishing standards that we had wanted. We began to scale down operations in terms of the quality of paper we used and of general appearance (by using one-color instead of three-color covers). All of this was hard as we had set out to create products that looked attractive.

The real question that has never been answered is do feminists consider the existence of our own presses and publications important enough to subsidize them? Unless the women's movement does support those, most of them will not go on existing. Many are, in effect, subsidized by a small group of people giving volunteer labor and money, and by their staffs having other jobs or receiving low salaries. But to live off those salaries, one has to have some savings or friends who are willing to help you out. So there's a number of ways we're indirectly subsidizing women's publishing. But we have to decide if it's important enough to become more systematic about support. Otherwise, it will simply be the projects with the best hustlers or the best connections or the most endurance that will survive.

F: Not only are women making fifty-seven cents to the men's dollar these days, but many women have children to support. When you're talking about trying to subsidize feminist presses you're also talking about a much smaller pool for the money to come from than there is in mainstream society. I think what I'm hearing is not so much that the vision failed, but that societal realities got it.

C: You put it in a nutshell. I don't think the vision has failed. The heart of the vision was that in order to build a movement and effect change we need vehicles for our own words, our expression, our graphics, our art, our own institutions. The vision of producing our own institutions, and particularly the importance of publishing as a tool for communication and for developing ideas, has not failed. The vision that we would be able to do it better if we controlled it ourselves is still true. The part of the vision that failed was our awareness of what it takes practically to make that possible. At Omaha, in an indirect way, we faced the fact that our vision of ourselves as the main culture was not realistic.

F: I think one thing it does is let us see ourselves, instead of reverting to that total invisibility from which we emerged with such a struggle. Print in particular is important for that sense that there is a community out there beyond individual problems.

C: You walk into a library and see the amount of feminist work that is available. It's a real high. I walk into your study and can get a lift just from seeing the women's books and magazines piled up. These are even more important in more isolated places. I've seen it on an international scale. A woman who is putting out a feminist magazine in Asia came to New York a few weeks ago, and I wanted to give her everything, because every publication gave her such a thrill. That visible product, that sense of your reality, is even more important when times are bad and for women who are isolated. In my traveling, the dog-eared copies I've seen of the things we sometimes take for granted have been a good reminder of the importance of our words.

We also have to recycle our energy. We have to recognize much more than we did in the '70s the necessary process of what I call "moving in and out." We need this both individually and as a movement. For example, I see myself moving into a popular-culture phase. I felt isolated; I felt at a certain point that the subculture was stifling me in areas that I needed to explore for making change. I had to get out more and interact with women who were not committed feminists, but who were at least open. I had to get out in the world and see what we were up against in a different way and try my ideas in more diverse environments. That wasn't just my missionary impulse to go out and convert; it was my sense that my own work was suffering from lack of exposure. I think we need to allow each feminist more space for her own rhythm, more space to say, "This is the period where I am consolidating my ideas within the subculture, and this is a time for trying them out in the popular culture," whether in writing, or activism of other forms.

I think that there's a cycle for projects as well. New presses arise like Persephone Press, which take on the role that, say, Diana Press or Daughters Inc. had five years ago. They are willing to experiment, to uphold the vision. Perhaps they'll do it more realistically. But even if they simply do it for a while, I'm beginning to see that a particular project or group or person or even country may carry the forward edge of feminism at a given moment, while the rest of us may be doing something else that keeps it alive.

F: Do you have any last words?

C: I think my last words for the future are to draw from the past—which is giving me a lot of sustenance lately. When I think about some of the hard times that we seem to be in for in the '80s, I'm sustained by remembering not only the Gertrude Steins and the Eleanor Roosevelts, but even more the Daughters of Bilitis, who started the lesbian publication *The Ladder*, which existed from 1956 to 1972. Those were years when very little existed for lesbians to read, but they kept that alive for all of us. They could go out of existence in 1972 because of the present wave of feminist and lesbian writing. History and our own work ebb and flow, but keeping alive the core of what we are about through those hard times has been done by women in our past, and their example can serve as guideposts for us in facing the future.

BUILDING FEMINIST THEORY:
THE STORY OF *QUEST*

I n the summer of 1974, while the FBI hunted for Patricia Hearst and female activists in France won abortion rights, a small group of feminists in Washington, D.C., published the first issue of *Quest: A Feminist Quarterly* on the theme "Processes of Change." *Quest* was born amid the enthusiasm of the women's liberation movement in the early '70s—a time that produced many feminist projects such as Olivia Records and the first feminist credit unions. The story of *Quest*'s development revolves around a dozen women in Washington, D.C., who struggled, with the help of many others, to bring to life a national journal of feminist political thought. But to talk about *Quest*'s early years involves several stories. It is a story of feminist theory and its evolution in the women's movement, of tensions between theory and action and between intellectual and activist demands. It is the story of a feminist group determined to create a nonauthoritarian work process based on feminist principles of cooperation and sharing of skills that would also meet the rigorous demands of publishing. It is a story about the effort to build a feminist institution with an independent economic base controlled by women.

This essay was published as the "Introduction," to *Building Feminist Theory: Essays from Quest*, Charlotte Bunch et al., eds. (New York: Longman, 1981).

Quest's stories reflect the 1970s spirit and struggles, successes and failures of the decentralized radical wing of the women's movement in the United States. While *Quest* continued to publish until 1982, this essay looks at the journal's initial years from 1973 to '79.

In its early stages, the women's liberation movement was fueled by our sense of discovery, our sense of sisterhood and unity among women. Consciousness-raising groups had provided a structure for exploring shared oppression and the camaraderie of the early zap actions had given us a powerful sense of our potential. But that unity was short-lived as we soon discovered our very real differences of class, race, sexuality, and politics. In 1972, just when the movement's political activity was expanding through marches and greater public visibility, internal schisms had divided women into small isolated units grouped around special interests and political priorities.

By 1972, Washington, D.C., had spawned two national radical publications, *Off Our Backs,* a feminist news journal, and *The Furies,* a lesbian-feminist analytical paper. As the nation's capital, Washington is a place where the line between local and national politics frequently blurs; the local women's movement was therefore very involved in national projects and debates. The movement was strong but fragmented, reflecting the tensions developing around the country between socialists and antileftists, straight feminists and lesbians, black and white women. This fragmentation was at its worst when two activists from The Furies (then recently disbanded) convened a citywide meeting to discuss what could be done to lessen the schisms in the movement and strengthen cooperation and power. That meeting led to the formation of a discussion group composed of diverse activists from various feminist projects—the Rape Crisis Center, Women's Legal Defense Fund, The Furies, and the Women's Center. Six months later, the group decided to start a national journal to explore issues of movement strategy and theory from an activist perspective.

As founders of *Quest,* we saw the journal as one part of developing viable strategies for political change, not as the ultimate goal of the group. Thus, we wrote in our statement of purpose: *"Quest* is not an end in itself but a process leading to new directions for the women's movement possibly including such concrete forms as regional or national conferences, a national organization or a political party." Karen Kollias elaborated on how we saw the magazine in the Introduction to the first issue (vol. 1, no. 1 [Summer 1974]: 3–4):

> Our goal is to promote a continuing, active search for ideologies and strategies that will bring about the most comprehensive change by the most effective and humane methods. . . . We are about open political forums. *Quest* wishes to explore differences and similarities in ideologies and strategies among the various segments of the women's movement. . . . We are about strategies. *Quest* wishes to contribute to the evolution of better strategy and tactics, to be a process for evaluating previous theory and practice. . . . We are about change. We assume that the women's movement, and those involved in it, consider complete and fundamental change as a primary goal. . . . We are about ideology. The time has come to expand feminist ideology. Differences in geographical location, race, class, sex preference, religion, age, and other factors must be included for a broader, more realistic ideology that moves toward a workable base for unity.

The activists who began *Quest* felt that political strength and clarity would come from exploring feminist analysis from a fairly wide range of viewpoints within the movement.* *Quest* was envisioned as a tool for the already committed, not as a mass-audience magazine. Its aim was to stimulate more political dialogue among organizers, researchers, writers, and activists in the women's liberation movement, in women's studies, in women's rights organizations, and in other social movements.

QUEST AS POLITICAL THEORY

The *Quest* staff was activist in temperament but viewed theory as important to the success of activism. We wanted to articulate a feminist theory out of the daily lives of women and the work of

*The initial *Quest* organizing group was Dolores Bargowski, Rita Mae Brown, Charlotte Bunch, Jane Dolkart, Beverly Fisher-Manick, Alexa Freeman, Nancy Hartsock, Karen Kollias, Mary-Helen Mautner, Emily Medvec, Gerri Traina, and Juanita Weaver.

the movement, and we wanted to direct that theory toward a workable strategy for the future.

We saw that a written analysis of concrete movement experiences, both successes and failures, was crucial to advancing feminist theory and developing strategies for change that built on previous work rather than on repeating previous mistakes. We invited activists to write about their ideas in political work, about their feminist principles, and about what happened when their strategies for change were put into practice. We felt that critical assessments of movement experiences were necessary to link theory and activism in the effort to meet intellectuals' demands for research, the substantiation of theoretical assertions, and organizers' needs for immediate solutions. *Quest*'s uniqueness lay in this struggle to be politically relevant to current issues *and* intellectually rigorous in developing the long-term implications of theory.

The staff of *Quest* considered certain questions of class, race, and sexual oppression, as well as strategic and organizational matters such as leadership, to be of paramount importance to this evolving theory. Our focus on these questions grew out of our own backgrounds, our experiences in the women's movement, and our knowledge of other struggles for change. For example, partly because many of us had worked in the civil rights movement in the 1960s, and partly because we lived in a predominantly black city, we saw issues of race as fundamental. Most of us were familiar with the literature on the black liberation movements, and several staff members maintained close contact with local politics and community organizations in Washington, D.C.

Our focus on the issue of class also grew out of our experiences. Over half of the original *Quest* group came from lower- or working-class backgrounds, and most of us had experienced the strains that class differences produced in the movement. We saw examining class not as a "male Left" imposition but as essential to the vitality and authenticity of feminism.

Lesbian-feminism was another central theoretical and political commitment for the original *Quest* staff, regardless of individual sex preference. Our understanding of the significance of lesbian oppression and our experiences in the bitter gay/straight split in Washington, D.C., convinced us that it was important to incorporate this political perspective into all aspects of feminist analysis, developed by lesbians and nonlesbians alike.

In addition, our various movement experiences led us to explore strategic issues such as conflict in the movement centered around questions of power, leadership, and organizational structure. For example, we felt that individual leadership should be encouraged and that problems with leadership should be openly discussed in the movement. This set us apart from many feminists who were anti-leadership at the time. We also insisted that we were not a "collective." We maintained that some responsibilities could not be shared and that addressing problems of power and responsibility went far beyond simple questions of collectivity. We wanted activists to tackle the tough problems underlying movement controversies over things like money, reformism, separatism, and socialism. Although we were generally anticapitalist, we thought that women should develop an analysis of socialism independent of the debates of the male Left in the United States, for the male Left had not only oppressed many women, but still treated "women's issues" as secondary.

In seeking to ensure that these and other issues would be covered in *Quest,* we decided to have a broad theme for each issue of the journal.* We developed an overall conception of each volume; then the four theme issues within it built on one another. For example, in the second volume, the four themes focused on aspects of change: the envisioning of a future society, the kind of revolution it requires, the organizations and strategies involved, and the role of leadership. The use of themes helped link theoretical and practical questions and highlight the connections between different issues.

Developing articles for *Quest* was a political education and a lively process for the staff. Manuscripts that sparked our interest were often discussed extensively and aggressively rewritten; movement organizers were interviewed, seduced, and cajoled to get their insights and operating theories onto paper. Many articles were written by women on the staff, often growing out of our discussions of the issues involved in the theme.

*The themes in volume I were Processes of Change; Money, Fame, and Power; The Selfhood of Women; and Women and Spirituality. The themes in volume II were Future Visions and Fantasies; Theories of Revolution; Organizations and Strategies; and Leadership. The themes in volume III were Kaleidoscope One (our first nontheme issue); Communication and Control; Work, Work, Work; and Race, Class, and Culture.

Each issue of *Quest* began with the staff identifying a theme area and forming a development committee, usually about eighteen months prior to publication. The development committee for each theme consisted of at least one *Quest* staff person and several other individuals, many desiring to work on one particular theme and some interested in working closely with *Quest* to "try it out." The development committee structure evolved over the first year as a way to meet several needs simultaneously. It brought new people and ideas into *Quest,* adding fresh experiences, perspectives, and enthusiasm. This approach also helped maintain a stable core of staff members while providing a gradual process for introducing to our group other women who might later join the staff.

The first responsibility of each development committee was to imagine all the questions that its chosen theme could and should address. It advertised the theme in advance, solicited articles, and reviewed all the copy received in order to make recommendations for consideration to the full staff. The full staff was then responsible for reading the recommended articles, for making final selections along with the development committee, and for assigning editors to work closely with each author. The staff might also direct the development of more manuscripts to fill gaps.

While copy development consumed much time, it was only one aspect of the production of the journal. Like many feminist projects, we saw our group's methods of dividing work and responsibility and sharing power and leadership as an important aspect of developing and testing feminist political theories. The mechanics of our process evolved to meet our unique needs. The following details are presented not as a blueprint for structure but to illustrate our belief that with trust and creativity, feminist projects can build effective structures based on participatory processes.

In the last two issues of our second volume (1976), we published a Report to the Readers describing the *Quest* process. In one issue, Jane Dolkart wrote for the staff (vol. 2, no. 4 [Spring 1976]: 41–44):

> In essence we have a system of shifting horizontal leadership based on our individual skills and time commitments. . . . We

see ourselves as equals in that we all perform essential tasks for *Quest,* but we do not see ourselves as identical. Each individual staff member must take responsibility for the work within some given area. In that work, she is delegated authority to make certain kinds of decisions and handles both the creative and mundane parts of the task. Thus, while we do not all do the same things, our division of labor is horizontal and no one does only the "best" or the "worst" parts of a job. . . .

Although we do not have a hierarchy, those who work full-time on *Quest* have more responsibility for and knowledge of the intricacies and problems of day-to-day operations, and therefore, have more decision-making authority. . . .

As the need and desire for additional staff developed, we had to set out more specific criteria for staff. We developed written criteria aimed both at evaluating persons interested in joining *Quest* (for example, extent of previous political experience, prior work with *Quest,* etc.) and at giving those interested an accurate picture of the commitment we would expect.

Clear work processes and explicit guidelines on which we built our structure combined with our common political goals were crucial to the success of our endeavor. Although in many cases friendships did develop, they were not all-important nor seen as mandatory in order to keep us working well together. Finally, our process also had to allow for our political needs as activists. Dolkart notes:

Since every minute of meeting time and of our lives could be taken up in the details and decisions related to producing a journal, we found that we had to insure that we kept in touch with politics generally, and with movement activity in particular. We decided to begin each of our weekly meetings with a one-hour political discussion, our subjects ranging from internal politics to more general political questions. Second, in an attempt to reach out more to the feminist community in D.C., we have conducted a political seminar following each *Quest* issue and are initiating a feminist political theory course. We are still struggling to develop more ways to keep ourselves actively involved with politics while maintaining *Quest* as a journal.

236

The Report concluded by recognizing that *Quest*'s political goals sometimes conflicted with the daily demands of producing the journal. Maintaining the journal took more and more time as we faced the economic realities of small businesses and publications in America. The building of a feminist business therefore became a central issue for us practically and politically. This reality for *Quest* reflected the situation of many feminist projects in the mid-1970s and points to the importance of the story of *Quest* as a feminist institution.

In the first half of the Report to our Readers, Beverly Fisher-Manick outlined the financial and organizational dilemmas *Quest* faced (vol. 2, no. 3 [Winter 1976]: 38–43):

> We set goals about quality, and we have largely stuck to those goals. We wanted a woman-produced journal that was readable, graphically pleasing, sturdy and of book quality. . . . We hoped to pay authors and artists adequate fees for their work, and we dreamed, eventually, of paying ourselves salaries for our work. We believe that feminist projects should support women at a decent living standard.
>
> As our financial statement illustrates all too clearly, the income from selling *Quest* does not, by itself, make these goals and dreams possible. Our expenses exceeded income in 1975, even after we had modified some of our goals.
>
> We need urgently to concentrate on promotion and fundraising but we do not have the time. . . . If we cannot raise the funds, then we face tougher decisions.

Fisher-Manick described those tough decisions and the difficulties not only of publishing on a low budget but also of doing the distribution and promotion necessary to make a journal succeed financially. She called attention to the contradictions in a movement that says it wants autonomy and self-determination yet does not or cannot support the few independent women's institutions that do exist. She related *Quest*'s need for support to the issues of how we live our politics through what we do with our resources:

Subscribing, ordering, buying, and promoting *Quest* are the most vital, ongoing ways to insure our survival. . . . You can promote us, urge others to subscribe, explain to them why it is important to subscribe, recommend it as a text in women's studies courses, and order it from us rather than Xeroxing it. . . . Get your local paper and magazines to review an issue. . . . With 10,000 subscribers *Quest* could pay three full-time salaries, rent office space, and continue to publish in the same style. With 1,500 subscribers, we cannot.

These kinds of pressures on feminist institutions have driven many projects out of existence. Yet, in spite of such pressures, *Quest* found ways to adapt and kept publishing a quality journal for eight years. It survived in large part because a committed feminist community sustained us through hard times. That community needed a place to express its individual and collective experiences in the work of creating political theory and social change. *Quest* provided one of the few places for that expression.

The group of activists who produced the first issues of *Quest* remained together as a core staff with few changes in personnel for almost five years. As we began to disperse, other women stepped forward to provide talent and energy to the endeavor. *Quest* produced its fourth volume amid gradual changes in staff and format, and with the fifth volume a largely new staff emerged. The transition involved dealing again with issues of power, leadership, and responsibility, with the new staff maintaining some of the previous group's process and creating forms of its own. But after the fifth volume was published, the financial pressures became too great and having failed to find a way to ensure its long-term survival, *Quest* ceased publishing in 1982.

QUEST IN PERSPECTIVE

Looking back at what we set out to do, *Quest*'s evolution shows some real progress and some failures. What is most important, *Quest* has contributed significantly to advancing the idea that there could be, and should be, specifically feminist theory and, especially among activists, that such theory is important to political action. We have challenged the limitations of popular labels and divisions in the movement, such as radical feminism versus socialist feminism, and have sought new feminist definitions of ourselves. In analyzing how class differences and heterosexism affected our assumptions and strategies as women, we have helped demonstrate that issues of class and lesbian feminism are integral to a comprehensive feminist analysis. But while we have affirmed the fundamental importance of issues concerning racism, we have been less successful in significantly exploring just how race and patriarchy are related and what an integrated analysis would look like in this area. Perhaps *Quest*'s greatest success has been in demonstrating the absolute necessity for feminists to examine critically the issues of organizational structure, power, leadership, and money as they affect our movement's growth and strategy. In all areas where we have explored the terrain of feminist theory, we have seen how much more work and discovery lie ahead.

Our work on *Quest* in its early years taught us many important lessons. We learned that the full development of the implications of feminism and the creation of a comprehensive feminist world view that combines theory and activism will take time—both the time to think and write about it and the time to engage in more struggles and experiments as women activists. *Quest* played a vital role in advancing that task, although our initial fantasy of having a solid new theoretical foundation on which to build a national organization dedicated to radical change was premature. In the ebb and flow of movement timing, the time did not ever seem right for creating the organizations we envisioned. Further, the constant demands of the magazine's daily survival affected our dreams of other pursuits, such as *Quest* study guides, political classes, *Quest* conferences, books, and *Quest*-inspired organizations. Since we had neither the time nor the resources to pursue these ideas, we learned, as women everywhere have learned, that the demands of economic survival establish the parameters for the pursuit of dreams. Understanding and expanding those parameters must be central to all our theories of liberation.

NOT BY DEGREES:
FEMINIST THEORY AND EDUCATION

The development of feminist theory and a rigorous analysis of society are more important for us today than ever before. Feminists need to understand the forces working against us, as well as to analyze our experiences as a movement, if we are to survive the antiwoman backlash and keep our visions alive. When feminists despair, burn out, or give up, it is often because the forces against us are strong and because our theoretical framework does not give us a sense of how individual activities contribute to significant victories in the future. A solid feminist theory would help us understand present events in a way that would enable us to develop the visions and plans for change that sustain people engaged in day-to-day political activity.

When I left the university to do full-time work in "the movement" in the 1960s, it didn't occur to me that I would return one day to teach or write feminist theory. Like many others who chose to become movement activists then, I felt that I was leaving behind not only the academic world, but also what I saw as irrelevant theorizing. However, as I experienced the problems of movement organizing when an overall analysis was lacking, felt the frustration of conflicts where issues were not clear, and observed people dropping out of political activity, I became aware of the critical

This essay first appeared in *Quest: A Feminist Quarterly*, vol. 5. no. 1 (Summer 1979).

role of theory in the movement. I began to see feminist theory not as academic, but as a process based on understanding and advancing the activist movement.

While my growing sense of the importance of theory applied to all my feminist work, the urgency that I felt about it became clearest during my involvement with lesbian-feminism. When the lesbian issue became a major controversy in the women's movement in the early 1970s, I realized that in order for lesbians to function openly, we would have to understand *why* there was so much resistance to this issue. It was not enough to document discrimination against homosexuals or to appeal to fairness. We had to figure out why lesbianism was taboo, why it was a threat to feminists, and then devise strategies accordingly. I saw that my life as a lesbian in the movement depended on, among other things, the development of a theory that would explain our immediate conflicts in the context of a long-term view of feminism. This theoretical perspective developed along with our activism, but it required us to consciously ask certain questions, to look at our experiences in and out of the movement, and to consider existing feminist theory in new ways. Through this process, new interpretations of the relationship between lesbianism and feminism, and new strategies for ending lesbian oppression emerged.

For example, as we examined feminists' fear of being called lesbians, we were able to confront directly the role that such name-calling played in the oppression of all women. Having a theory about lesbian oppression did not tell us what to do tactically, but it did provide a framework for understanding situations, for placing them in a broader context, and for evaluating possible courses of action. This experience showed me that theory was not simply intellectually interesting, but was crucial to the survival of feminism.

THE FUNCTIONS OF FEMINIST THEORY

Theory enables us to see immediate needs in terms of long-range goals and an overall perspective on the world.* It thus gives

*There are many approaches to theory, and those interested in exploring more about how theory is constructed should look at the literature of political philosophy. Another model for feminist theory similar to the one that I discuss in this paper was developed by Judy Smith of the Women's Resource Center, in Missoula, Montana.

us a framework for evaluating various strategies in both the long and the short run, and for seeing the types of changes that they are likely to produce. Theory is not just a body of facts or a set of personal opinions. It involves explanations and hypotheses that are based on available knowledge and experience. It is also dependent on conjecture and insight about how to interpret those facts and experiences and their significance.

No theory is totally "objective," since it reflects the interests, values, and assumptions of those who created it. Feminist theory relies on the underlying assumption that it will aid the liberation of women. Feminist theory, therefore, is not an unengaged study of women. It is an effort to bring insights from the movement and from various female experiences together with research and data-gathering to produce new approaches to understanding and ending female oppression.

While feminist theory begins with the immediate need to end women's oppression, it is also a way of viewing the world. Feminism is an entire world view or *gestalt,* not just a list of "women's issues." Feminist theory provides a basis for understanding every area of our lives, and a feminist perspective can affect the world politically, culturally, economically, and spiritually. The initial tenets of feminism have already been established—the idea that power is based on gender differences and that men's illegitimate power over women taints all aspects of society, for instance. But now we face the arduous task of systematically working through these ideas, fleshing them out and discovering new ones.

When the development of feminist theory seems too slow for the changes that we seek, feminists are tempted to submerge our insights into one of the century's two dominant progressive theories of reality and change: democratic liberalism or Marxist socialism.* However, the limitations of these systems are increasingly obvious. While feminism can learn from both of them, it must not be tied to either because its greatest strength lies in providing an alternative view of the world.

The full implications of feminism will evolve over time, as we organize, experiment, think, analyze, and revise our ideas and strategies in light of our experiences. No theory emerges in full

*For more discussion of this problem and of nonaligned feminism as a response to it, see "Beyond Either/Or: Feminist Options," pp. 46–60.

detail overnight; the dominant theories of our day have expanded and changed over many decades. That it will take time should not discourage us. That we might fail to pursue our ideas—given the enormous need for them in society today—is unconscionable.

Because feminist theory is still emerging and does not have agreed-upon answers (or even approaches to many questions), it is difficult to work out strategies based on that theory. This difficulty can lead feminists to rely on the other theories of change or to fall into the "any action/no action" bind. When caught in this bind, one may go ahead with action—any action—for its own sake, or be paralyzed, taking no action for lack of a sense of what is "right." To escape this bind, we must remember that we do not need, and indeed never will have, all the answers before we act, and that it is often only through taking action that we can discover some of them. The purpose of theory, then, is not to provide a pat set of answers about what to do, but to guide us in sorting out options, and to keep us out of the "any action/no action" bind. Theory also keeps us aware of the questions that need to be asked, so that what we learn in each activity will lead to more effective strategies in the future. Theory thus both grows out of and guides activism in a continuous, spiraling process.

In pursuing feminist theory as an activist, I have become increasingly aware of the need to demystify it. Theory is not something set apart from our lives. Our assumptions about reality and change influence our actions constantly. The question is not whether we have a theory, but how aware we are of the assumptions behind our actions, and how conscious we are of the choices we make daily among different theories. For example, when we decide whether to put our energies into a rape-crisis center or into efforts to change rape laws, we are acting according to certain theories about how service projects and legislation affect change. These theories may be implicit or explicit, but they are always there.

A MODEL FOR THEORY

Theory doesn't necessarily progress in a linear fashion, but examining its components is useful in understanding existing political theory as well as in developing new insights. In the model

I have developed, I divide theory into four interrelated parts: description, analysis, vision, and strategy.

1. Description: *Describing what exists* may sound simple, but the choices that we make about interpreting and naming reality provide the basis for the rest of our theory. Changing people's perceptions of the world through new descriptions of reality is usually a prerequisite for altering that reality. For example, fifteen years ago, few people would say that women in the United States were oppressed. Today, the oppression of women is acknowledged by a large number of people, primarily because of feminist work which described that oppression in a number of ways. This work has involved consciousness-raising, as well as gathering and interpreting facts about women in order to substantiate our assertions. Description is necessary for all theory; unfortunately for feminism, much of our work has not yet gone beyond this point.

2. Analysis: *Analyzing why that reality exists* involves determining its origins and the reasons for its perpetuation. This is perhaps the most complex task of theory and is often seen as its entire function. In seeking to understand the sources of women's oppression and why it is perpetuated, we have to examine biology, economics, psychology, sexuality, and so on. We must also look at what groups and institutions benefit from oppression, and why they will, therefore, strive to maintain it. Analyzing why women are oppressed involves such things as sorting out how the forms of oppression change over time while the basic fact of oppression remains, or probing how the forms of oppression vary in different cultures while there are cross-cultural similarities.

Analysis of why something happens sometimes gets short-circuited by the temptation to ascribe everything to one single factor, such as capitalism or motherhood. In developing an analysis, I find that it is useful to focus initially on a phenomenon in a limited context and consider a wide range of factors that may affect it. Then, as that context is understood, the analysis can be expanded. Above all, we need not feel that we must answer the "why" of everything all at once with a single explanation.

3. Vision: *Determining what should exist* requires establishing principles (or values) and setting goals. In taking action to bring about change, we operate consciously or unconsciously out of certain assumptions about what is right or what we value (principles), and out of our sense of what society ought to be (goals). This

244

aspect of theory involves making a conscious choice about those principles in order to make our visions and goals concrete. We must look at our basic assumptions about such things as "human nature" and how it can be changed, about the relationships of individuals to groups, about whether men and women are essentially different, for example. We may choose not to address some of these issues yet, but since every action carries implicit assumptions, we must be conscious of them so that we do not operate out of old theoretical frameworks by default. The clearer we are about our principles—for example, whether we think that women should gain as much power as possible in every area, or believe, instead, that power itself should be eliminated—the more easily we can set our long-term goals. Immediate goals can then be based on an assessment of what can be accomplished that may be short of our long-term vision, but moves toward, not away, from it. Visions, principles, and goals will change with experience, but the more explicit we make them, the more our actions can be directed toward creating the society we want, as well as reacting to what we don't like.

4. Strategy: *Hypothesizing how to change what is to what should be* moves directly into questions of changing reality. Some people see strategy not as part of theory, but rather as a planning process based on theory. But I include strategy here in its broadest sense— the overall approach one takes to how to accomplish one's goals. The descriptive and analytic process of theory help develop a more systematic understanding of the way things work, but they usually do not make obvious what one should do. Developing a strategy requires that we draw out the consequences of our theory and suggest general directions for change.

Like the other aspects of theory, this involves a combination of information-gathering and creative speculation. It entails making judgments about what will lead to change—judgments that are based both on description and analysis of reality, and on visions, principles, and goals. Developing a strategy also involves examining various tools for change—legislative, military, spiritual—and determining which are most effective in what situations. There are many questions to consider, such as what sectors of society can best be mobilized to carry out which types of action. In working out which strategies will be most effective, the interaction between developing theory and actively experimenting with it becomes most clear. For in all aspects of theory development, theory and activism continually inform and alter each other.

USING THE MODEL

This four-part model for theory can be used in many ways. In my feminist-theory classes, we have tried to understand different theories by outlining how various authors address each of its developmental parts. For example, we take Shulamith Firestone's *Dialectic of Sex* and discuss her approach to description, analysis, vision, and strategy. Then we compare her ideas in each area with those of other radical feminists, in an effort to see the common tenets of radical feminism, the important areas of disagreement, and the strategy implications of those differences. We then take the same approach to socialist-feminist authors, compare them to each other and to radical feminist works, and so on.

Another way to use this approach to theory is to examine possible ways of addressing a specific issue in terms of these processes. For example, on the issue of reproductive freedom, we can use theoretical work to understand the implications behind various strategies. Considerable work has been done detailing the variety of ways in which women lack control over reproduction, from forced sterilization to negligence in the development of contraceptives. Several analyses of why women do not have control over our bodies have been suggested. These range from the idea that men fear women's powers to create life and therefore compensate by controlling reproduction, to the proposition that capitalism is the primary cause because it must control the number of workers produced, to the view that the Catholic Church is the dominant perpetuator of this situation because its control over reproduction and matters of family life is central to its power. Most analyses also look at which institutions are most influential and which are most vulnerable to change, and the relations between them—e.g., how the Catholic Church affects hospital and government policies.

There are considerable differences of opinion about how reproduction should be treated. Some feminists argue that women should have absolute control over our bodies and reproduction at all times and in all circumstances. Others contend that there can be some legitimate limits on an individual woman's control; in the case of abortion, for example, limiting a woman's right to abortion on demand to the first trimester. Some argue that the state should prescribe standards of control that "protect" women such as the requirement of a thirty-day waiting period for any sterilization; and still others hold that a woman's control must be subordinate to the obligation of government to supervise overall population growth.

The practical consequences of these differences in theory become clear when strategies for gaining women's reproductive rights are discussed. Even among those who agree that women's lack of control over reproduction is central to our oppression, there are differences in strategy based on differences in analysis and vision. Those who think that the Catholic Church is the primary enemy of women's reproductive rights may focus on efforts to remove Church influence on the state, the fight against religious tax exemptions, and so on, while those who see multinational corporations as the primary controller of population issues would focus on them. The controversy among feminists over whether having the government require a thirty-day waiting period for all sterilizations would protect women or further abridge our rights to control our bodies illustrates how disagreement over vision and goals leads to different strategies and often to conflict over what we will demand.

This example, though simplified here, illustrates how the four-part model in particular, and theory in general, can be used to clarify practical political problems. When we understand the basis of our disagreements and the nature of the forces against us, we are better equipped to come to some agreement or to realize when compromise may not be possible. Theory helps clarify how things work and what our choices are, and thus aids in determining where to put our energies and how to challenge the sources of our oppression most effectively.

Theory is also a tool for passing on the knowledge we have gained from our life experiences and movement projects. Feminists need to analyze personal experiences as well as political developments—to sort out our initial assumptions about goals and analysis, to look at the strategies we used and why, and to evaluate the results in terms of what could be learned for the future. Making such feminist analysis accessible to others usually involves writing it down, which brings us to feminist education.

My approach to teaching feminist theory assumes that it is part of an educational process that is connected to the feminist political struggle. As such, feminist theory underlies all feminist education: a course on women artists, when taught from a feminist perspective, for example, should not only include the work of particular artists but also a political analysis of why women's art has not received proper attention. Feminist theory should be present in this way throughout a feminist curriculum, but it also needs to be taught as a separate subject where political theories can be explored in depth.

A feminist theory course begins with teaching the basic skills of how to read, analyze, and think about ideas. The course must also give information about existing feminist theory, about how that theory affects our lives, and about where to go to learn more theory. To get students personally involved, a teacher must challenge them to develop their own ideas and to analyze the assumptions behind their actions.

These are the central tasks of teaching feminist theory as I see them, after doing it in a variety of settings since 1970. I have taught women in universities and women's centers and summer institutes, in public and private institutions, as undergraduates, graduates in women's studies, seminarians, and feminist activists, and I have worked on transmitting theory through feminist publications. What I have found in all these cases is that women's problems with theory most often grow out of their trouble with thinking about ideas, and their view that their own thoughts and experiences are not important enough to be the basis of theory. Or, to put it in a slightly different way, many women have difficulty both in systematically pursuing thoughts and in believing that what they think makes any difference. These problems with thinking and with believing in the importance of one's thoughts and experience are related.

When teaching feminist theory, one must counter such attitudes and find ways to encourage women to think systematically about the world. Our society trains only a few people to think in this manner, mostly those from the classes it expects to control the social order. Certainly most women are not expected to take control and, in consequence, are not encouraged to think analytically.

In fact, critical thinking is the antithesis of women's traditional role. Women are supposed to worry about mundane survival problems, to brood about fate, and to fantasize in a personal manner. We are not meant to think analytically about society, to question the way things are, or to consider how things could be different. Such thinking involves an active, not a passive, relationship to the world. It requires confidence that your thoughts are worth pursuing and that you can make a difference. And it demands looking beyond how to make do and into how to make "making do" different—how to change the structures that control our lives. My goal in teaching feminist theory is to provoke women to think about their lives and society in this way.

To counter women's negativity toward and fear of theory, it has to be presented as something with practical consequences for one's life and as something that can be made accessible to anyone. One of the ways women misunderstand, and thereby avoid, theory is manifested in the "too hard/too easy" paradox. Many women assume that theory is esoteric and concerns matters that are removed from daily life. As a consequence, they regard something as properly theoretical only if it is very abstract and they don't understand it very well—implying that it can't be real theory unless it is "too hard" for them to grasp. The flip side of this attitude is wanting all theory to be "easy"—implying that if it requires reading slowly, or returning to it later, or looking up words in the dictionary, then it is of no use. Both attitudes prevent a realistic approach to theory. Reading and writing theory is not easy, but it can be done, and it can be made comprehensible.

Underlying some women's difficulties with theory are problems of literacy—of reading, writing, and thinking. Without the basic skills of reading and writing, women face limits on how actively they can engage in theory. In my experience, people who do not see reading and writing as basic are usually those who can take them for granted.* Revolutionary movements have almost always seen developing a general literacy as one of their most important tasks. Yet, in this country, where we assume that most of us can read and write, it is often overlooked. In fact, not only are many

*Discussing the relationship of literacy to politics is not unique to feminism. The topic has been widely debated in political circles, and for recent opinions, I recommend "The Politics of Literacy," a special issue of *The Radical Teacher*, no. 8 (May 1978).

people illiterate, but we are also rapidly moving into a generally postliterate era.

Reading and writing are valuable in and of themselves, and women should have access to their pleasures. Beyond that, they are vital to change for several reasons. First, they provide a means of conveying ideas and information that may not be readily available in the popular media. For example, the ideas of women's liberation first spread through mimeographed articles that were passed around long before it was possible to get the attention of the mass media—and with more clarity than that with which the mass media later portrayed feminism. Second, reading and writing help develop an individual's imagination and ability to think, whereas much of mass culture, especially television, pacifies and encourages conformity rather than creativity. (Studies of the effects TV has on children, such as the way it emphasizes the immediate dramatic moment at the expense of reflective thought, have demonstrated these consequences.) Third, an individual's access through reading to a variety of interpretations of reality increases that person's capacity to think for herself, to go against the norms of the culture, and to conceive of alternatives for society—all of which are fundamental to acting politically. Fourth, reading and writing aid each woman's individual survival and success in the world, by increasing her ability to function in her chosen endeavors. And finally, the written word is still the cheapest and most accessible form of mass communication. This makes it useful to those who have limited resources. Feminists should, of course, use other mediums as well, but I emphasize the political importance of literacy because it is often overlooked. When we recall why literacy is important to movements, it becomes clear that we should neither assume that women are already literate, nor ignore the value of teaching women to read, write, and think as part of feminist education.

TEACHING TECHNIQUES

In most of my courses, I have not had to teach the basic skills of reading and writing so much as the skills of reading and writing *critically* as part of learning to think in new ways. There is no one method for thinking and there is no one way to teach it. I have used several techniques to encourage thinking and to provide women with tools for analyzing the world.*

I begin by introducing the four-part model of theory, and then encourage students to use the model in looking at everything around them, as well as in reading "theory." For example, in one classroom exercise I pass out a variety of feminist and nonfeminist women's magazines. Each student examines one during class and uses the four-part model to tell the rest of us what theoretical assumptions are embodied in that magazine: what is its view of reality for women? What does it imply about how, why, or whether that reality needs to change? What are its approaches to those changes? What values does it espouse? The exercise can be adapted to popular movies or TV series, to comic books—anything. The point is to demystify theory by showing that theory underlies everything and does not exist only in books. At a simple level, the exercise also makes a student aware of how she thinks and analyzes for herself.

There are many situational assignments that enable students to explore the link between theory and action or that require them to think through the strategic implications of a theoretical position. For instance, one can set up a specific situation and assign people theoretical positions within it. The situation might be a women's center board of directors meeting where it has to be decided how to use a $20,000 gift it has just received. This situation can be designed leaving the students to devise their own options, or it can be narrowly defined so that students must choose between a given set of options. At a Washington, D.C., Feminist Alliance workshop on theory, for example, the group had to choose between using the money for a lesbian mother's defense fund, dividing it equally among groups affiliated with the organization, or using it for office space and staff for the organization.

Once a situation is defined, each student is assigned a theoretical position to represent in the discussion: she must be an anarchist-feminist, a liberal-feminist, or a particular person whose theories have been studied, such as Elizabeth Cady Stanton or

---

*There are volumes of literature on teaching the basis of how to read and write. The most useful exploration of teaching reading and writing along with political and analytic skills is Paulo Freire's *Pedagogy of the Oppressed* (New York: Seabury Press, 1970). Freire describes an educational process that is similar to consciousness-raising.

Juliet Mitchell. After the exercise, we discuss why each thought that a particular theory would lead to a certain position on the issues and what questions it raised for her.

Another variation on the situational approach is to break into small groups, assign each a particular identity, and ask each to take positions on certain issues: e.g., you are a socialist-feminist women's union and you must decide whether to join with other groups to demand wages for housework. After we study various feminist theories, I have turned the situation approach around by giving students a particular issue to resolve in which they represent their own opinions, asking, for example, "do you favor a wages-for-housework demand?" Afterward, we discuss what assumptions and theories they found themselves using to arrive at a decision.

The situations can be varied any number of ways and carried out in a few minutes or over several weeks. I have often found that what may have seemed abstract when first discussed in class comes alive during these exercises. The exercises also train students to think systematically and help them to gain confidence in applying theory to real life situations.

To get students to think creatively, a teacher must convince them that they should not try to figure out the "right" thing to say. Those most oriented toward politics seek the "correct line," while those oriented to the academy seek the "correct answer." The effect is usually the same. Concentrating on what is "right" or expected stymies creative thought. I often create situational assignments and give examples in my lectures where there is clearly no right answer, but rather a number of options that depend on deciding between different approaches and values instead of finding the so-called truth. Getting away from the right answer or correct line mentality is particularly important in a theory course because comprehending theory and its role depends so much on understanding the importance of interpretation and speculation. Since theory is primarily about interpreting reality, it depends on leaps of perception, speculation, and imagination—most of which get stifled by trying to be "correct."

I want to see women creating more theory, and to do this I have used techniques in the classroom that come out of my experiences in seeking women to write theoretical articles for *Quest: A Feminist Quarterly*. To assist someone in her efforts to put her analysis on paper, we have found it useful to ask for responses to other articles or to provide concrete questions to address. In my classes, I initially asked for term papers in which students were to analyze a particular topic, but this generally meant that they pulled together some facts with others' opinions and did not make their own efforts at analysis. Now I require a journal in which students outline the basic ideas of all the readings assigned to the class and give their responses to those ideas. This approach has yielded both more originality and more systematic work on classroom readings. I now provide specific questions for papers to address and/or position papers to respond to, rather than free-form topics. These approaches help students work out what they think, just as they enable activists who seldom write to record insights and analysis that would otherwise be lost. Giving someone something to start with besides a blank page helps her to write.

The crux of teaching feminist theory is getting women to analyze and think about others' ideas as well as to develop their own. I also want to teach specific feminist theories, and most of the classroom time is used in lectures and discussions of such theories. But I have found that giving information is the easiest part of teaching. The real challenge is to teach skills and inspire an interest that enables students to understand that content more fully during the course, and to take that understanding with them into the rest of their lives.

FEMINISM, BLACKS, AND EDUCATION AS POLITICS:
A CONVERSATION WITH BETTY POWELL

C*harlotte:* Feminist education occurs in a variety of different places, in university and nonuniversity settings. But one of the questions I am particularly interested in is how education involves a certain attitude toward life—some people are educators as a central way in which they perceive the world and go about their lives both inside and outside a classroom. For as long as I've known you, you have been one of those people. I've heard you refer to yourself as a feminist educator, a black lesbian educator. You have said that your perception of education and its importance to the lives of women politically is based on your experience as a black woman, coming out of a black tradition of seeing education as important to the race. Can you talk about how you came to see yourself as an educator?

Betty: I probably started referring to myself as an educator only in the last five or six years, although I've been teaching for nineteen years, but the attitude you refer to is something that has always been there—from the first time I stepped into a classroom,

This essay was first published as "Charlotte Bunch and Betty Powell Talk About Feminism, Blacks, and Education as Politics," in *Learning Our Way. Essays in Feminist Education,* Charlotte Bunch and Sandra Pollack, eds. (Trumansburg, N.Y.: The Crossing Press, 1983). It was condensed from a sixty-page transcript of a four-hour conversation.

in kindergarten. There was this sense of educating oneself and educating the world that was seen as part of lifting up the entire race in the black culture of the forties. We had our little graduation in my kindergarten in 1945 in a Negro section of town in Miami, Florida—St. Agnes. One of our themes was faraway places, and while singing our hymns in five-year-old voices, I remember the Father lifting me up and saying, "Young lady, you will go far. You will go far places for us." The belief was that every person who could was going to use everything that education had to offer in order to go that distance, not only for yourself but also for the race. Education was the way out, but it was also a way of being. For example, as a central part of the culture, the church was a place where you tithed for all of the Negro colleges four or five times a year. We understood that as we were giving money at St. Paul's Church on that particular Sunday, people in Negro churches all over the South were also giving money for the schools. So we had a strong sense of contributing to the community through tithing for the education of the race. I believe this grew out of the leap to embrace education immediately after emancipation.

The educator was such an important person in the community that I remember thinking it was something I could never be. I teach a foundations course in the School of Education at Brooklyn College—the history, philosophy, sociology, and psychology of education. In covering the sociological aspect, I teach black history within education and language by using a photographic essay book by Francis Benjamin Johnston, the nineteenth-century photographer. This is her book of photographs (1890) of the Hampton Institute in Hampton, Virginia, one of the first black colleges in the United States. Her photos capture that total dedication and commitment to education as the vehicle for lifting the race— students sitting at rigid, almost reverent, attention in their math classes, their science classes. The philosophy of education at Hampton Institute was a hands-on approach combining manual with intellectual training. So you see six- or seven-year-old girls and eighteen- and nineteen-year-olds in long dresses hanging out in the lumber yards and in the fields taking notes. Those images are so real to me because they reflect what I experienced as a child growing up. The concept that education was important was integrated into the race through the schools and the churches.

Charlotte: You describe the educator in the Southern black community when you grew up as someone of very high status, an important person because education was valued. When we look at U.S. society today, education doesn't have that value in mainstream white America, and yet it is still used by every class to pursue its interests. The upper class certainly uses education as a tool—Harvard and Stanford, for example, are clearly meant for training the upper class, usually white males, to control the world. When I was in college, I realized for the first time that some people are actually taught how to make things happen with the assumption that it is their responsibility and right to influence and control the world.

Betty: From the point of view of blacks, it's not being trained to control the world but to have more control over how we *survive* in the world: expanding our access to things in the world and our economic well-being. But education was also about moral and spiritual well-being. It was very much understood that we were to be trained to be morally and spiritually effective in the world.

When it came to the gay civil rights movement, I brought this consciousness and approach as an educator with me. Here I was, thirty-two years old, embracing my feminism and my lesbianism at the same time, realizing that I loved this woman and that meant I was a lesbian and the world doesn't like lesbians. So I said: "What, are you crazy? How can we go out and tell them about this? We've got to make them understand." That was totally out of my black consciousness, my black being. The sixties had given me an increased consciousness about blackness, but the attitude was already there, especially growing up in the South. I knew we had to set the world straight; we had to inform the world where it is ignorant, where it is morally stupid. There was just no question about the fact that one has to educate. I use the Latin definition—*educare*—to lead forth, to lead forth the truth that is there within the environment and within the person.

For me, when you do know something about the reality of the world that those who stand in ignorance do not know, then you can't *not* educate. That's not an arrogant posture. It's simply about reality. If you're black, you know things about reality that whites do not know because you have experienced being black. For example, if you're black, you know that your brain is not smaller; you don't smell—you *know* that. And certain people are acting, standing in their ignorance, like you have a smaller brain. So clearly there is a dialogue of education that has to take place; you've got to lead forth the truth out of this ignorance. It was very easy for me to make that leap immediately around gay rights. I knew that I didn't have two heads, and that I was not this evil person attacking kids and so forth. And I knew you've got to lead people away from their ignorance and prejudice. So I immediately found myself on stages at the Gay Academic Union and doing television shows about being a lesbian. From the beginning, I spoke about the linkages between the black liberation struggle, the feminist movement, and the gay civil rights struggle. Talking about that was really preaching and teaching to me. In fact, preaching and teaching are synonymous to me.

Charlotte: When I first met you, I felt this immediate connection to what you were doing, but I didn't know what to call it. Now we talk about seeing ourselves as educators and communicators, but since neither of us is a classroom teacher of women's studies in the traditional sense, most people don't think of us as feminist educators. Yet, what is at the heart of feminist education to me is this very concept you're now talking about: looking at the world and feeling the need to call forth people's better instincts, to challenge people's ignorance and make them examine it; and to call forth, in particular from women, the ability to do something about the world. I realize that a lot of my approach to politics as education comes from becoming politically aware and receiving my earliest political training in the civil rights movement in the South. Much of my approach to feminist education has been modeled on a Southern black education model—that combination of being the educator/teacher/activist/preacher. Until I met you and heard you calling yourself a black educator, I didn't realize the degree to which my attitude had its origins in the black Southern experience.

Betty: As we're talking, I get clear how the whole concept of education (education almost doesn't fit sometimes)—this passion for changing the person and changing the world—was there from the time I was five years old, making little speeches at my mother's social club on Sunday afternoons. These black ladies were sitting there, fanning themselves and waiting to hear and see this little child being well trained to give little speeches that had morals. There was a special kind of urgency and importance to having the truths that we knew sprinkled throughout our lives. In church we got it, in school we got it, in the social clubs and community activities we got it; it just permeated everything. We were being taught and groomed to teach in ways that were not formal—just to stand up and give a speech. I gave a lot of speeches.

Charlotte: Another issue I want to discuss is the assumption that people are educable, that people can be changed by being engaged with other views of the truth. I think that approach is important for any kind of political movement. When I look at what goes on with feminists, there seems to me to be some who approach a situation and say: all right, whatever is wrong and ignorant here, we have to figure out a way to help people see it differently. And then there are others who say: those dumb idiots, let's forget about them. I think it's important for a political movement to see education as very political because if there is any hope for the human race, we have to believe that people can change.

One of the struggles that goes on with feminists, as it has with blacks, is over our effort to maintain a belief in a different kind of power for change than force and militarism. The question of education becomes central to political strategy, therefore, because we are dependent on the process of convincing and changing people. To get the changes we want, we've got to convince enough people to be willing to work to make that possible: first, the education of one's community to feel good about ourselves and to stop our own self-hatred; and second, the education of our communities in the tools for change.

You teach education and linguistics, not women's studies or black studies, so you don't teach the content of our oppression directly. Yet I know you are teaching oppressed people how to have tools to take control of their lives and to do something in the world. How do you bring that perspective into your classes?

Betty: My field is linguistics applied to education, so I deal with foreign-language students, or anthropology-sociology students who want to learn the basic application of language to culture. I also teach the foundations course. But no matter what I am teaching, my primary goal is to get the students to see beyond any of the givens that they have, any of the constructs they have about language or history or philosophy of education. It's not the content of the subject but *how* you know, how you get at knowing, that I teach.

Students are used to saying: tell me what to do, and I'll take down all the notes. What I try to do is engage them in their own learning, have them participate in their learning. There are lots of classroom strategies for that. People have basically been miseducated by the culture. One of my most important tasks is to try to strip away the blinders: to try to get them to imagine another way of learning, another way of seeing, another way of being. Then I teach the actual content, which involves a lot of alternative-educational techniques and breaking down barriers between teacher and students.

The mode of questioning is very important when you look at feminist education. I try to create different visions and a new way of looking at the world in my classrooms. I also realize that students need guidance, so I am constantly with them: "Why don't you try another question or just a little piece of it." "If you're going to stop right there, you haven't gone far enough." I do this sort of guidance with everything. In feminist education, we need to develop techniques of helping people see differently and question in ways that are not just rejecting what *is* but developing and learning to go beyond it.

Charlotte: I've mostly taught feminist theory, and one of the main struggles that I've encountered in doing this is how to teach people to think. Particularly, I struggle with how to teach women to think because women have been socialized to be passive, to please people rather than raise questions, to not use our minds actively. How do you teach someone to put down the book, put away all the pat answers, and just think? I had a history teacher in college who said that for his test, we were not to memorize anything in the books, but simply to read them and sit down and think about them. It terrified me, but it also made a lasting impression on me. How do you teach thinking?

Betty: Serious thinking is missing from the culture. While I don't want to get into lamenting on a cosmic level, we must note that within this culture there is a giving over of ourselves to technocracy. We want to be technicians around everything, whether it's a philosophy course or the practice of medicine. Most kids in college in America today are not coming there because they want to think; they are coming to get training or a degree for jobs. Both men and women are terrified if someone tells them to think because nobody has ever taught them how to do it. When we talk about feminist education, we're doing so in a culture that, even within its most literate institutions, doesn't foster a lot of serious, original thought. Women resist thinking because the culture is so resistant to it. Clearly, this situation is part of the challenge of feminist education—to recognize there is no way that we can move forward without really thinking and analyzing. So much power can emanate from the kind of purposive thinking we're talking about.

I've had the idea of creating cells nationwide where we think for half an hour together; we would all do it at the same time. What if we knew that Thursday evening all across the country there were three hundred cells that were meeting with maybe five or six or even ten or fifteen women in each cell focusing on the same issues. I tell you, the power would be enormous.

This idea has been with me since I did a paper in college on racism—or prejudice, which is what we called it then. I lived in an interracial house and after I had written the paper, I gave a speech in which my point was that we won't conquer prejudice just by black folks talking about it to whites. I had a very clear sense, on one level, that resolving racial problems was really about white people getting together and doing it among themselves. And so my whole thing was to organize cells in every community, and once a week, people would come together and they would really deal with racism. That was 1959 and my nineteen-year-old vision was just so unclouded: if all over American white people were meeting once a week and dealing with this stuff, thinking about racism and analyzing racism and talking about racism, then change would occur.

Charlotte: It's fascinating to me that you had this vision in 1959. Almost ten years later, when I was working in Washington, D.C. (where I had gone to do community organizing in the black community), we—white folks—realized that what we had to do was education in the white community. We started the Center for Emergency Support, which did white-racism discussion groups in the suburbs. They were your little cells. But our approach to doing those sessions was linked to the fact that we had lived in the black community and still had the authenticity of the sixties civil rights experience. We talked about race based on the education about racism that we had been given by the blacks we worked with. When black people say "We can't go on educating whites for the rest of our lives," I recognize this as a woman and a lesbian. What's crucial is that the education process beget more education. As whites, we were able to teach another set of white people, but the process began with interracial interaction, that initial education that we got from black people.

At some points, education about oppression does seem to require what Frances Doughty calls *mandatory presence*. It requires the presence of someone from the oppressed group, at least to get the process started, whether that's blacks with whites or gay people making contact with straight people. For example, we know that what changes heterosexuals' minds most about homosexuality and affects their homophobia is knowing "one." That has to occur, and yet none of us want to spend our entire time being the lesbian taken to lunch. While most of us can do a certain amount of that educating, we have to set up processes so that the people we educate will be educating others. We have to say, now that you understand homophobia or now that you understand racism, you must take that back to the rest of your people so they will change also. Each of us has to pass that education on. That's where your concept of education as an ongoing part of daily interaction is so important, and so different from what most schools teach.

Betty: It was at the Racism-Sexism Conference cosponsored by Sagaris and the National Black Feminist Organization in 1977 that I first encountered the concept of mandatory presence. One of the themes there was looking at how each of us could do things very positively around race and sex after the conference. It was emphasized that you cannot always have this mandatory presence, and when it is not there, it does not mean that you do not deal with the racism issue. The assumption was: after the conference, we're counting on you to raise these difficult issues in every arena of your life.

Charlotte: If we could teach this approach, people might understand better that after you've had a primary learning experience about oppression, you have to become the presence yourself, whatever your race, sex, sexual preference, nationality, or class.

Not only does our culture not support these ideas, but it also has perpetuated, if not created, the very problems themselves. For example, our culture treats differences as something to be afraid of, something to distrust. Look at the myths about black people, the myths about homosexuals, the myths about women. All involve terror and distrust of someone who is different from the dominant norm—the other.

Education involves breaking down those fears. It's not just providing information about the inequality of women or the inequality of blacks. It's not just letting people know that some people get a bad deal. It's also speaking to that fear of difference, that absolutely irrational and yet deeply imbedded terror of the other in our society. Fear, insecurity, and hierarchy are so entrenched that if someone is different from you, immediately there is a need to rank them as better or worse; to worry that they're going to get you; or that there's something very terrifying about their life-style. If we could learn from differences to see that they make life interesting, then those differences would open us all up for greater possibilities. More important than anything that I learned about the facts of racism in the sixties, as an eighteen-year-old in the white South, was the discovery that there was a whole different way of seeing the world. Race wasn't just about being oppressed; it was also about perceiving the world differently, interacting with it in various ways that we now call cultural differences.

One task of feminist education, then, is to teach people to understand the differences in how things are viewed: differences based on race, class, sex, sexual preference, religion, culture, as part of the substance and variety of human experience. This is not to say that we are going to approve of everything just because it's not part of the dominant culture, but we do see learning from differences as positive. So, Betty, concretely, you've got all kinds of different people in your classes at Brooklyn College. How do you teach them to understand diversity?

Betty: The first thing I do in all of my classes is start breaking down the barrier between teacher and student, and the barriers between students. Brooklyn College is in an urban setting. My class this summer had black women, one Haitian male, Jewish women and men, one Hispanic female, Italian men and women, and very few WASPs. In terms of class, there was a wide range of experiences.

First, I have them introduce themselves and say one thing that they're really good at. I begin with "I'm Betty Powell, and I am very good at teaching, but I'd like to be better at tennis." So they start immediately having to come with their person to the classroom, not just their heads. Part of dealing with difference is to begin to have each person expose her- or himself so we can see what we are here, what's the configuration. Then they must say who the people were before them. If this is a hard task, I say, "Just imagine if there were eighty-six students and you had to remember them all." It immediately engages them. First, they get a little uptight. I point out that education is about paying attention, and what we're doing now is introducing ourselves to each other, so they should pay attention. An initial appreciation of who each person is starts developing just by saying that's so-and-so and that's what they do.

Then, I do other exercises where they interact with each other, depending on the particular subject. A number of these are autobiographical things, such as giving three instances of having learned something, how they learned it, who they learned it from, where they were in terms of their family, environment, neighborhood, schooling. They write down these things and then share them in small groups. A lot of breaking through differences is having students share the commonality of their experiences. The variations on those commonalities for a Jewish kid growing up in Brighton or a black kid growing up in Crown Heights are also great. Seeing that our experiences are very different, yet the same, is something I consider vital.

In terms of classroom techniques, feminist education can draw a lot from the human potential movement within education. We don't have to reinvent the wheel. There are many texts, programs, and workshop materials, dealing with ways to increase self-concept within the classroom, or techniques for enhancing the setting of cultural differences. The Teachers/Writers Collaborative* has a lot of this kind of material.

*Teachers/Writers Collaborative, Inc., 84 Fifth Avenue, New York, New York 10011.

Charlotte: You were teaching innovative education before you became a feminist. In what ways has being a feminist affected your teaching?

Betty: First, it's made me more convinced about the importance of getting people to question assumptions and to break down their own concepts. It strengthened my conviction that if we are to learn, we do need to work differently and to learn to see differently. Second, my references to women and the condition of women in life come into my teaching all the time. Since I don't teach "women's subjects," I announce very clearly that they'll have to get used to the fact that I am an ardent and vocal feminist. Some are a little anxious, and comments go back and forth about that, but the consciousness gets set up within the first week.

As we're discussing the philosophy or sociology of education, I point out that it's been men who have projected these modes of thinking that we're talking about. Women have only just begun to give their vision of how we ought to be educated. Obviously, therefore, much is lacking and there's lots of room for my students to give their input. Thus, while it's not a course on feminist education, it's very clear that they have got to respond in a way that's more enlightened.

Another illustration is how I discuss pronouns after they submit their first paper. I say, "Some of you really struggled very hard with those pronouns, didn't you, using s/he." Some write it once or twice and then don't know what to do, and some of them don't do it at all. I tell them that as a linguist, I know that the problem has not been solved, that it's very difficult, but that they have to be conscious of it. They have to decide the best way to handle pronouns in their writing. Sometimes I'll give them an example or indicate a preference, but the main point is that they have to decide something about it.

Having established that kind of awareness in the first few weeks, I am free to make reference any time to women or to the lack of women in this place, or to the condition of women when you talk about adolescent development, and so forth. All of my topics give me room for making observations, or having them make observations, that clearly come out of a feminist consciousness. Most young women really do appreciate having that space to make their own comments about this or that.

Because feminism is so much a part of me, there's no way that I can teach without me or my students being affected by it. There is nothing that you can say for any length of time without running into sexism, so I just open it up every time and see where it takes us.

Charlotte: What you're doing teaching as an explicit feminist in the Education Department is injecting feminist education into that part of the curriculum. Unfortunately, a lot of women, especially those who are not white or middle class, are either afraid of women's studies or see it as frivolous or irrelevant to them. Unless we get feminist education into ongoing courses like yours, especially in fields like teaching where there are a lot of women, we're not going to reach these women.

How can feminist education be more relevant to the lives of Third World women in a place like Brooklyn College?

Betty: As a black woman, I know that black women in ever-increasing numbers are articulating what it means to them to be feminists and what their concerns are. Yet it's still difficult, and feminism continues to be looked on by many Third World women as not addressing the major concerns of their lives. Black women in college today, by and large, are not imbued with the same sense of education as an ideal that I had when I went to college. The culture has changed in these twenty years, and the culture today instructs them to get in there and get that piece of paper in order to get a job. That's a broad generalization, of course, and I do meet many students who just really want to learn. At any rate, it is very important for feminist education to deal with issues of racism and the insights of Third World women and have that in the curriculum. Women's studies also needs to have a consciousness of the particular situation of the black and Third World women students on the campus, so that effective outreach can be made to them. There are many specific things one could do, like coordinating student programming with the Black Studies Department or with Puerto Rican studies. Such programs need to start with some topic that's very interesting to the students, like sexuality, but the agenda would be to talk about women's studies and what it can give them. Then you can have Third World feminists like me talk; that is my role. In a sense, it's kind of token, but it's an important visibility and presence. For women students to see a black or an

Asian-American faculty member saying, "I am a feminist," is important.

Charlotte: Following up on that, I think that women's studies and feminist education must take into account the life experience of women of different race and class backgrounds, which may affect what they want out of a course. For example, in a working-class college, where many students come from poor schools, I've found that what women often want to learn first is how to read and write, as a necessary prerequisite to doing women's studies. So, teaching women to read and write can be feminist education. If feminists act as if learning those skills is not very important, we've lost many women already.

To reach those who aren't already feminists, it's crucial to know what each woman feels she needs to survive better in the world. Then we can both address that need and teach a critique of patriarchy through relating to that need. If we know why someone is taking a course, we can move from that starting point to a greater understanding of what feminism has to say or needs to know in that area.

Betty: Yes, if we don't pay attention to those needs, it only reinforces some women's suspicion that feminism is irrelevant to their lives. When a young black woman is screaming that she has got to learn to play this society's game, that she's got to learn how to survive in this world, a women's studies course that disdains this, misses her. A lot of my colleagues will complain that the students can't read and write, but they won't put any energy into changing that.

The important message to get across is that feminist education is not, and must not be, just the education of the few elite so that they can go out and play with the boys. That's crucial. We can't move into the next phase of the contemporary women's movement without such an understanding, or without a significant number of Third World women really committed to feminism. But with such an approach and a broad base of feminist support, so much more is possible in the world. This is our challenge.

GLOBAL FEMINISM

he material presented in this section reflects my ongoing interest in making global connections and in understanding the international dimensions of our lives. While the student Christian movement and the antiwar movement in the '60s and early '70s provided my first global experiences, the essays here stem primarily from a later period when I sought to create such connections in a feminist context.

In 1976–77, I explored the issues of global feminism through editing a special issue of *Quest: A Feminist Quarterly*. Most of this section however focuses on organizing activities around the United Nations Decade for Women from 1975 to 1985. This includes looking at the Decade and its consequences both in the United States and in the Third World, as well as reporting on international feminist gatherings and the UN events themselves. One essay is based on organizing an international network against female sexual slavery and traffic in women, which grew out of the 1980 Copenhagen World conferences. The section ends with the third pamphlet in my "Feminism in the 80's" series, which discusses how to relate local feminist initiatives to a global feminist perspective, and with my reflections on directions for feminism after the 1985 end-of-the-decade conference in Nairobi, Kenya.

267

WOMEN AND WORLD REVOLUTION

hen I became a feminist in the late 1960s, I was already active in the movement against the war in Vietnam. The following pieces from speeches and articles between 1968 and 1972 reflect my efforts to bring together feminist analysis and anti-imperialist concerns. Although these are related to Vietnam in a past decade, there are parallels to the questions feminists are raising about the war in Central America in the 1980s.

JEANETTE RANKIN WOMEN'S PEACE BRIGADE

(These paragraphs from a speech at the Jeanette Rankin Women's Brigade for Peace National Congress on January 15, 1968, give the flavor of this period.)

Three years ago when I first demonstrated against the Vietnam War, I thought that it was just a bad mistake in U.S. policy that if we protested enough, would be remedied. Since then, we have seen many disturbing events—U.S. intervention in the Dominican Republic, the militaristic reaction to black riots at home, the further escalation in Southeast Asia, and so on. Today it is clear that we not only protest ruthless slaughter in Vietnam but also must examine why that "mistake" has not been easily remedied. We must see Vietnam, not as an aberration, but as a logical extension of U.S. foreign policy.

269

It is this policy, to which the United States has committed our national energy in lives and dollars over the past twenty years, which we must reverse if we are to stop both the war in Vietnam and the Vietnams of the future. This involves three interrelated factors: first, we must look at how the U.S. is embarked on a policy, not of defense, but of offense—of world domination and control, what one poet calls "Pentagonolia." Second, we should consider those Third World nations that have become the battle-ground for our struggle for domination, where the effects of our policy are most clear and disturbing. And finally, we must realize the domestic results of this policy, specifically a "war" against dissent and social change that we see vividly in the ghettos today and in the coercive use of the draft and the recent indictments of antiwar leaders.

The most obvious cases of U.S. power used for domination are military: intervention in the Bay of Pigs, green berets in Bolivia, U.S.-backed coups in Iran and Guatemala, and so on. The net result of these activities has been to put the U.S. on the side of dictatorships and repression throughout much of the Third World. The policy of domination cannot be defined only in military terms, however. It also operates through economic pressure and the involvement of the U.S. in the everyday affairs of other nations. This type of presence is seen most clearly in Latin America, which has been dominated by the U.S. for over a century, and is experiencing an increased U.S. presence or "Vietnamization" in recent years.

Given the present direction of our government's policies, we cannot trust it for information much less to develop the alternatives that are needed. The imperative on us—this room full of women—is great. We cannot wait passively to see what 1968 will bring; we must begin now to determine what '68 and '69 and '78 and '79 will look like.

We must escalate our efforts—research, organize, act, and do it over and over. Bringing change in foreign policy involves not so much influencing top decision makers in Washington, but building a massive base of people at the local level who demand the necessary changes. We must develop new responses that put human priorities first, that attack racism and domination at home and in foreign policy, that redefine our interests and the role of the U.S., not as world policeman, but as part of a more humane order internationally.

270

Where traditional modes of politics such as lobbying have failed, we must turn to new styles of action. The most pressing things today are direct action and resistance to what we consider wrong. These are already organized around such issues as the draft and war taxes. We must find areas that affect women's lives around which to organize direct confrontation with the system and through which to build a larger base of activists.

Indeed, the task ahead will take nothing short of a lifetime. These may be hard times when we grow discouraged, but we have only begun a serious political struggle, already being waged in other places, over the future of man (sic). We can not retreat; rather we as women must develop strategies to discover effective action that leads the American public to define a new future for our nation. We must make clear that the choice before our nation is between making the U.S. more of a garrison state or turning to new directions at home and abroad. This must be a choice put before every local community and determined by the people, not the government. It is our job as women in the twentieth century to put choices before our people and to point to directions for our country if it has the will and the courage to undergo fundamental changes in many aspects of its life.

VIETNAMESE WOMEN IN REVOLUTION

(In May 1970, I went on a trip to North Vietnam with another woman and two men sponsored by the Mobilization Committee to End the War. I was already involved in women's liberation and sought to understand more about women's situation in Vietnam while there. The following excerpts are taken from a report on my trip in "Asian Women in Revolution," *Women: A Journal of Liberation,* vol. I, no. 4. [Summer 1970].)

The women of Vietnam are in the midst of their own process of liberation and they identify that process at this stage with defeating the United States and building socialism. Whether or not the process of liberating women will in fact be completed without another struggle going on between the men and women in society is a question for the future. From its inception, the Vietnamese Communist party proclaimed women's equality as one of its goals and created a Women's Union for this purpose. For most, therefore, the concept of women's liberation was introduced into their lives by the party.

The main instrument for women's liberation is the Women's Union. Its two goals are: defending the interests of women, and organizing and raising their political consciousness. We asked what do they do with the women. One of the first things they said is to help women overcome their inferior complex. They talk to women and offer them training so that they realize they can become active and part of the developing society. One way that they inspire confidence is through "emulations" in which women who have become part of the national struggle are held up as examples of the potential strength of women. In every village, the Union is responsible for educating the women about the war, socialism, and women's rights. They set up training schools to give women technical skills. They hold sessions about health to promote hygiene and give out birth control information. They promote the idea of a three-to-five child family, as compared to the traditionally larger one. They also hold sessions to discuss how to choose a husband and what women can expect and demand of husbands in the new society.

The marriage laws passed in 1960 outlawed polygamy and gave women rights equal to men in the family, divorce, and property ownership. The main strategy for bringing equality to the family is to industrialize housework. It is stated in the constitution that housework, canteens, child care, and home services should be handled communally. Day care exists for about 50 percent of the children from around four months old and up. The other 50 percent often stay with aunts or grandmothers in extended families. We visited a kindergarten for children of the most active women cadres in Hanoi. It was a well-organized boarding school with four young women teachers and one old man for ninety children aged three to five who stayed all week and went home on weekends. However, most kindergartens are day schools.

The other areas of the program for women's liberation are achieving equality in fighting, in labor, in party leadership and administration, and in management of the society. Several laws were passed and services set up, such as paid maternity leaves for women workers, toward these goals. The Women's Union is also responsible for understanding the needs of women in their villages and interpreting these to the government.

While it seems that much is being done to increase women's status and participation in North Vietnamese society, male supremacy still exists. One would not expect them to have eliminated it in twenty years, nonetheless it is useful to look at some of the problems. The first important question is whether the advances made will continue or be turned back, as in Algeria after the war for liberation ended there. We asked women what they expected, and most knew what work they wanted to pursue. Since the society has a tremendous rebuilding job to do requiring their labor, there is no reason why women should be sent home.

There are three areas in which the women we talked to felt their revolution was not yet complete: in women's self-image, in politics, and in the family. Male supremacy is also still embedded in the militia. While women carry guns and fight, they are not major military forces in the North and are never sent to the front. We asked why and were told: "If we send women to the front, who would take care of the country back home, industry, agriculture, children?" Production and life at home are, of course, important, but there is no question that going to the front has greater status. It is called the greatest thing one can do for one's country, and yet, women are excluded from participating.

There is a male/female job hierarchy with women more concentrated in "light" work that is less well paid than "men's heavy work." Women also appeared at times to be viewed more as supporters and entertainers for the men who were the heroes. In North Vietnamese films, women were writing letters or doing embroidery for their husbands at the front, or taking up the jobs that men left behind. Children were inheriting these attitudes, as we saw, in a kindergarten where the girls did songs and dances for us but no boys participated. We asked why, and they said that girls like to do songs and dances, but boys like to fight and do other things.

The problem that affected us most was the lack of women as public spokesmen (sic). There was often a representative from a women's organization, but she usually did not speak except when we talked about women. Representatives from other groups such as ethnic minorities and youth were almost all male. Even more troubling was what seemed a patronizing attitude toward women's progress: "We're really proud of how far our women have come." Since women did not have an independent movement prior to the party, this attitude is understandable, but it revealed that men think women have to earn equality rather than that they deserve it already.

The most positive attitude that Vietnamese women communicated to us was that their lives were significant, not for individual glory but for what they could contribute to the struggles of their country. While they still face many problems, they have moved from a state of servitude under feudalism to one of vital participation in society in a short time, and they face the future with confidence. They also believed that women could change the course of history for the benefit of all. This was expressed by a Buddhist nun in Vinh City who told us that she was sure if the women in the U.S. understood what was happening in Vietnam, they would stop the war.

RISE UP, MY SISTERS

(In December 1970, the Washington, D.C., Women's Anti-Imperialist Collective, along with groups in other cities, edited an issue of *Off Our Backs* [vol. I, no. 15] on women and imperialism. The following selections illustrate our initial efforts at forging links between anti-imperialist struggles in the world and the women's movement, including the newly emerging gay and lesbian groups.)

Bursting forth from the resistance of oppressed peoples comes a consciousness of our strength and our potential for creation. We use the word "life force" to symbolize this life-oriented politics, based on people's determination to take control of their own lives. Too often in the midst of the atrocities perpetrated by U.S. imperialism, we forget that we are not only trying to bring down a system but that we are also moving toward a new world, a new woman and a new man, a new life for all people. Revolution is the acting out of this spirit—it is the process which liberates our consciousness and affirms our humanity. It is this life force which gives us the will and energy to fight and do what we know is necessary to defend what we are building and becoming.

Today we are expressing this life force throughout the world, sometimes loudly as in Southeast Asia, at other times quietly as in a women's consciousness-raising group, in a jail cell where Ericka Huggins (a black female political prisoner in jail in New Haven) writes letters, or in the cane-cutting fields of Cuba. The contrast between the emerging revolutionary forces and the dying old order can be seen all around us. . . .

Struggle between life and death has gone on for centuries, but now this battle has reached a new peak of intensity. We see it in the struggle to survive of Third World liberation movements both in the United States and abroad. We see it in the lives of more and more white people, especially among youth, women, and gay people. Today we see life force bursting forth from women. The women's liberation movement has developed from women coming together, out of isolation, to understand and end our oppression. As we have to take control of our lives, we have encountered the powerful forces of the society that hold us back and we have seen that we must fight these to survive. We have learned that all relationships based on power, on dominance and subordination, produce loneliness, dependency, self-hate, and do not allow us to grow. In the very process of struggling against these oppressions, we have experienced more and more the life force within ourselves and our sisters. This life force is a flowering of creativity, joy, trust, and love that we never knew before. . . .

The life force released by the women's movement is making it possible to respond to the emerging life force among gay women. Our gay sisters are raising our consciousness about love, sexuality, and human relationships. We are learning about love for a sister that is good, happy, sad, difficult. Knowing that love between women is sometimes happy and sometimes difficult demystifies the whole concept of love, changes it from a thing that must follow a script to something that lets us discover each other. . . .

Gay people came together to resist their own oppression but as that consciousness grows into something beyond resistance, it opens up space for all of us to deal with things in addition to homosexual love. We are freer to understand how we treat each other on every level, to throw out all those assumptions that separated us and held us down. Life force is that which makes us first rise up against our oppressor, and is also released by the act of rising up. We are responsible for nurturing this life force, for it must be our future.

OUT NOW: FEMINISTS AND THE VIETNAM WAR

(By 1972, I stopped trying to link the feminist and anti-imperialist movements and chose instead to look at issues of war and imperialism from the vantage point of the women's movement. These extracts are from my explanation of this decision in *The Furies,* vol. I, no. 5 [June–July 1972].)

Of course, being anti-imperialist and antisexist go hand in hand: both are evils created by white male domination of the world. But the conquest of women took place so long ago that it is taken for granted as the natural way of life. Meanwhile, women who remain enslaved are drawn into these battles of men over race, nation, and class and have never succeeded in putting our interests first. Few of these battles between men have significantly altered the oppression of women. None has eliminated male supremacy.

In developing a feminist analysis of society, we must include a critique of imperialism and link the Vietnam War to other forms of domination. But for feminists at this time, there is a conflict between building our movement and spending time actively working against the war. Whenever we have tried to combine these in the past few years, we have sacrificed feminism. This time, we must build a movement that brings these together from a feminist viewpoint—that doesn't sacrifice women and is ultimately strong enough to challenge all imperialisms. Feminists must concentrate on developing a women's ideology, program, culture, and movement. If we don't make ending male supremacy our priority, no one else will.

Two years ago we tried to create actions and programs that combined feminism and anti-imperialism, but we soon found ourselves working mainly on the war, out of touch with the women's movement, and with no significant time to think about feminist strategy. We were not able to build a feminist movement from the anti-imperialism work wc were doing. I realized that women had learned more about the connections between sexism and world imperialism when we were working on the problems of birth control, which had grown out of our own needs, than we were learning from antiwar work.

Men have carried on endless struggles over race and nation, using women and keeping us in servitude. This will not change until women demand it—with our lives. This begins quietly with every feminist's decision how to spend her time, what struggles will be her priority. We must develop a world view and strategy for change that deals with the other forms of imperialism, but we must do so from a feminist perspective. Only this kind of attack can hope to end all forms of imperialism. Our oppression does not give us the luxury to dabble in worthy causes without developing an overall strategy that attacks sexism as well. We must choose to win this time.

AN INTRODUCTION
TO INTERNATIONAL FEMINISM

n the summer of 1964, I made my first trip outside of North
America. I participated in a work-study project sponsored by
the Japanese YMCA where we discussed "Our Responsibility
in a Changing Asia." I was one of the few participating Westerners; half the participants were Japanese, and most of the others were Asians. Therefore, everything we did and discussed
was from a Japanese, or at least Asian, perspective, and experiencing that difference changed my life. At first I was completely disoriented. Gradually, though, I learned that the world,
its problems, and even how one discusses them, look quite dif-
erent when viewed from another culture, from other countries
and life experiences. To say that this is true, however, and to
experience its truth often are very different. *Spending time* in
another country is not the only (or even a guaranteed) way to
come to understand this phenomenon; but *having to function* in
a completely different cultural context can be one of the most
effective ways to learn this lesson—as the Third World women
who critiqued the U.S.-sponsored conference on Women and

"An Introduction to International Feminism" was published as the Introduction to the
"International Feminism" issue of *Quest: A Feminist Quarterly,* vol. IV, no. 2 (Winter
1978).

Development held at Wellesley College (1976) have observed.*

Since that summer, I have traveled to other places, met people from many other societies, and discovered more about the cultural differences within this country itself—and I have also learned a great deal about imperialism. But still, I will never forget that shock and the changes in my perception of "reality" that came with having to function in a different frame of reference. As a movement, feminists in the United States need to experience that shock. We have necessarily begun our analysis in light of our own experiences, but our perspectives have also been limited by that view. As our movement and its analysis have matured over the past few years, it is particularly important that we listen and talk across national boundaries. This is not an easy task, but we hope that this international issue of *Quest* will be an eye-opener and a significant contribution to the difficult but essential process of building a sustained international feminist dialogue.

When *Quest* began planning its future themes in 1974, a special "international" issue was proposed. We rejected the idea at that time because we wanted to integrate articles from all over the world into each issue rather than segregating them into one. We thought that it would not be necessary to have a special theme in order to include feminist perspectives from elsewhere. We were wrong. In our first three years, we published only a few articles written by women outside the U.S. We discovered that we were not able to attract such articles unless we made a particular effort by concentrating an entire issue on feminist perspectives from other countries.

When the development committee for this issue convened, our first problem was how to describe our intent. We wanted articles about women's struggles toward the development of feminism—by whatever name they called it. But we did not want articles simply describing the state of women's oppression throughout the world because other publications are already providing that information. Yet, we realized that understanding the context in which ideas and actions develop is integral to understanding the feminism of other countries. We also realized that while many women outside the U.S. are forced to know something

---

*See "A Critical Look at the Wellesley Conference" by Nawal El Sadawi, Fatima Mernissi, and Mallica Vajarathon, *ISIS International Bulletin*, no. 3 (April 1977).

about our culture because it is exported everywhere, not many women in the U.S. know much about other countries.

Calling the issue "International Feminism" we solicited articles covering three major areas of focus: (1) What kinds of feminist or women's activities, movements, and concerns are generated by different national and/or cultural conditions? How do these differ and what—if any—seem to be common themes in women's concerns internationally? Can we talk about the global oppression of women—its causes and cures—in any universal terms? What cross-national networks of women are developing? (2) How do particular governments, economic structures, and social systems affect women's lives in work, childrearing, sex, and so on? What role do nongovernmental forms of social organization—such as ethnic, tribal, or religious groups, or trade unions and political parties—play in affecting women's lives, either in conflict or in cooperation with the government? (3) What theoretical, strategic, and programmatic developments are taking place that are vital to an international feminist audience? Why are issues such as "development," the economic function of women, lesbian oppression, or race and class analyses important internationally, and what is their significance for women in various situations?

Ambitious questions, we knew, but ones that we hoped then, and still hope, will provoke discussion and future work. Despite the focus of our questions, most of the articles we received were about the state of women's oppression in various countries. And many of those were written by American and European women *about* Third World women. We had initially decided not to print articles by Westerners about the Third World in order to avoid the cultural bias and problems of "us" writing about "them." Nevertheless, many of these articles were informative, and through consideration of this dilemma, we became aware of the need for the development of a political/ethical perspective on how and when feminists can write with integrity about women in other cultures.

We have learned a great deal about the problems of "internationalism" and about the common questions that feminists face. Two related themes are most significant: first, all issues are indeed feminist issues, and second, a certain instinct for a common perspective ties us together, although we do not yet have an analysis providing the cohesive element. If feminism is to be perceived

280

globally as a viable concept, it must not limit itself to a narrow definition of women's concerns. Feminism is not about a list of issues. Rather, it is about developing a particular perspective on *all* matters that touch our lives. Women in different countries clearly have different priorities; but if feminism is a universally applicable perspective, it will provide a framework for all those concerns, no matter how diverse. And there is among women a certain impulse toward such a common feminist perspective; its existence—in not yet fully articulated terms—is clear throughout the manuscripts we have received.

We are, then, a movement of many common experiences and instincts, but one that has not yet given birth to a common language and analysis. Still, it is the presence of that impulse which fuels the search for that common language and analysis and gives us hope that, indeed, some form of global feminist perspective is developing.

In working on this issue, certain questions kept recurring: how does the feminist movement relate to Marxist or class movements—both in theory and practice? What is the role of women's revolution within nationalist movements? What is the significance for women of what have been called "development" plans for the nonindustrialized countries? What do *we* consider signs of progressive "development" or advance for women in any culture? How do we respect the self-determination of previously colonized countries and also articulate our criticisms of antiwoman practices within them? How has the oppression of women in industrialized countries taken a subtle and insidious turn that is sometimes exported as "women's emancipation," and how can we prevent that exportation without reinforcing the more traditional forms of female oppression? And of course, finally, what are the origins of our oppression in every culture, and how are they related: what are strategies for eradicating sexism, and how much can we transfer strategies from one culture to another?

While producing this issue, we have experienced some of the practical problems of communicating internationally. Most of us in the U.S. are English-language chauvinists. We are not familiar with trying to understand something not written in our native tongue, and we are used to having access to an abundance of material in our own language. We not only take language for granted, but are also cut off from many important feminist writings because we have not sought to read or have translated the feminist literature not available in English. Reading material written outside of the U.S. made us aware of how often our own writing is based in American experience and jargon that assumes it is international, but is in fact parochial and inaccessible to other women. For these reasons, we considered printing each article in this issue in its original language and leaving it to you, the readers, to discover the problems of translation, but we decided the content was too important to risk such an experiment.

Finally, the process of putting this issue together reminded us of the tenuous hold we have over any of life's resources, including our channels of communication. We are utterly dependent on male international systems, such as the postal service, for our communications. This dependence has caused us problems and taught us that patience is essential in dealing on an international scale.

This issue only begins to touch the areas that must be explored before international feminism is a living reality. Its purpose is to contribute to awakening a greater concern for exchange among women throughout the world. Such an exchange must be based on seeing ourselves as equals—women engaged in creating an international dialogue grounded in our respect for both our common and our differing experiences.

DEVELOPING STRATEGIES FOR THE UNITED NATIONS DECADE FOR WOMEN

The United Nations declared 1975 International Women's Year (IWY), and held its first World Conference on Women that year in Mexico City, Mexico. Delegates at the IWY conference passed a plan of action and called for a UN Decade for Women. The UN General Assembly then declared 1976–85 as the United Nations' Decade for Women: Equality, Development, and Peace. In 1980, a UN Mid-Decade Conference to appraise the progress of women thus far was held in Copenhagen, Denmark, and in 1985, the UN held its End-of-the-Decade World Conference on Women in Nairobi, Kenya. At each of these conferences, nongovernmental organizations (NGOs) affiliated with the UN organized parallel events, open to anyone, to discuss the status of women; the NGO event in 1975 was called the IWY Tribune and in '80 and '85, the NGO Forum. The following are excerpts taken from pieces that I wrote about the 1975 and 1980 conferences.

U.S. FEMINISTS AND INTERNATIONAL WOMEN'S YEAR

(This is from an article written with Frances Doughty and published by several U.S. feminist periodicals in preparation for the 1975 IWY. I did not go to Mexico City and worked instead to help the National Gay Task Force Women's Caucus send Frances as our representative.)

There has been much confusion over plans for the UN International Women's Year conference in Mexico City, June 19–July 2. We have tried to sort out some facts and evaluate radical feminist and lesbian participation in it. First, the official UN conference is for government representatives and security will be tight; efforts by feminists who are not credentialed to get in are probably useless. The other conference planned through the nongovernmental organizations (NGOs) of the UN is open. There will be two large rooms that seat two thousand persons each with translation facilities and mikes on the floor. There will also be numerous small rooms without translation facilities. The conferences do not claim to be feminist events, but we think that some radical and lesbian feminist presence at the NGO Tribune is vital, while not making it our movement's priority. We have written to the organizers of the Tribune requesting space for lesbians to make a presentation, and those who go might hold special workshops there.

In order for U.S. feminists to be most effective at IWY, the situation in Mexico City must be considered carefully. Most countries, except for the United States, Canada, and Mexico will be represented by relatively few women, either sent by governments or who can afford the high cost of going on their own. Therefore, large numbers of women attending from the U.S. presents problems. No matter whether the individual is conservative or radical, she will be part of an overwhelming U.S. presence that will be resented by many. This is the reality of American cultural and economic imperialism.

Therefore, U.S. feminists should consider seriously whether to go to Mexico City at all and what our presence there means. Some of our suggestions are:

1. Groups from particular cities or projects might choose to send only one woman to present your concerns, rather than allowing a situation where those who can afford it are the ones to go.

2. Individuals going to Mexico primarily for a vacation should consider the impact and problems caused by massive numbers of U.S. Americans outnumbering other women present and reconsider where to spend your vacation.

3. People considering taking actions in Mexico should remember that it is not primarily U.S. women, but Mexican feminists who will suffer any repercussions of what we do there.

4. Above all, those who do go (and some radical and lesbian

feminist presence is important) should keep in mind that all U.S. citizens are from an imperialist country and our behavior, even as feminists, often reflects that. For example, English-language domination will be an issue, and priority should go to sending women who speak other languages. In our workshops, we should provide translation and remember that we are at an advantage verbally if all conversations are conducted in English.

Feminists should go to listen as much as to show the world what our idea of feminism is. We should take the time and opportunity to hear what women of other countries tell us about their lives—both their oppressions and strengths. Those strengths are often ones that have been socialized out of most white, middle-class women, and we therefore often fail to recognize them in others.

If feminists attend the Tribune with such a consciousness and if the number of U.S. Americans is not overwhelming, there should be many chances to learn and to share politics, experiences, and insights with other women. Without this consciousness, however, we play into the hands of U.S. imperialism and confirm the stereotype of the arrogant American. Men around the world already use that to denounce "women's lib" and to keep "their women" divided from us. We must show the women themselves that we are not simply American feminist chauvinists, and then real learning and exchange can take place.

DEVELOPING STRATEGIES FOR THE FUTURE: FEMINIST PERSPECTIVES

(In June 1979, I was the U.S. participant in an international workshop, "Feminist Ideology and Structures in the First Half of the Decade for Women," sponsored by the United Nations Asian and Pacific Centre for Women and Development (APCWD) in Bangkok, Thailand. I helped write the section of the workshop report on "Goals of the Women's Movement," which sought to develop a working definition of feminism that could be used globally. I then coordinated a follow-up international workshop co-sponsored by APCWD and the Women and Development Unit of the University of the West Indies. Like the Bangkok meeting, this was also a small, regionally diverse group of women who met for almost a week, this time in Stony Point, New York, in April of

1980. Both of these workshops published papers in preparation for the 1980 world conferences in Copenhagen. The following is the "Issues Paper" I wrote with Peggy Antrobus of the West Indies and Shirley Castley of Australia, summarizing the Bangkok paper and raising questions from it as a starting point for discussion at the Stony Point workshop.)

Section I: Goals of the Women's Movement

Summary:

The Bangkok paper begins by defining feminism in terms of two long-term goals:

1. First, the achievement of women's equality, dignity, and freedom of choice through women's power to control their own lives and bodies within and outside the home, and,
2. the removal of all forms of inequity and oppression through the creation of a more just social and economic order, nationally and internationally.

This section then discusses the relationship of feminism to other political movements, to the creation of new visions and structures for the world, and the ways in which feminism has often been distorted, keeping women from different cultures separated from each other.

Issues:

1. The Bangkok workshop defined feminism in terms of goals; it has been suggested that a working definition of feminism that would correspond to those goals might be:
   a consciousness of factors that create women's subordination and a commitment to work towards changing them.
   Does this definition of feminism along with the Bangkok definition of goals provide a useful beginning as a shared definition of feminism?
2. While there are a variety of different feminist ideologies, are there common points shared by all or most of them? How do various ideologies account for differences among women in terms of class, race, religion, life-styles, rural-urban environment, political convictions, etc.?
3. How does feminism relate to other political ideologies and move-

286

ments, such as socialism or movements for national liberation? How does this vary according to particular local and regional conditions?

4. How is feminism changing women's self-concepts? What kinds of new visions is it creating for how we live our lives? (How has the women's movement affected the struggles and visions of other movements for social change?)

5. As women's opportunities increase and their roles and responsibilities broaden, what are the effects on men, families, and other basic institutions? What are the critical adjustments that take place?

6. While acknowledging that there are conflicts of interest among women, what are the commonalities in women's experiences that cut across various class, cultural, and religious differences? For example, the Report of the Experts' Group meeting held in October, 1979, called by the UN Secretariat for the Mid-Decade conference stated:

"How are we to understand, both at a conceptual and a strategic level, the relationship between the universal problem confronting women and the problems that particular groups of women face in different countries? In this document, we have started from the assumption—already present in the Mexico Declaration of 1975—that women universally face some form of subordination. Indeed, a long range historical analysis makes it clear that women everywhere, and at all times, have shared work, wars, and exploitation equally with men, but they have rarely, if ever shared equally in power or in the benefits of given social situations."

Are there further common points?

Section II: Redirecting Social Processes

Summary:
This section reflects on the powerful institutionalized social processes in society. The family, education, industrialization and development, employment structures, law and the media were all discussed in terms of their functions as obstacles to the full potential of women and also as possible positive agents in the task of changing society's values.

Reformist and revolutionary approaches were discussed in

order to identify possible strategies for achieving such social change.

Issues: (Part A)

1. The major social processes identified in the Bangkok paper which serve to institutionalize women's oppression are role socialization, economic processes, legislation, education, employment, the family, and the media. Are there any other processes or institutions which should have been identified? How can these processes and institutions which are vehicles of oppression be used *by* women to create the kind of social justice and equality which is needed?

2. Are there institutions and social processes which operate at the international level, such as the imperialism of multinational corporations, that affect women in various countries in different but related ways? How can women develop strategies that take into account these international dimensions?

3. The Bangkok paper talked of reformist and revolutionary strategies. How can we strengthen and deepen our analyses and prescriptions for the strategies we require?

(Part B)

The issue of women in development has many facets which makes it relevant not only to women in Third World countries and marginalized groups of women in the "developed" countries but also to women and men, to planners and policy makers, the world over. It raises questions of definition, content, and style which expose its complexity and make it a central issue for feminists. Further, we need to examine what are feminist perspectives on the concept of development.

1. The most common definition of "development" as industrialization and economic development makes it an exclusive Third World concern: yet, even then, women who represent more than half the human resources are seldom perceived as part of the solution. Women's participation in the process of development must be enhanced, both as beneficiaries and as contributors; but do strategies to "integrate women into development" adequately reflect women's own perceptions of what development is or should be?

2. Must equality between men and women wait for economic development? Would removal of poverty solve the problem of women's

288

disadvantages? Conversely, can poverty be eradicated and development fully achieved if there is widespread sex discrimination?

3. The concept and goals of development have been reassessed over the past twenty years with the increasing recognition of the inadequacy of economic growth alone for ensuring benefits to all members of society. A distinction has been made between "growth" and "development" which acknowledges that for development, social goals (the quality of life) must be pursued simultaneously with economic growth, thus extending the relevance of the issue to "developed" countries as well. Many Third World feminists have called for an integrated approach to development as "progress with distributive justice." In this sense, is it possible to speak of development without equity? And can the issue of equity be separated from that of development?

4. At the international level there are calls for a New International Development Strategy (the NIDS), and a New International Economic Order (NIEO). Is the women's issue part of this impetus? Will women benefit from the NIDS and NIEO?

5. The existence of a women's movement in the so-called developed countries indicates that economic industrial development alone does not bring equality and dignity for women. How can women in countries whose primary energy is going towards economic development prevent a repetition of this problem and ensure that equality for women goes hand in hand with economic development?

6. National revolutionary leaders or newly independent countries sometimes claim as part of the cultural integrity of their freedom the right to impose or reimpose 'customary' yokes on women. How can women establish their own freedom while still maintaining respect for the culture of their country?

Section III: Government Structures and Institutions

Summary:

This section describes the various forms of national structures which have been established by governments to improve the status of women, integrate women into development, or monitor and advise on policies relating to women. It critically examines some of the problems inherent in such government structures and outlines some of the ways in which the problems identified could be overcome. The functional roles of national machineries are explored along with the kinds of structural links with other institutions and women's groups, which need to be established in order to maximize effectiveness.

Issues:

1. To what extent do the strategies already adopted by governments to improve the status of women and broaden their participation in national life reflect a feminist perspective?

2. How can women ensure that special national machinery is sensitive to their real needs and priorities? How can women working in bureaucracies or on National Commissions, etc., ensure that they retain contact with women at all levels of society?

3. The UN document prepared for the Mid-Decade conference, *Review and Appraisal of Policies and Plans to Integrate Women in National Life 1975–78,* states in part:

   It can be stated as a general proposition that the simplistic faith in such machinery evident five years ago has been considerably tempered by experience. Specifically, the divergence between the formal charters of the machinery and their actual impact in affecting policies has been very wide in most member states. In some instances the establishment of national machinery has had adverse effects. Thus in situations where governments are not committed to the integration of women in development, the fact of the establishment of the institutions *formally* mandated to represent women's interests has been cited as the proof of *substantive* commitment. Such institutions have also been identified as the exclusive legitimate bridges between the government and the grass roots, and have served to preempt popular women's demands initiated outside the bureaucracy.
   Are these accurate reflections? If so, what needs to be done to change the situation?

4. How do various types of governments and socioeconomic systems affect women's lives and the ways in which national machineries might operate or be effective?

5. What efforts can be made to utilize other major institutions (e.g., unions, churches, private associations, etc.) to help women gain more influence over government policies and programs? What kinds of linkages are necessary between women's organizations

and various efforts to bring change through national machinery and other established institutions?

Section IV: Role of the Women's Movement and Organizations

Summary:

This section of the Bangkok Report notes that ultimately the realization of feminist goals depends on the organizing of an independent movement of active women's groups at all levels of society, and particularly at the grass roots. It identifies three critical aspects of building a women's movement:

1. conscientization of women about their oppression and how it can be altered,
2. training women in various skills necessary for creating social change, and
3. mobilizing women's strengths personally, politically, and economically to bring about change.

Issues:

1. To what extent and through what means do NGOs and women's movements have the opportunity to affect government policies? How can their potential for doing so be increased? When is it necessary, as the Bangkok paper notes, to work with forces in opposition to governments rather than with existing governments?
2. What progress is being made towards involving nongovernmental institutions (such as trade unions, political parties, cooperatives, etc.) in organizing women to achieve power over their own lives and in society? How can these institutions and various types of traditional women's organizations be utilized further in the conscientization of women towards feminist goals?
3. What resources are necessary for women's groups to develop a broad-based movement? What are the problems and advantages associated with utilizing government channels for training and organizing women?
4. What models for conscientization, mobilization, and training have been successfully developed in different contexts? How have these varied according to class, race, and geographic differences among women? What can women learn from these to make our efforts more effective?
5. What kinds of change does feminism imply for men and families

and how can women's groups develop strategies to help with that transformation at both the individual and the institutional levels?

6. Are there common perspectives for organizing women based on women's work in the home, in agriculture and in industry; concern for the health, adequate nourishment, and living standards of all individuals; protection of the environment; need for child care and decent education for all children; belief in all women's rights to control our bodies, our sexuality, and our reproduction; the necessity to end violence against women in all its forms—rape, wife beating, female slavery, etc.

7. Can these or other issues provide the basis for greater international cooperation among women? How can women's movements in different countries develop more direct communication in order to understand each other better, share resources, exchange information and insights, and strengthen all of our efforts?

WHAT NOT TO EXPECT FROM THE UN WOMEN'S CONFERENCE IN COPENHAGEN

(This article was published in *Ms.* magazine [July 1980] in preparation for the 1980 Mid-Decade Conferences.)

At the midpoint of the decade, the UN has called another world conference on women, in Copenhagen, Denmark, July 14–30. As in Mexico City, a variety of women's events, including a forum sponsored by nongovernmental organizations, will be held simultaneously.

The official goals of the UN's conference are to assess the progress and problems of women since the 1975 World Plan of Action, focusing specifically on the areas of health, education, and employment. The agenda also calls for consideration of women under apartheid, the rights of Palestinian women, and women refugees.

In preparation for this conference, eighty-six governments and various UN-related agencies responded to a questionnaire about women's status; and a number of reports have evaluated women's progress in the theme areas, as well as in government planning and politics. The documents reveal, to no one's surprise, that while women's status has improved slightly in a few areas such as antidiscrimination legislation, and while the issue of women's rights has gained greater recognition internationally, little actual change has occurred in women's daily lives. (In fact, we are far from achieving even legislative equality, much less the demands of a broader feminist agenda.) The conference will therefore consider a new program of action, which calls for basic changes at the local, national, and international levels.

This, at least, is what the UN World Conference on Women is *supposed* to be discussing in Copenhagen. But we know from past experience that the UN is hardly a feminist forum.

The most important fact and limitation of the official Copenhagen conference is that it is a meeting of government-appointed representatives. Aside from a few official observers from UN agencies or nongovernmental organizations, some two thousand delegates will be chosen by the governments of the UN's 146-member nations and their actions and votes will be directed by those governments. The resolutions that pass will therefore represent only that amount of feminist perspective or rhetoric that has been accepted by existing patriarchal governments—which is to say, not very much.

Copenhagen will reflect the political tensions of competing state powers, and will be used, both internationally and domestically, by governments to promote their own images or needs. While the concerns of women cannot be divorced from other political and economic questions, this usually means that various national interests take precedence over more feminist perspectives on women's needs. One Mexico City resolution, for example, focused on a denunciation of Zionism without discussing particular effects on women of the Mideast situation—and the Palestinian issue will probably be handled similarly in Copenhagen.

In the case of the United States, President Carter will no doubt choose and use the U.S. delegation to support his administration. The State Department has established its own Secretariat for the conference and has held various regional meetings and sought domestic input in the three areas of health, education, and employment. But these meetings were by invitation only, had no official relationship to delegate selection, and will not determine the content of the position papers presented to the UN conference by our government.

The process demonstrates how different this conference is from the U.S. National Women's Conference held in Houston, Texas, in 1977. While the Houston conference was also government-sponsored and produced a Plan of Action, it was a meeting of democratically elected individuals, not of government-appointed delegations. There was room for significant grass-roots participation and feminist organizing around the conference agenda.

While it is important to understand that Copenhagen is a government conference about women—not a women's conference—it can still serve a valuable function. Governments will make public statements on their policies toward women and can thus be held accountable. In addition, we will have a measure of how much the pressure of women's movements around the world has affected what governments at least declare should be done for women.

As in Mexico City, a variety of additional women's events will be held along with, but outside of, the official UN conference. The central event will be the Forum, officially sponsored by forty nongovernmental organizations (NGOs), such as the World YWCA, the Afro-American People's Solidarity Organization, and International Planned Parenthood. Since most of the pressure for women's rights historically has come from outside of governments, and policy is often determined in response to the climate and pressure created by movements and NGOs, the issues and strategies discussed in the Forum will certainly reveal as much about the future directions of feminism internationally as the government conference. The Forum also gives feminists a chance to use the occasion and attention of the UN conference for international exchange and learning.

The Forum's program will give special attention to the mandates of the call of the UN Decade—equality, development, and peace—as well as to the three official themes of health, education, and employment. Two additional topics will focus on racism and sexism, and refugees and migrants. While the Forum will not necessarily be a feminist body, it will probably incorporate a wide range of feminist concerns—from violence against women to multinational corporations; from lesbianism to literacy; from women in development to women in minority groups. Formal panels are planned, but much of the activity will take place in workshops, seminars, and informal gatherings. Emphasis will be given to topics of concern in more than one country and to the participation of women from Third World countries.

At home, feminists can use any media attention given to Copenhagen to reassert that the women's movement is alive and expanding globally. But, with Mexico City as our example, we know that the media may ignore or misrepresent the substance of the events or focus on whatever political dissension emerges. At least three women's media projects are hoping to ensure that accurate news gets to as many women as possible. The Forum will publish a daily newspaper covering the events at both the UN Conference and the Forum. A Satellite Communications Project, initiated through the Women's Institute for Freedom of the Press, plans to broadcast news and events to public television and radio stations in the United States and other countries. And a number of women's publications and feminist writers are getting press credentials and plan to pool information in order to publish news and analysis from a feminist perspective in both established local papers and feminist publications.

Although the United Nations won't be offering a feminist conference this summer, the meeting clearly provides the occasion for global consciousness-raising and even the exertion of moral force. And feminists who are in Copenhagen can make invaluable international connections.

WHAT THEY DID NOT TELL YOU ABOUT COPENHAGEN

(Following the 1980 world conferences on women, I wrote a report published as part of a Women's International Press Service packet. This piece is an adaptation of that article which appeared in *Signs: Journal of Women and Culture in Society,* vol. VI, no. 4 [Summer 1981], where it was published as a response to "A Feminist View of Copenhagen" by Irene Tinker, *Signs,* vol. VI, no. 3 [Spring 1981].)

While I agree with Irene Tinker that women must improve their networks, sharpen their tactics, and insist that their special needs be inserted in every relevant UN debate in order to have an impact on the United Nations in the future, I disagree with her view that the events in Copenhagen were more negative than positive, and I believe that feminism was advanced there in spite of the UN's patriarchal attitudes and structures. Feminist discourse about the significance of Copenhagen is particularly important, since the media's headlining of sensational divisions over the Middle East substituted for substantial coverage, much less analysis, of what did happen there. The divisions and conflicts were real, but they coexisted with, and sometimes led to, valuable cross-cultural experiences, insights, and connections as well.

The official UN World Conference proceedings were controlled by the competing interests of the 145 patriarchal governments who attended, but the spontaneous applause that greeted a few outspoken delegates' pleas on behalf of women pointed to the potential for connections that many women felt and that some made on the sidelines. Such individual contacts and some of the proposals included in the Programme of Action that were not featured in the press were probably the best results of the conference. The program calls for greater involvement of women in all aspects of development planning, for changes in the international economic order particularly as it affects women in poverty, for special attention to migrant and refugee women, for an end to the exploitation of the prostitution of others and to the traffic in persons, for a commitment to higher standards of female nutrition and water sanitation, for the establishment of refuges for battered women; and it adds consideration of areas of women's oppression, such as sexual violence, that were not included in the Plan of Action passed at the first UN World Conference on Women in Mexico City in 1975. The problem with these proposals is of course implementation. The conference reports assessing progress made since 1975 toward improving women's status indicate that few governments have moved in more than token ways toward implementation of the plan, and in many areas women's status has deteriorated. The political will to implement these proposals does not yet exist. Women can however use the Programme of Action as a tool in pressuring for government and international agency action.

Some have complained that the UN Conference was "politicized" by discussion of other than "women's issues," but this misses the point. Feminism is political and it must address every possible issue of concern to human life, including the Middle East conflict. Further, women's oppression is interrelated with political, economic, and social conditions and cannot be solved in isolation from these. The problem was not that the conference was "political" but that it did not consider issues from a feminist political perspective or even in terms of how they specifically affect women. By relying on existing national and political divisions, it avoided dealing seriously with either the specifics of women's oppression or a feminist critique of "other issues," such as the economy, racism, war, and patriarchal nationalism.

The showdown around issues of the Middle East demonstrated that maintaining a hard line on national positions and keeping traditional alliances intact was more important to both the PLO-Arab block and the Israeli-U.S. side than creating a plan for women. Further, this focus on areas of international conflict provided governments with a way of avoiding discussion of the facts of female oppression both globally and within their own countries. Many industrialized countries hid behind a narrow definition of "women's issues," thus expressing concern for the plight of poor women in developing societies without accepting responsibility for the role that corporations and governments in rich countries play in oppressing women in other countries as well as in their own. Meanwhile, many Third World governments focused on legitimate grievances about the international economic order as a way to avoid examining various aspects of female oppression within their own societies.

There were no governments willing to put the interests of women first at this conference. There were, however, individual delegates who tried to introduce discussions of issues such as sexism, as one of the causes of discrimination against women. The Russian delegate gained notoriety for claiming that sex discrimination did not exist in his country because it was illegal and that sexism did not exist because the word was not in his language. Meanwhile, one of the Russian feminist exiles was holding a press conference on the lawn. Some argued that sexism was not as significant as racism and would end with the end of poverty anyway; a Third World woman wrote with irony about how the male delegate from India proclaimed that since he had experienced colonialism, he knew that it could not be equated with sexism.* A compromise footnote stated that in a group of countries discrimination on the grounds of sex is called sexism. Government doubletalk on women's equality was well illustrated when the British delegate explained that his country was not signing the UN Convention on the Elimination of All Forms of Discrimination

*Rubina Kahn, "Women: Contradictions at the World Conference on Women on Sexism," Inter Press Service Copenhagen Coverage, issue 7 (July 31, 1980).

against Women at this time because it takes UN conventions very seriously.

Still, there was a seriousness about Copenhagen and the way that governments sought to use and control the issue of women that indicated that the potential power of women as a constituency has been recognized. There were more high-level officials in Copenhagen than in Mexico, and generally governments kept a tighter rein over delegates, exhibiting more sophistication about how to use the conference. If Copenhagen can be taken as a measure, feminism has barely begun to change patriarchy's power structures, but it has increased world consciousness of women as a potential power bloc—a consciousness that can be used against feminism as well as for it.

Unlike the official UN conference, the NGO Forum had no central agenda or sessions. Its diversity, passion, openness, and largely honest conflict were a refreshing counterpoint to the tightly scripted UN arena. The majority of the eight thousand women from a hundred twenty-seven countries at the Forum came, often at great expense, to meet women from other countries, to exchange stories and strategies, publications and products, and to make connections for future work. The intensity of the Forum sessions and the determination of small knots of women gathered in every available corner testified to the reality of a movement among women globally. It was not unity around a set of issues but it was solidarity and respect for diversity as women sought to define our problems and possible solutions. The strength and the limitations of the Forum lay in this diversity and decentralization.

The atmosphere at the Forum was that of "Let a Hundred Flowers Bloom." While there were official panels set apart in the Library School where the conflicts of the UN's "real politick" often dominated, these were not the heart of the Forum. Its life was in the hundreds of small workshops and numerous sub-groups that formed around common interests, such as the Danish-sponsored women and development room, the continuous roundtables on women's studies, or the international feminist networking area in Vivencia. Low-profile networking became the hallmark of the Forum as women in workshops talked seriously about their concerns and strategies, and made plans for future organizing.

The decentralization of the Forum, however, created a sense of fragmentation and reinforced our immediate powerlessness to alter the UN agenda. Several demonstrations at the UN conference were held on various issues, but efforts to create a united voice were consistently frustrated. Without any opportunity to meet together and sense the power and diversity of the eight thousand women present, cohesion was missing and it was difficult to assess how much unity might have been possible. Since the format of the Forum did not demand that conflicts be resolved, some were never openly aired, but many issues did surface for discussion during the second week. Regional caucuses convened to demand consideration of topics, such as nuclear testing in the Pacific; and issue groups formed to raise problems such as racism in the women's movement. Caucuses and networks tended to gather around regional/cultural identity or on the basis of political ideologies or areas of interest.

Just as the term *sexism* became controversial in the UN conference, an important point of identity and source of conflict at the NGO Forum was the term *feminist*. Most of the forum activities did not use the word, but comments about it flew around the halls. The debate was brought out into the open by a quote highlighted in the *Forum '80* newspaper that read: "To talk feminism to a woman who has no water, no food, and no home is to talk nonsense." Sessions debated this view of feminism, and finally, a group drew up a refutation of it stating that "feminism is a political perspective on all issues of concern to human life" and calling for a meeting to discuss "feminism as a political perspective that reaches beyond patriarchal political divisions and national boundaries." The ensuing session drew over three hundred women from many countries and addressed the difficulty of defining feminism across regional and cultural lines, as well as the tasks of creating feminist analysis, programs, and power to bring change.

Since women control little of the world's money, opportunities to gather internationally are rare, and the UN provides one of the few arenas where women from Third World as well as from industrialized countries can meet. While not feminist-oriented events, the UN conference and the NGO Forum did provide the occasion for global consciousness-raising, for learning more about where women stand in relation to ruling powers, and for making invaluable connections. If the UN holds an end-of-the-decade conference in 1985, stronger networks for international feminist influence should be organized to counter the governments' manipulation of women. And if those networks are possible, their emergence will have been assisted by Copenhagen, which above all resulted in more women thinking creatively about feminism and the need to organize in order to bring change. As a woman from Latin America said, "Before Copenhagen, I was not at all interested in feminism, but after seeing how governments and the UN treat women and what has and has not happened in the Forum, I am now considering the potential of feminism seriously." For many, that was a good place to end the Forum and to begin postconference work on building an independent force for feminism globally.

PROSPECTS FOR GLOBAL FEMINISM

I have chosen to talk of global feminism, not international feminism, because I see feminism as a movement of people working for change across and despite national boundaries, not of representatives of nation-states or national governments. As a people seeking change, we must move beyond the concept of nation-state, which is another expression of patriarchy whereby groups battle for domination over each other on the basis of geographical territory. Instead, we must be global, recognizing that the oppression of women in one part of the world is often affected by what happens in another, and that no woman is free until the conditions of oppression of women are eliminated everywhere.

When talking of feminism, we also need to be clear what we mean by the term, which, as the Forum in Copenhagen demonstrated, is often misunderstood. While I do not want to see a narrow "correct line" on feminism emerge, it is important for women to develop some general understandings of the concept so that it is not defined by the media and other sectors of the Establishment. To date, Western mass media have dominated in con-

This essay was written for *Sammen er vi Stoerke*—an international anthology on the Forum published in Denmark in 1981; it was published in English in *Quest: A Feminist Quarterly,* vol. V, no. 4 (Spring 1982).

trolling the images of feminism and have tended to portray feminism either as the prerogative of a few token women rising to the
top of corporate structures or as the province of a group of crazies
who simply can't live a "normal" life. These distorted stereotypes
are meant to keep women both in industrialized countries and in
the developing world from identifying with a movement that in
fact asks very basic, root or radical, questions about existing structures of society, and particularly about the injustice of all forms
of domination, whether based on sex, sexual preference, race,
class, age, religion, or nationality.

This problem was discussed extensively at an international
workshop held in Bangkok on "Feminist Ideology and Structures
in the First Half of the Decade for Women," sponsored by the UN
Asian and Pacific Centre for Women and Development in June
1979. In that workshop, we chose to affirm the term "feminist"
and to define it for ourselves, rather than to allow the media to
frighten us away from it or to divide us through stereotypes and
name-calling. The workshop then defined feminism in terms of
two long-term goals:

1) The freedom from oppression for women involves not only equity,
   but also the right of women to freedom of choice, and the power
   to control our own lives within and outside of the home. Having
   control over our lives and our bodies is essential to ensure a sense
   of dignity and autonomy for every woman.
2) The second goal of feminism is the removal of all forms of inequity
   and oppression through the creation of a more just social and
   economic order, nationally and internationally. This means the
   involvement of women in national liberation struggles, in plans for
   national development, and in local and global struggles for change.

On the basis of our definition, it is clear that feminism *is* and
must be a *transformational politics* that addresses every aspect of
life. It is not simply a laundry list of so-called women's issues such
as child care and equal pay. While these issues are important,
feminism is not a new ghetto where women are confined to concerning ourselves about only a select list of topics separated from
the overall social and economic context of our lives. Similarly,
feminism is not just "add women and stir" into existing institutions, ideologies, or political parties. Yes, feminists want more

power for women, but we desire more than simply "equality" within a system of injustice: we seek a change in existing institutions and a new approach to power in our lives. Thus, for instance, the problem with the UN official conference in Copenhagen was not that it was "politicized," but that it failed to consider issues from a feminist political perspective or even in terms of how they were specifically viewed by or affected women.

Developing feminist political perspectives on issues such as the New International Economic Order, the nuclear arms race, or the international slave traffic in women is still work in progress. We have much to do in order to demonstrate the potential of feminism for providing new ways of viewing the world that can help build a just future. In approaching this task, feminists can draw on the insights of our movements, but we are primarily building from the base of experience and analysis begun by women in motion politically in many countries. This experience is diverse and rich. In building a global politics we must link and affirm the struggles and insights gained from feminist demands on a variety of fronts: from woman's fight to control her body through reproductive freedom to her demands for control through adequate standards of nutrition and sanitation to her right to define and embrace her own sexuality to her demand for an end to violence against her body and her mind. We must show that violence to and degradation of the body are connected to alienation and exploitation at work; we must demonstrate that a world committed to domination at its intimate core in the home more readily accepts ever-escalating levels of domination and imperialism not only between peoples but throughout all its structures. Thus, through examining and struggling to end the oppression of women, feminism is providing new insights into various forms of domination, new visions for how societies might exist without injustice at their core and new energy for working to bring these visions into reality.

In the formation of a transformational feminist politics that is global in perspective, the particular issues and forms of struggle for women in different situations will vary. Nevertheless, we must strive to understand and expand the commonality and solidarity of that struggle. Doing this requires that we recognize the social forces that divide women from each other—forces such as race, class, sexual orientation, colonialism, poverty, religion, nationality—and work to end the forms of oppression that are based on these factors. Yet fighting on these fronts should go hand in hand with challenging oppression on the basis of sex—not before or after, but as a single struggle with many faces.

One problem that feminists confront is how to value cultural diversity without allowing it to be used to justify traditions that are oppressive to women. Cultural imperialism from the dominant world powers often worsens women's status and certainly offers little of benefit to women in developing countries; moreover, the experience of women in the Western world illustrates the inadequacy of the Western mode of "development" as a humane model for others. At the same time, efforts by some males to justify the continuation or adoption of practices oppressive to women by labeling them "resistance to Western influence" is also onerous to feminists. Most cultures as we know them today are patriarchal. Hope for the future therefore requires that women create new models, allowing for diversity and drawing from the best of the past, but refusing to accept any form of domination in the name of either tradition or modernization.

To make global feminist consciousness a powerful force in the world demands that we make the local, global and the global, local. Such a movement is not based on international travel and conferences, although these may be useful, but must be centered on a sense of connectedness among women active at the grass roots in various regions. For women in industrialized countries, this connectedness must be based in the authenticity of our struggles at home, in our need to learn from others, and in our efforts to understand the global implications of our actions, not in liberal guilt, condescending charity, or the false imposition of our models on others. Thus, for example, when we fight to have a birth control device banned in the United States because it is unsafe, we must simultaneously demand that it be destroyed rather than dumped on women in the Third World.

Too often international contact takes place only between the experts of government or of the university and not among the activists involved in creating and maintaining a political struggle. For instance, I have found that most women in developing countries only get to meet U.S. women who are considered experts on their regions, and rarely have contact with local feminists with whom they might exchange ideas and experiences on organizing projects or protests. This lack of contact is unfortunate since feminism in the U.S. is primarily a decentralized, indigenous people's struggle and has much to learn from women elsewhere as well as to offer from its own endeavors. It is this diverse local base of feminism that needs to develop a greater global awareness and be connected to women in struggle around the world if the feminist perspective is to advance.

If any lesson was clear in Copenhagen, it was that a global feminist movement will only come through people connecting to people, not from governments. The Forum gave us a hint of how powerful such a movement could be as well as a taste of the conflicts and creativity inherent in such a possibility. The challenge is great, but so are the stakes. The crisis of survival on our planet demands that we take the risk of trying to develop a global feminism that can add to the forces for sanity and justice at work in the world.

STRATEGIES FOR ORGANIZING AGAINST FEMALE SEXUAL SLAVERY

ollowing the 1980 World Conference in Copenhagen, three of us *(myself, Shirley Castley, and Kathleen Barry) agreed to organize a global meeting on the issue of traffic in women and female sexual slavery—a topic that had received considerable response in sessions we had organized during the NGO Forum. It took us three years to raise the money to bring thirty women to such a meeting and to identify local women from all regions of the world who were working in this area. The workshop was held in Rotterdam, The Netherlands, from April 6–15, 1983. The following article is from the report of that workshop,* International Feminism: Networking Against Female Sexual Slavery, *Barry, Bunch, and Castley, eds. (New York: International Women's Tribune Centre, 1984).*

One of the major tasks of this international workshop focused on strategies for action against female sexual slavery and the functions of an international feminist network. We began this by listing and discussing the major themes, problems, and strategies that had emerged during individual presentations from each region and from resource people. The resource presentations provided participants with a basic level of information in such areas as trafficking in children, sexual torture of prisoners, prostitute organizations, the human rights community, and the workings of the UN.

Our discussion of strategies initially centered on what is a feminist approach to countering the exploitation of women in prostitution and of violence against women (rape, incest, sexual mutilation, battery, pornography, and torture) in the context of patriarchal society. We looked at the various ways in which these issues are connected to the treatment of women in all areas, to cultural attitudes toward female sexuality, and to oppression by class, race, militarism, and neocolonialism.

After some general discussion, we identified three major areas where we wanted to do more work in depth: 1) Legislation and Prostitution; 2) Violence and Sexuality; and 3) Institutionalization of Female Sexual Slavery. We chose this division of the topic because it provided the working groups assigned to each area with both the theoretical problems involved in the issue and with practical questions of strategies for action. Further, each topic included both national and international concerns and each related to an area where there are existing groups or constituencies with related concerns that we might work with. Each group then considered strategies for combating female sexual slavery in their area generally, and strategies for developing an effective international network in that area as well. A fourth working group, formed to begin outlining the basic platform and structures for an international network, will be discussed later in this chapter.

In the following pages, I outline the issues taken up by the three topical working groups. These groups each consisted of between five and nine people who deliberated together for one to one and a half days and then presented a short, written report to the larger group. The reports were amended and agreed to in principle by the workshop groups as a whole, which then adopted them as part of the network. Following the groups' instructions, I have edited them and provided some additional commentary based on my notes and the tapes of the discussion.

LEGISLATION AND PROSTITUTION

This working group was concerned with our position on national legislation relating to prostitution and to the oppression of women in other areas, such as marriage laws, which contribute to forcing women into prostitution. In this regard, it sought to develop strategies that would oppose the institution of prostitution, but not penalize the individual women in prostitution. When we distinguish between the institution of prostitution and the individuals within it, it becomes clear that legal action should focus on prosecuting the sex industry—procurers, pimps, travel agencies, and other exploiters of women—rather than on the victims of this exploitation. This group also discussed how the network could relate to international agencies, UN conventions and resolutions, and international human rights groups concerned with aspects of female sexual slavery.

The group's report begins with a statement regarding our concept of law. The following is a summary of the group's work: laws are instruments that control the lives of people; laws are formed according to the understanding and beliefs of legislators (primarily men) and the dominant economic system. In a patriarchal society, laws are always favorable to men, maintain the subordination of women, conserve the status quo, and legitimize the existing economic, political, and racial systems.

Laws, however, can also be instruments that facilitate the process of change and advance the situation of women. This is true, particularly when women committed to women's rights participate in the formulation of laws, and when they recognize the strengths and weaknesses of legislation and how it can be utilized to promote human rights. In some instances, laws can serve as a means of protection for women, although so-called protective legislation has also been used to limit women's activities.

In many countries, in addition to the recognized legal systems, there exist customs and customary law, patriarchal in nature, that are used by the dominating groups to control the lives of women and other oppressed people. Such customary laws and civil and penal codes constitute another legal system that suppresses women and their basic right to self-determination. In this regard, we make special reference to the oppressive character of marriage and divorce laws, dowry, bride price, child marriages, racial discrimination, immigration laws, abortion laws, and employment legislation. The situations for women that are created by these laws often contribute to pushing women into prostitution. Customary laws and civil and penal codes thus reinforce and perpetuate the double standard of morality established by religious beliefs.

Prostitution is often a logical form of survival in a patriarchal society in which women are considered as private and public property and are reduced to sexual objects. Patriarchal ideology divides women into "madonnas" and "whores" in order to control the lives of women at all levels of society. This is the fundamental coercion that objectifies women's bodies and reduces sex to a commodity. Whether women are forced into prostitution or choose it, they are under the control of the system. This control encompasses every aspect of women's lives.

Laws relating to prostitution reinforce the patriarchal system and its control over women. These laws become part of the institutional apparatus that maintains control over all women. By condemning women who do what a male society demands as "necessary," prostitution laws force women to stay within the institution of prostitution, even when they want or attempt to leave it.

The legal system of prohibition of prostitution treats women as criminals and puts the onus of blame or punishment on them, while not penalizing pimps or customers. The legalization of prostitution, however, still focuses on the women who are controlled and manipulated by regulation; legalization also legitimizes the male society's contention that prostitution is inevitable and that men have the right to women's bodies. Both prohibition and legalization further the dependency of women in prostitution on pimps—individual or the state—and on the police who have power over their lives.

The only adequate solution in terms of legislation that concerns the women in prostitution themselves is decriminalization of prostitution per se. Decriminalization makes the act of prostitution itself neither legal nor illegal, thus removing the focus and punishment from the individual women in prostitution, while still not legitimizing the institution of prostitution. While working for the decriminalization of the act of prostitution itself, we must also call for the strengthening and application of laws against the exploitation of prostitution by procurers and pimps, against the trafficking of women and children, and against all forms of sexual violence. All existing laws regarding prostitution, soliciting, vagrancy, and so on need to be reexamined and amended from this perspective. Decriminalization of prostitution and prosecution of the exploiters of the prostitution of others are both called for in the 1949 United Nations Convention for the Suppression of the Traffic in Persons and of the Exploitation of the Prostitution of Others, and in the 1981 United Nations Convention for the Elimination of All Forms of Discrimination against Women.

1. Study the existing legal system regarding prostitution, in particular, and women in general, in each country, in order to compile a complete picture of the legal situation of prostitution and female sexual slavery on a national and global level.
2. Seek the abolition of discrimination against women in all laws dealing with employment, education, and other areas of public life.
3. Work toward legislation that guarantees women equal rights in marriage and divorce laws.
4. Work for the decriminalization of prostitution per se and the strengthening of laws that oppose the enslavement of women by pimps and prosecute those involved in all forms of trafficking of women.
5. Initiate and support efforts to combat police harassment of women in prostitution and efforts that promote the prosecution of violent crimes against women in prostitution. Seek an end to all discriminatory measures against women in prostitution.
6. Work to provide refuge centers and supportive services aimed at assisting women to escape or leave prostitution.
7. Cooperate with organizations which are committed to addressing these issues from a perspective that is compatible with our feminist network.
8. Establish permanent relationships with international governmental organizations and nongovernmental organizations dealing with the problems of prostitution, trafficking in women and children, and female sexual slavery.
9. Provide necessary information and consulting services to nations requesting such services who seek to make improvements in their legislation and services related to prostitution and violence against women.
10. Promote investigation into international trafficking of women, sex tourism, etc.

VIOLENCE AND SEXUALITY

This working group considered violence against women—rape, battery, incest, pornography, sexual mutilation—and how these relate to prostitution and trafficking in women. It also looked at issues of female sexuality, how this is manipulated and controlled in patriarchal society, and how to assure women's rights to sexual self-determination without condoning the exploitation of female sexuality. Related concerns included how female dependency, particularly economic dependency, and traditional customs often contribute to the vulnerability of women to sexual abuse.

The following are the group's conclusions: violence against women is intimately connected to the power relationships that exist between men and women in a patriarchal society. The power that men exercise over women engenders violence, and fear exists as the basis of all forms of violence against women.

In discussing the issue of violence against women, an understanding of the concept of sexuality is essential. Two questions must be raised: 1) how has sexuality been defined in a patriarchal society? and 2) what is the definition of sexuality that we must adopt as the basis of our network against female sexual slavery?

Patriarchal definitions of sexuality have resulted in the objectification of women as either sex objects or reproductive units. In our view, a redefinition of sexuality must reject this notion of sex as a commodity, and understand sexuality as a means through which people can relate to each other as human beings and not as beings of a specific sex. We uphold women's freedom of sexual choice. We feel that an acceptance of sexuality from only the perspectives of reproduction or of women as sex objects for men to use is an expression of patriarchal ideology that has mutilated female sexuality.

Women are victims of many forms of domination by men that are exercised through the structures of sexism, racism, and classism. Therefore, attempts to address the situation of violence against women must incorporate strategies that look at specific problems within the larger context of creating structural changes in society in all these areas.

We understand that there exists *one* universal patriarchal oppression of women which takes different forms in different cultures and different regions. However, all these diverse expressions of patriarchal oppression like sexual mutilation, rape, pornography, torture, forced marriages, etc. mutilate women. Economic dependency generates psychological and emotional dependency in women, and all such forms of dependency reinforce each other, making women more vulnerable. The creation of dependency on all levels results in violence against women occurring in a variety of forms, that is, through the body, through the mind, in the workplace, in education, etc.

We must understand and recognize the commonality of patriarchal oppression experienced by all women if we are to devise a common strategy to eradicate female sexual slavery. We feel that it is necessary to devise strategies at two levels: strategies to create and maintain an international network; and, strategies to begin communication among regional and local groups regarding the issues raised by the network.

In relation to strategy-building at the international level, we recommend that our network be built upon existing structures such as CAMS (International Commission for the Abolition of Sexual Mutilations). We point out that organizations based in the so-called First World are viewed with a great deal of hostility and suspicion by Third World women, and this factor should be taken into consideration when deciding on the location of the network's base of operation.

The second level of strategy-building in the regions must take into consideration specific regional needs. After a review of the major problems that need to be addressed in various regions, and the difficulties involved in addressing these issues due to political, cultural, and religious factors, we have come up with the following strategy recommendations.

Strategies

1. To make the different forms of violence against women and their relationship to female sexual slavery more visible in all our countries, since they are frequently kept hidden.
2. To make these issues visible by using different tactics to raise what are often suppressed as "undiscussible" issues in certain countries. For example, if it is particularly difficult to discuss a certain form of female sexual slavery in one country, a woman in that country might disseminate information about what is happening in that area in a neighboring country. This might have the effect of helping to open up avenues for discussion about that issue in her own country.
3. To communicate with and utilize the resources of other regional and local groups and organizations in order to reach people with information about female sexual slavery and what can be done to combat it.

312

4. To work with immigrant women who could provide information about the situations of women in their own countries that they had to leave. These women could also be channels through which information about the exploitation and violence against women could be sent back into the countries of their origin.

5. To establish training centers for women (prostitute and pre-prostitute) in nontraditional fields and to create intermediate shelters for prostitutes that provide them with practical services and protection from pimps. In addition, we need to pressure other groups, including governments where appropriate, to support these centers and to help ensure that these women will find employment after they receive job training.

6. To insist on nonsexist, coeducational education from primary school level for all, and to change the content of text books especially with regard to their attitudes towards women and girls. Whenever possible, women's groups should establish communication with school teachers and parent associations about these issues.

7. To make contact with women in the media, and through them, develop ways to use the media to expose violence against women and how it can be prevented.

8. To start campaigns on specific issues of violence and female sexual slavery on an international level which would be coordinated by the network but organized according to the specific conditions of each region and country.

9. To adopt International or National Days Against All Forms of Violence Against Women. This would create a greater sense of solidarity among women globally and allow the organization of national and international campaigns each year. This strategy has been used successfully in Latin America, where for several years, groups have organized such a day on November 25. This date commemorates the death of three sisters from the Dominican Republic who were raped, tortured, and killed during the Trujillo regime. The group invited others to consider this date or to adopt another, appropriate to their region.

INSTITUTIONALIZATION OF FEMALE SEXUAL SLAVERY

This working group was concerned with strategies to combat specific forms of female sexual slavery and prostitution that are institutionalized as parts of other patriarchal interests. It consid-

313

ered the effects of militarism, military bases, and war conditions on sexual violence against women; it looked at the sexual torture of women prisoners; and it discussed the growing phenomena of organized sex tours and mail order brides as current examples of how women's bodies are being systematically sold.

These are the group's conclusions: in looking at how female sexual slavery is institutionalized throughout society from the local to the international levels, it is clear that domination and violence against women is linked to the domination of people generally through militarism, racism, and economic exploitation. All of these are manifestations of a patriarchal ideology that legitimizes the right of one group to dominate another, usually by means of coercion and physical violence—beginning in the family and escalating to global warfare. Throughout all of these forms of domination, the sexual exploitation of women persists.

This report focuses on the particular forms of female sexual slavery that have arisen as part of the present economic world order and the military power that sustains it. These practices are, however, simply the latest manifestations of female sexual slavery, which has had many different forms in other cultural and economic conditions. Further, the structures that oppress women today are often based on remnants of feudalism or of traditional customs that have become even more oppressive when combined with the prevailing economic conditions, which are manipulated for the benefit of a powerful few.

The internationalization of capital and the international division of labor have further exploited women through various kinds of sexual enslavement, not only locally, but also on a transnational level. The national security ideology, a patriarchal ideology that sees the state as fatherland, absolute and supreme, with the right to unquestioning obedience of its citizens, is the justification for much of this exploitation. A blatant expression of this ideology is the use of military power to protect the interests of transnational corporations through military bases and intervention in strategic places. Local dictatorships assure political stability to foreign investments through military repression and so-called democratic states exert control through police and intelligence networks.

A more subtle form of exploitation occurs through "development" schemes imposed on the Third World by financial institutions such as the World Bank. Many countries have gone into enormous debt through national policies geared toward the industrialized world's interests such as tourism, transnational corporations, and the export of human labor. In this world economic order, women are more than ever exploited as cheap labor in agriculture and industry, as prostitutes for the military and in the "service" sector, and as migrant workers in foreign countries, many of whom are forced into prostitution. In a patriarchal culture, this political economic thrust has intensified the control and abuse of women in an organized way by business, governments, and the military.

A particularly hideous example of how these oppressions combine is the torture of women by the modern military state. Since the military is based on the masculinist values of power, physical domination, and public authority, it sees women who oppose it as threatening to its masculine defined hierarchy. There is, therefore, a distinctive pattern of sexual torture for a female political prisoner, aimed at violating her personal worth and sense of human dignity as a woman. This torture involves sexual enslavement in a situation from which she cannot escape and in which she suffers sexual attacks upon her body and her psyche.*

Militarism is symptomatic of a male-dominated society that uses violence and power to control others. One form of its enslavement of women is the demand for bodies to cater to men's "rest and recreational" needs. Prostitution has proliferated around military bases and ports for many years, and with it comes violence against these women. Women forced into military prostitution become dependent on the base and their relations to the rest of the culture are often destroyed. Military prostitution and violence against women is exacerbated during war situations such as that in Lebanon. In Asia, mobile field brothels were funded by American dollars during the Indochina war where there was practically a prostitute for every GI.

Many victims of military brothels have been transferred to duty as prostitutes for tourists. Sex tourism is the "buy-and-sell" of women's bodies for sexual service to men as part of tourist activities. It is one of the growing institutions of female sexual exploita-

*For a fuller discussion of this form of sexual slavery see Ximena Bunster, "The Torture of Women Political Prisoners: A Case Study in Female Sexual Slavery," in *International Feminism: Networking Against Female Sexual Slavery,* Barry, Bunch, and Castley, eds. (New York: IWTC, 1984), pp. 94–102.

tion which governments use to obtain foreign currency and which airlines, hotels, travel agencies, and local pimps use to make profits. It is international both in trafficking women's bodies from one country to another and in receiving support from governments in both receiving and sending countries. It combines sexual oppression with class and race discrimination since it primarily involves the selling of Third World women.*

Marriage by catalog where brides are ordered by photos is another example of economic and sexual exploitation of poor women. "Happiness without Barriers" and promises of fidelity and docility are some of the slogans used by commercial matchmakers who profit from such marriages. Pictures of women from the Third World with their vital statistics are presented as commodities to male clients. Many of these women are later forced into prostitution.

Strategies

This group began with a general principle underlining all its strategies: the focus of our work on these issues must be on exposing and bringing an end to the sex industry and exploiters of women, not on limiting the rights of women. Our approach respects the rights of movement of women and guards against a growing tendency to harass and restrict women (especially Third World women) traveling alone or in groups.

1. Seek international recognition of the right of a woman to determine the nature and extent of her sexual activity as a political right. Any woman seeking to escape from sexual violence or enslavement should be recognized as a political refugee and afforded protection and asylum as such. This status must include a woman's right to self-defense when under physical attack.

2. Investigate and expose the international trafficking of women in the sex industry, the procurement practices—such as deceptive advertising for employment and phony marriages, and the exploitation of women in particularly vulnerable situations such as migrants, displaced persons, and refugees. Enlist human rights and church groups to assist in this exposure and in confronting the transnational institutions which are investing in trafficking directly

*For more on sex tourism and military prostitution, see Yayori Matsui, "Why I Oppose Kisaeng Tours," ibid., pp. 64–72.

and which control development options in Third World countries which contribute to women's vulnerability.

3. Demand the creation of alternative plans for the development of national economies that do not exploit women's bodies in the sex industry or in production. Challenge the national interests which profit off the sexual exploitation of women.

4. Conduct public education campaigns about these practices through utilizing the media and through dialogue with groups that have common concerns. Develop lists of sympathetic media and of those who exploit sexual topics and share this information with women through the network. Develop media guidelines about who to debate and in what circumstances.

5. Create awareness—particularly among peace, labor, political groups—of the connections between sexual enslavement, violence, militarism, and torture of women in such situations as: in jails— whether incarcerated as political or regular prisoners; by police or terrorist forces in society; as prostitutes controlled by pimps or brothel keepers; in refugee camps or hamlets; in military or war settings; on the job as workers and as union organizers.

6. Bring international attention and pressure to bear on individual cases of female sexual slavery. Local groups must give feminist interpretations to cases and determine what outside support is useful. The network can then be used to mobilize petitions and telegrams of support or to send media observers to trials or to expose crimes against women in other areas.

7. Take direct action at the points of contact with the sex industry such as demonstrations at airports where tours leave or at travel agencies; picket and harass agencies or individuals involved in these practices; campaign against and remove racist and sexist advertisements, posters, publications, etc.

8. Provide humanitarian services to women in exploitative situations and challenge local agencies and governments to provide for these.

9. Work toward a long-term end to militarism, economic, racial, and sexual exploitation and the patriarchy that sustains all forms of domination.

THE NETWORK

The fourth working group outlined points that formed the basis for discussion and decisions about the focus of the network, how it would function, and what its relationship would be to existing

organizations and groups. This was approached with the understanding that this network is part of a global movement of women
who seek to abolish patriarchy and all forms of domination,
whether by sex, race, class, religion, or nationality. As such, our
network does not see itself as working in isolation but rather as
taking on particular tasks within this larger feminist struggle.

The International Feminist Network Against Female Sexual
Slavery and Traffic in Women will focus on the issues of violence
and exploitation of women through the use of female sexuality.
The primary manifestations that this network will address are
prostitution, trafficking in women, sex tourism, and their relationship to violence against women in rape, sex mutilation, incest,
battery, forced marriages, dowry and bride wealth, pornography
and the torture of political prisoners. We recognize further that,
particularly in certain regions, some of these issues must be approached in relation to other concerns, such as sexual harassment,
the exploitation of women's work, female poverty, racism, and the
denial of women's right to choice in matters of sexuality and
reproduction. It was agreed, therefore, that while it is important
to narrow our focus enough so that we are not attempting to take
on everything at once, we also recognize that female sexual slavery
is integrally related to so many issues that we cannot separate our
work against it from a consideration of these as well.

The network will be based on the directions set out in the
reports and strategies of the three working groups on: Legislation
and Prostitution; Violence and Sexuality; and the Institutionalization of Female Sexual Slavery. In considering our concept of
feminism, we see it primarily reflected in the analysis and strategies of these reports. Beyond the reports and such general statements about the goals of feminism as stated in the document
"Developing Strategies for the Future: Feminist Perspectives," we
recognize that feminism needs to be expressed in different ways in
different cultural contexts.*

In considering how individuals would relate to the network, it
was felt that there must be general agreement with our political
approach as outlined by the working groups and with the central
focus of the network on female sexual slavery. Beyond this core
of agreement, we seek to approach the meaning of feminism with-

*See "Developing Strategies for the United Nations Decade for Women," p. 283–300.

out forcing consensus on every issue, particularly given the different conditions and development of feminism in various countries. However, it was also stated that, while everyone might not agree on all issues, no one publicly identified with the network could be working actively against feminist issues that are of great importance to many in the network, such as abortion and lesbian rights. These two controversial issues were discussed as examples precisely because they were not major themes of our network, but they do highlight the difficulty of working globally when the consciousness about, and sense of priority around, certain feminist concerns, differs from region to region as well as among different individuals, often depending on cultural or religious assumptions.

Another dilemma discussed was the importance of acknowledging cultural differences while not adopting double standards based on them. The specific conditions in each country make it necessary to work in different ways and often on different priorities, but we cannot say that certain oppressive practices are okay in some places but not in others. While traditional customs or current imperialism sometimes make the conditions of exploitation of women in prostitution different in Third World countries than in industrialized ones, we cannot say that such exploitation is tolerable in one place and not in another. For example, just because many women in developing countries are in poverty, with few job options, does not excuse the violence against and coercion of them by sex tourism. Nor, on the other hand, do we accept the notion that Third World women in prostitution need our assistance while European and North American women trapped by pimps are not worthy of our concern.

Another area in which we reject a double standard is in relation to heterosexual and homosexual prostitution. While our network is focused on the abuse of women and therefore deals primarily with heterosexual crimes against women, we do not condone homosexual exploitation of prostitution. But we also do not, as many imply, see homosexual abuse as worse than heterosexual abuse. For example, the sexual violation of children by adults is neither worse nor less onerous if it is done by men against boys than if it is done by men against girls.

This network is not a hierarchical organization with an international headquarters at the top and local chapters, but rather a means of assisting, linking, and coordinating work done by many organizations, individuals, and grass-roots groups. It will be centered in the regions. It is hoped that groups and individuals will use the network to help circulate information nationally and internationally and thus assist us all in finding out what others are doing. The network can also be used by regional groups to help coordinate actions from region to region or internationally to facilitate days of protest or meeting around particular concerns. Further, the network can provide linkages for local or regional groups to international agencies and/or to other regional groups.

In discussing how the network would function, we were concerned with the problem of how to have a viable network with access to resources and major lines of communication without centering it in the Western industrialized countries. Given that this network is just beginning and has few centralized resources, our decision for now was to work primarily through the regions and by utilizing existing regional and international groups. The hope was expressed that each region would devise a structure appropriate to its situation and that, eventually, there would be a documentation and coordination center in each region.

Finally, the participants agreed that in the next two years, the emphasis of the network will be on organizing groups and actions in local communities and in the regions. We will seek to develop global strategies primarily through the evolution of regional activity and/or from interaction among the regions. This approach to organizing the network will be evaluated in 1985 at the time of the United Nations End of the Decade Conference on Women scheduled for Nairobi, Kenya. At that meeting, some participants from Rotterdam and other contacts who work with the network in the ensuing years will gather to review the progress of the network and to organize for further action against female sexual slavery.*

*Several meetings of the network were held in 1985 in Nairobi. It was decided to continue working primarily at the regional and local levels, while maintaining some international communication through these groups and via existing international organizations such as ISIS and the International Women's Tribune Centre.

UN WORLD CONFERENCE
IN NAIROBI:
A VIEW FROM THE WEST

A s a white feminist from the United States, I go to the world conferences on women to be held in Nairobi, Kenya, in July committed to the idea that global feminism is not a luxury activity for an elite but a necessity for effective action. Feminism demands learning about other women's lives and how we are interrelated, even in our diversity. While the strength of the women's movement is in its decentralized organizing at the local level, we must put that in a global framework. At a time when we in the West are seeking new directions and assessing women's conditions in every country, we can gain ideas and inspiration from the actions, accomplishments, analysis, and imagination of our sisters elsewhere.

The UN World Conference on Women and the NGO Forum '85 provide both opportunities and challenges to Western feminists. Whether or not one goes to Nairobi, this can be a time when we Americans, who are often limited in our understanding of other parts of the world, can open ourselves to change and look beyond the assumptions of our ethnocentric culture. We can engage in this process by participating in local events around global concerns, reading articles by women from other cultures, and questioning the impact of our country on other peoples.

This article was first published in *Ms.* magazine (June 1985).

It is important to view the world conferences not in isolation, but in the context of the larger process by which feminism is growing and flourishing worldwide. During the past decade, women have organized around an ever-increasing number of issues. Feminists in Latin America have held regional conferences to strategize against patriarchy in all aspects of their lives from the church to the economy, from literature to the family. We've seen hundreds of thousands of European, Pacific, and North American women organize in opposition to nuclear arms and militarism. International feminist gatherings have deliberated on everything from women's health and work to sexual violence and book publishing—in countries as diverse as Senegal, The Netherlands, Sri Lanka, Colombia, England, and India. Regional and local events that reflect geographic and cultural linkages abound.

As the depth and breadth of women's activities increase, we see the myriad of possibilities for feminism to influence the twenty-first century, especially in relation to race, class, and culture. These developments should have center stage in Nairobi so that the world can see the richness and diversity of women's visions today.

With the hope of having such an influence at the conferences, women have been meeting in strategy sessions and developing papers and proposals. Along with official UN regional meetings, initiatives have been taken by women outside of government to influence both the UN and NGO agendas. A number of meetings, with international representation, to develop a feminist approach to Nairobi have taken place. For example, the Development Alternatives with Women for a New Era Project (DAWN), made up of twenty women from five continents, has written a book on women's visions of development. Regional gatherings have been held; one brought women from seventeen countries together under the auspices of the Asian Women's Research and Action Network. This group is preparing an alternative Asia/Pacific report that reflects women's own evaluations of the decade's impact on their lives. There have also been specific topical events—the African Women Speak Workshop in Sudan worked on a unified message on the eradication of female circumcision. Here in the United States, a number of local and national meetings have also been held. Several have reflected the high level of interest in Nairobi among women of color. The African-American Women's Political

Caucus, for example, gathered more than three hundred women to develop strategies and statements for 1985.

The 1975 World Conference in Mexico City not only raised awareness of women's concerns and special needs worldwide; it also spawned a number of national and international programs and events. In countries where local women's movements had not yet emerged or where nongovernment resources were scarce, many of these programs provided vital lifelines. Although most governmental initiatives were not feminist in orientation, many women, especially in the Third World, credit them with providing the space for their development and work as feminists. The many meetings held in preparation for Nairobi and the diversity of groups and interests they reflect amply demonstrate that women's networking, exchanges, and global actions have significantly developed since 1975. Today the range of activities, especially in the Third World, emphatically counter the idea that feminism is a uniquely Western development.

Unfortunately, women's concrete gains in economic and political status are appallingly behind the goals of 1975. The majority of the world's women are no better off than they were then. The ugly truth is that women are an ever-increasing percentage of the poor. Few governments have acted systematically on the specifics in the World Plan of Action. The number of women with political power in government has not significantly increased during the decade. Even within the UN itself, there has been little improvement. The Ad Hoc Group on Equal Rights for Women in the UN has protested the lack of advancement of women to top-level positions, and has exposed considerable sexual harassment. Further, both the 1977 UN World Water Conference and the 1984 World Population Conference had minimal female representation, demonstrating the lack of attention paid to women even on "soft" issues like water and population, much less in areas like science and disarmament.

Despite all this, the good news is the growth of women's awareness and political activism. Since 1975 we have put issues like sexual violence and child nutrition on the political agenda in our countries for the first time. And despite the very real cultural and ideological conflicts among women, many groups have found a common basis for global work, particularly around concrete issues such as violence against women, health, rural development, and women's studies.

Still, it is naïve to assume that Nairobi will be free from conflict. Within government conferences, divisions along traditional nationalistic and political lines are inevitable. Previous world conferences sadly demonstrated that fact. While the Mexico City conference raised consciousness about and hopes for women, the Mid-Decade Conference in Copenhagen brought out specific conflicts between women and the realities of working inside patriarchy. Focusing specifically on health, education, and employment, the Copenhagen agenda also called for consideration of women under apartheid, the rights of Palestinian women, and women refugees. Although a substantial program of action for the second half of the decade was produced, the much-publicized showdown over the Palestinian question and the equation of Zionism with racism in the resolutions overshadowed everything else.

The trouble with this debate was not, as some suggested, that it was an inappropriate topic for a women's conference; any issue of human life deserves our analysis. The difficulty was that the debate made no attempt to consider these issues specifically from women's perspectives. Instead they were used to divide women and mirrored the traditional male political lines of the UN General Assembly as did every vote taken. Hard-line positions and alliances were more important both to the pro-PLO–Arab bloc and to the Israeli-U.S. side than was creating a progressive plan by and for women.

The conflicts that arose in Copenhagen illustrate the most important fact about UN conferences: they are meetings of government-appointed representatives whose actions are directed by the world's patriarchies. So while there were more female delegates to Copenhagen than to Mexico City, they generally were required to vote the state line, which prevailed over feminist perspectives. This traditional patriarchal approach to international discussions allows governments to deflect attention from their own responsibilities for perpetuating female subordination, while stifling the possibilities for innovative solutions to national and global problems. Simply put, no government, including our own, puts women's interests or perspectives first. One of Nairobi's many challenges will be moving beyond the patriarchal mold.

Just as the rise of the women's movement in the Third World

has been one of the decade's triumphs, it also additionally challenges Western women. Most of these movements have evolved in a context of economic stagnation, political instability, and extreme poverty. In this environment many women find it impossible to separate women's issues from the overall economic and political conditions. The world's economic crisis and its effect on women's lives and options will be an important discussion at the Nairobi conferences. When issues such as the famine in Africa or the role rich countries play in exploiting the Third World inevitably arise, some Westerners may feel uncomfortable. We must strive to move beyond discomfort to action. Although women have not generally created U.S. economic, political, and military policies, we must take the responsibility to challenge them in terms of their effects on the rest of the world.

The beginning point at both conferences must be that *everything* is a woman's issue. That means racism is a woman's issue, just as is anti-Semitism, Palestinian homelessness, rural development, ecology, the persecution of lesbians, and the exploitative practices of global corporations. Domination on the basis of race, class, religion, sexual preference, economics, or nationality cannot be seen as a mere additive to the oppression of women by gender. Rather, all these factors help to shape the very forms of that oppression. Even lesbianism, which has been so negatively portrayed and used by patriarchal powers to divide women, can be discussed productively in an atmosphere of mutual sharing.

The challenge we face in Nairobi is to work to transcend cant and patriarchal manipulation and transform tensions into meaningful dialogue about how various political issues affect our lives. Hopefully, the NGO Forum, which is nongovernmental and open to all, will provide women with just such an opportunity. Since it has no official decision-making power and does not take positions on issues, the Forum could be a place for a truly feminist discussion of these issues.

Carmen Barroso, a Brazilian feminist researcher, at a preparatory meeting for Nairobi, stated the challenge: "If we are to have an impact, we have to find ways to build alliances among ourselves. We cannot repeat past errors of pretending to avoid political definitions, especially in an international forum. Instead of lamenting the politicization and engaging in the naïve hope of finding some trick to escape politics, we should try to understand that we have a common identity. In the last part of this twentieth century we have rebelled against the current state of affairs in gender relations and helped to develop what is perhaps the most dynamic social movement of our times. . . . We need to acknowledge the political nature of our relationships within women's networks . . . devise ways to deal more constructively with the tensions among ourselves."

Governments tend to be antifeminist, and much of the media—if past experiences are any guide—relish stories that show women divided and ridicule feminism. We cannot control the media or the hostility of UN or government officials. But we can work to build global alliances that counter some of their divisive effects. We can enhance the sensitivity of Western women to the legitimate grievances that Third World women have toward the West, and we can support and strengthen feminism in the Third World.

To that end, here are some specific ways that Western women, especially whites, can prepare for Nairobi. First, we should be acquainted with some of the ideas and literature coming out of the women's movement in the Third World, as well as from Western women of color. There are abundant sources available in English in the United States, as well as information published in many languages, which can be found in women's publications, centers, and bookstores. It is particularly urgent to learn about African women's struggles, whether in the famine-ridden north or the apartheid-bound south. Wambui Otiemo, chairperson of the Maendeleo Handicraft Cooperative Society in Kenya, made this appeal to American women: "Please, sisters, do not pay us lip service. Take these problems as your own and act on them. It is only through this kind of understanding that equality can be achieved in the world."

Another useful preparation is to meet with women who have different perspectives. For example, groups of Jewish and black Americans in New York and Arab and Jewish women in California are meeting to discuss the issues that divided women in previous conferences. While recognizing that women cannot solve in one decade problems that men have perpetuated over thousands of years, we know these efforts are important for creating a more productive basis for feminist dialogue.

One of Nairobi's more serious limitations is that many of the

326

women from groups independent of governments and other male-controlled institutions cannot afford to go. On the other hand, this is still one of the few places that women can gather internationally and make contact with one another. For some, this is one of their only legal opportunities to leave their country, and for others, hearing about the conference afterward is the only time they learn about women elsewhere.

Those of us who go to Nairobi need to be open to change, to learning, and to having our assumptions challenged. This does not mean denying our own ideas and experiences or feeling guilty or defensive about the circumstances of our lives. If we believe in our own authenticity we can offer welcome insights and information in the context of mutual sharing. None of us should assume that we have the superior answer or the universal truth about feminism. Americans in particular need to be aware of the fact that we are not *the* leaders of the world movement, nor should we act as if we are.

I take quite seriously those women who emphasize that the initiatives and connections this decade has fostered are vital and must not be lost after 1985. I go to Nairobi committed to the necessity of global feminism and excited by the promise of learning more from other women because I believe that the greatest hope for life in the next century lies in the number of women's voices that are being raised where once there was silence.

BRINGING THE GLOBAL HOME

O ne of the most exciting world developments today is the emergence of feminism all over the globe. Women of almost every culture, color, and class are claiming feminism for themselves. Indigenous movements are developing that address the specific regional concerns of women's lives and that expand the definition of what feminism means and can do in the future.

This growth of feminism provides both the challenge and the opportunity for a truly global women's movement to emerge in the 1980s. But a global movement involves more than just the separate development of feminism in each region, as exciting and important as that is. Global feminism also requires that we learn from each other and develop a global perspective within each of our movements. It means expansion of our understandings of feminism and changes in our work, as we respond to the ideas and challenges of women with different perspectives. It means discovering what other perspectives and movements mean to our own local setting. Any struggle for change in the late-twentieth century must have

An abridged version of the third pamphlet in the Bunch series on "Feminism in in 80's," this is taken from several speeches and was published by Antelope Publications (Denver, Co.) in 1985.

a global consciousness since the world operates and controls our lives internationally already. The strength of feminism has been and still is in its decentralized grass-roots nature, but for that strength to be most effective, we must base our local and national actions on a world view that incorporates the global context of our lives. This is the challenge of bringing the global home.

A global feminist perspective on patriarchy worldwide also illustrates how issues are interconnected, not separate isolated phenomena competing for our attention. This involves connections among each aspect of women's oppression and of that subordination to the socioeconomic conditions of society, as well as between local problems and global realities.

To develop global feminism today is not a luxury—it requires going to the heart of the problems in our world and looking at nothing less than the threats to the very survival of the planet. We are standing on a precipice facing such possibilities as nuclear destruction, worldwide famine and depletion of our natural resources, industrial contamination, and death in many forms. These are the fruits of a world ruled by the patriarchal mode—of what I call the "dynamic of domination," in which profits and property have priority over people, and where fear and hatred of differences have prevented a celebration of and learning from our diversity.

Feminists are part of a world struggle that is taking place today over the direction that the future will take. Crucial choices are being made about the very possibilities for life in the twenty-first century—from macro-level decisions about control over resources and weapons to micro-level decisions about control over individual reproduction and sexuality. At this juncture in history, feminism is perhaps the most important force for change that can begin to reverse the dynamic of patriarchal domination by challenging and transforming the way in which humans look at ourselves in relation to each other and to the world.

LEADERSHIP VERSUS CONTROL OVER WOMEN

Global feminism is emerging as part of a process in which women everywhere are demonstrating a growing determination to be actors who participate in shaping society rather than to remain victims. Yet, as women's potential as a newly activated constituency is recognized, more groups are competing over who will lead—or, all too often, control—women's political energies. Governments, political organizations, and political parties are seeing the usefulness of organizing our support for their politics. The patronizing attitude of male powers who view women as needing to be "directed" is reflected in manipulative expressions such as "mobilizing" women's votes or "harnessing" women's labor power. Still, many male-dominated groups are well organized and successful in offering a direction for women's energies and frustrations. If feminists do not provide leadership that can activate large numbers of women on our own behalf, we will find that women will be—as we so often are—separated by existing male-defined political divisions.

This situation has been clearly demonstrated throughout the United Nations Decade for Women. In 1975 at the UN International Women's Year Conference in Mexico City, most governments and the media generally treated the conference as a joke and/or as a perk for their wives or whichever women they owed a favor. A Plan of Action with measures to improve women's status was passed, but the process was not taken too seriously by male power structures.

By 1980, however, when the UN held its Mid-Decade Conference on Women in Copenhagen, the mood had changed. Not that governments were now profeminist—none of the existing patriarchal powers are feminist to any real extent, although some certainly treat women better than others. The difference in 1980 was that they no longer considered it amusing for women to talk together about politics. They saw it as potentially threatening. Therefore, governments sought to keep this second conference under tight control.

Most government officials and many UN bureaucrats see their political, economic, and social power, their jobs and their lifestyles, as dependent on maintaining the existing divisions in the world. They are not about to let a bunch of idealistic women get out of hand and shake up the way they rule. In the nongovernmental (NGO) events held simultaneously with the UN Conferences in Mexico and in Copenhagen, there were pockets of discussion and networking that brought women together across male political lines. While this was not powerful enough to change the UN conference, it did point the way toward such possibilities, which were realized further at the NGO Forum in Nairobi in 1985.*

If women are prepared—even determined—to get "out of hand," it is possible to come together across male divisions. To do this does not require, as some have suggested, that women avoid "politics" and "male issues," but that we redefine these from women's perspectives. Feminists must provide new ways of looking at political struggles. We must imagine other approaches in every area, including such difficult problems as the Arab-Jewish conflict, apartheid in South Africa, or the international debt that is crippling economies in Latin America.

If feminists are to provide such leadership and political direction in the coming years, we must recognize and believe in the potential power of women and in the potential of feminism as a politics emerging from women's experiences. To challenge the dynamic of domination at all levels, from the home to the military, and to demand a world based more on cooperation than on conquest, would indeed be revolutionary. Patriarchal powers see feminism as a threat because they recognize just such a potential for women to organize outside of male control and value systems. They are committed to preventing that possibility and will use every opportunity to keep women divided. Unless we see this potential as clearly and organize around it, feminism will be limited in its impact on the structures that control most women's lives.

To talk about how feminism can provide such leadership, I need to reassert the basic premise on which all of this rests: global feminism exists. Feminist activity and thought are happening all over the world. There is much diversity among us and no agreed-upon body of doctrine or central organization. Yet, there is a similarity in our approaches and in our fundamental questioning of society. While the particular forms that women's oppression takes in different settings vary and often pit some women against others, there is a commonality in the dynamic of domination by which women are subordinated to the demands, definitions, and desires of men.

You can see this commonality in the numerous feminist periodicals in the Third World, as well as in the West, that have emerged during this decade. These discuss a variety of issues from

*See "Reflections on Global Feminism After Nairobi," pp. 346–352.

reproductive rights to female poverty, from legislation to sexuality, from violence against women to the violations of the military. You can see it also in the local, regional, and international gatherings that have been held among activists, academics, policy makers, health practitioners, social workers, and community leaders, from Sri Lanka to Switzerland to Senegal. A good illustration was the Second Feminist Encuentro (Meeting) for Latin America and the Caribbean, where over six hundred women gathered in Lima in 1983 to discuss patriarchy in the region in relation to a list of some nineteen proposed topics and still had to keep adding to the agenda. The vitality and breadth of feminism are also seen in the myriad of grass-roots projects, centers, demonstrations, celebrations, and meetings where women voice their demands for a greater say over their lives. Here, too, they take the time and space to plan together how to develop visions into reality.

A GLOBAL VIEW OF FEMINISM

The excitement and urgency of issues of global feminism were brought home to me at a Workshop on Feminist Ideology and Structures sponsored by the Asian and Pacific Centre for Women and Development in Bangkok in 1979. Women from each region presented what they were doing in relation to the themes of the UN Decade for Women. In doing this, we realized the importance of the international male-dominated media in influencing what we knew and thought about each other before we came to Bangkok.

We saw how the media has made the women's movement and feminism appear trivial, silly, selfish, naïve, and/or crazy in the industrialized countries while practically denying its existence in the Third World. Western feminists have been portrayed as concerned only with burning bras, having sex, hating men, and/or getting to be head of General Motors. Such stereotypes ignore the work of most feminists and distort even the few activities the media do report. So, for example, basic political points that women have tried to communicate—about what it means to love ourselves in a woman-hating society—get twisted into a focus on "hating" men. Or those demonstrations that did discard high-heeled shoes, makeup, or bras, as symbolic of male control over women's self-definition and mobility, have been stripped of their political content.

Thus, women who feel that their priorities are survival issues of food or housing are led to think that Western feminists are not concerned with these matters. Similarly, media attempts to portray all feminists as a privileged elite within each country seek to isolate us from other women. The real strength of feminism can be seen best in the fact that more and more women come to embrace it in spite of the overwhelming effort that has gone into distorting it and trying to keep women away.

By acknowledging the power of the media's distortion of feminism at the Bangkok workshop, we were able to see the importance of defining it clearly for ourselves. Our definition brought together the right of every woman to equity, dignity, and freedom of choice through the power to control her own life and the removal of all forms of inequalities and oppression in society. We saw feminism as a world view that has an impact on all aspects of life, and affirmed the broad context of the assertion that the "personal is political." This is to say that the individual aspects of oppression and change are not separate from the need for political and institutional change.

Through our discussion, we were able to agree on the use of this concept of feminism to describe women's struggles. While some had reservations about using the word "feminism," we chose not to allow media or government distortions to scare us away from it. As one Asian pointed out, if we shied away from the term, we would simply be attacked or ridiculed for other actions or words, since those who opposed us were against what we sought for women and the world and not really concerned with our language.

In Copenhagen at the 1980 NGO Forum, the conference newspaper came out with a quote-of-the-day from a Western feminist that read: "To talk feminism to a woman who has no water, no home, and no food is to talk nonsense." Many of us felt that the quote posed a crucial challenge to feminists. We passed out a leaflet, "What Is Feminism?," describing it as a perspective on the world that would address such issues, and we invited women to a special session on the topic. Over three hundred women from diverse regions gathered to debate what feminism really means to us and how that has been distorted by the media and even within our own movements.

The second challenge we saw in the quote was that if it were true and feminists did not speak to such issues, then we would indeed be irrelevant to many women. We therefore discussed the importance of a feminist approach to development—one that both addresses how to make home, food, and water available to all and extends beyond equating "development" with industrialization. Terms like "developing nations" are suspect and patronizing. While we need to look at the real material needs of all people from a feminist perspective, we can hardly call any countries "developed." For this reason, while I find all labels that generalize about diverse parts of the world problematic, I use "Western" or "industrialized" and "Third World," rather than "developing" and "developed."

Recently at a meeting in New York, I saw another example of confusion about the meaning of feminism. Two women who had just engaged in civil disobedience against nuclear weapons were discussing feminism as the motivating force behind their actions, when a man jumped up impatiently objecting, "But I thought this meeting was about disarmament, not feminism." It was the equivalent of "to talk feminism in the face of nuclear destruction is to talk nonsense." Such attitudes portray feminism as a luxury of secondary concern and thus both dismiss female experience as unimportant and limit our politics. They fundamentally misconstrue feminism as about "women's issues" rather than as a political perspective on life.*

Seeing feminism as a transformational view is crucial to a global perspective. But to adopt a global outlook does not mean, as some feminists fear and male politicos often demand, that we abandon working on the "women's issues" that we fought to put on the political agenda. Nor does it imply setting aside our analysis of sexual politics. Rather it requires that we take what we have learned about sexual politics and use feminist theory to expose the connections between the "women's issues" and other world questions. In this way, we demonstrate our point that all issues are women's issues and need feminist analysis. For example, we must show how a society that tacitly sanctions male violence against women and children, whether incest and battery at home, rape on the streets, or sexual harassment on the job, is bound to produce people who are militaristic and believe in their right to dominate others on the basis of other differences such as skin color or

*See section on "transformational politics" in "Going Public with Our Vision," pp. 69–71.

nationality. Or we can point out how the heterosexist assumption that every "good" woman wants to and eventually will be supported by a man fuels the economic policies that have produced the feminization of poverty worldwide. This refusal to accept a woman who lives without a man as fully human thus allows policy makers to propose such ideas as keeping welfare payments or even job opportunities for single mothers limited since they "contribute to the destruction of the family."

The examples are endless. The task is not one of changing our issues but of expanding the frameworks from which we understand our work. It means taking what we have learned in working on "women's issues" and relating that to other areas, demanding that these not be seen as competing but as enabling us to bring about more profound change. To use the illustration above, to seek to end militarism without also ending the dynamic of domination embedded in male violence at home would be futile. And so, too, the reverse: we will never fully end male violence against individual women unless we also stop celebrating the organized violence of war as manly and appropriate behavior.

MAKING CONNECTIONS

The interconnectedness of the economic and sexual exploitation of women with militarism and racism is well illustrated in the area of forced prostitution and female sexual slavery. It is impossible to work on one aspect of this issue without confronting the whole socioeconomic context of women's lives. For example, females in India who are forced into prostitution are often either sold by poverty-stricken families for whom a girl child is considered a liability, or they have sought to escape arranged marriages they find intolerable. In the United States, many girls led into forced prostitution are teenage runaways who were victims of sexual or physical abuse at home, and for whom there are no jobs, services, or safe places to live.

In parts of Southeast Asia, many women face the limited economic options of rural poverty; joining assembly lines that pay poorly, destroy eyesight, and often discard workers over thirty; or of entering the "entertainment industry." In Thailand and the Philippines, national economies dependent on prostitution resulted from U.S. military brothels during the Vietnam War. When that demand decreased, prostitution was channeled into sex tourism—the organized multimillion-dollar transnational business of systematically selling women's bodies as part of packaged tours, which feeds numerous middlemen and brings foreign capital into the country. In all these situations, the patriarchal beliefs that men have the right to women's bodies, and that "other" races or "lower" classes are subhuman, underlie the abuse women endure.

Feminists organizing against these practices must link their various aspects. Thus, for example, women have simultaneously protested against sex tourism and militarism, created refuges for individual victims who escape, and sought to help women develop skills in order to gain more control over their lives. Japanese businesses pioneered the development of sex tourism. Feminists in Japan pioneered the opposition to this traffic. They work with Southeast Asian women to expose and shame the Japanese government and the businesses involved in an effort to cut down on the trade from their end.

On the international level, it is clear that female sexual slavery, forced prostitution, and violence against women operate across national boundaries and are political and human rights abuses of great magnitude. Yet, the male-defined human rights community by-and-large refuses to see any but the most narrowly defined cases of slavery or "political" torture as their domain. We must ask what is it when a woman faces death at the hands of her family to save its honor because she was raped? What is it when two young lesbians commit suicide together rather than be forced into unwanted marriages? What is it when a woman trafficked out of her country does not try to escape because she knows she will be returned by the police and beaten or deported? An understanding of sexual politics reveals all these and many more situations to be political human-rights violations deserving asylum, refugee status, and the help that other political victims are granted. As limited as human rights are in our world, we must demand at least that basic recognition for such women, while we seek to expand concern for human rights generally.

In these areas as well as others, feminists are creating new interpretations and approaches—to human rights, to development, to community and family, to conflict resolution, and so on. From local to global interaction, we must create alternative visions of how we can live in the world based on women's experiences and needs in the here-and-now.

336

In sharing experiences and visions across national and cultural lines, feminists are inspired by what others are doing. But we are also confronted with the real differences among us. On the one hand, our diversity is our strength. It makes it possible for us to imagine more possibilities and to draw upon a wider range of women's experiences. On the other hand, differences can also divide us if we do not take seriously the variations on female oppression that women suffer according to race, class, ethnicity, religion, sexual preference, age, nationality, physical disability, and so on. These are not simply added onto the oppression of women by sex, but shape the forms by which we experience that subordination. Thus, we cannot simply add up the types of oppression that a woman suffers one-by-one as independent factors but must look at how they are interrelated.

If we take this approach, we should be more capable of breaking down the ways in which difference itself separates people. Patriarchal society is constructed on a model of domination by which each group is assigned a place in the hierarchy according to various differences, and then allocated power or privileges based on that position. In this way, difference becomes threatening because it involves winning or losing one's position/privileges. If we eliminated the assignment of power and privilege according to difference, we could perhaps begin to enjoy real choices of style and variations of culture as offering more creative possibilities in life.

The world has been torn apart by various male divisions and conflicts for thousands of years and we should not assume that women can overcome and solve in a short time what patriarchy has so intricately conceived. The oppressions, resentments, fears, and patterns of behavior that have developed due to racism, classism, nationalism, and sexism, are very deep. We cannot just wish them away with our desire for women to transcend differences. Above all, we do not overcome differences by denying them or downplaying their effects on us—especially when the one denying is in the position of privilege.

A white woman can only legitimately talk about overcoming differences of race if she struggles to understand racism both as it affects her personally and as she affects it politically. A heterosexual can get beyond the divisions of sexual preference only by learning about both the oppression of lesbians and by acknowledging the insights that come from that orientation. A U.S. American must understand the effects of colonialism before she can hope for unity with women beyond national boundaries. Too often the call to transcend differences has been a call to ignore them at the expense of the oppressed. This cannot be the route of global feminism. We can only hope to chart a path beyond male divisions by walking through them and taking seriously their detrimental effects on us as women. This examination of and effort to eliminate other aspects of oppression does not come before or after working on sexism—it is simultaneous.

A crucial part of this process is understanding that reality does not look the same from different people's perspectives. It is not surprising that one way that feminists have come to understand about differences has been through the love of a person from another culture or race. It takes persistence and motivation—which love often engenders—to get beyond one's ethnocentric assumptions and really learn about other perspectives. In this process and while seeking to eliminate oppression, we also discover new possibilities and insights that come from the experience and survival of other peoples.

In considering what diversity means for a global movement, one of the most difficult areas for feminists is culture. In general, we affirm cultural diversity and the variety it brings to our lives. Yet, almost all existing cultures today are male-dominated. We know the horrors male powers have wrought over the centuries in imposing one cultural standard over another. Popular opposition to such imposition has often included affirmation of traditional cultures. Certainly none of our cultures can claim to have the answers to women's liberation since we are oppressed in all of them.

We must face the fact that in some instances male powers are justifying the continuation or advocating the adoption of practices oppressive to women by labeling them "cultural" and/or "resistance to Western influence." Feminists must refuse to accept *any* forms of domination of women—whether in the name of tradition or in the name of modernization. This is just the same as refusing to accept racial discrimination in the name of "culture," whether in the South of the USA or in South Africa. Feminists are seeking new models for society that allow for diversity while not accepting the domination of any group. For this, women in each culture must sort out what is best from their own culture and what is oppressive. Through our contact with each other, we can then challenge ethnocentric biases and move beyond the unconscious cultural assumptions inherent in our thinking.

In taking into account and challenging the various forms of domination in the world, we do not necessarily accept existing male theories about or solutions to them. We must always have a woman-identified approach—that is, one of seeking to identify with women's situations rather than accepting male definitions of reality. Such a process enables us to distinguish what is useful from male theories and to see where feminist approaches are being or need to be applied to issues such as race, class, and culture. Further, in a world so saturated with woman-hating, it is through woman-identification, which involves profoundly learning to love women and to listen for women's authentic perspectives, that we can make breakthroughs in these areas.

We confront a similar dilemma when examining nationalism. From a feminist perspective, I see nationalism as the ultimate expression of the patriarchal dynamic of domination—where groups battle for control over geographic territory, and justify violence and aggression in the name of national security. Therefore I prefer the term "global" to "international" because I see feminism as a movement among peoples beyond national boundaries and not among nation-states. Yet, nationalism has also symbolized the struggle of oppressed peoples against the control of other nations. And many attempts to go beyond nationalism have simply been supranational empire-building, such as the idea of turning Africans into "Frenchmen." Further, in the context of increasing global control over us all by transnational corporations, many see nationalism as a form of resistance. In seeking to be global, feminists must therefore find ways to transcend patriarchal nationalism without demanding sameness, and while still preserving means of identity and culture that are not based on domination.

THINK GLOBALLY, ACT LOCALLY

A major obstacle that feminists face in seeking to be global is our lack of control over the resources necessary for maintaining greater contact worldwide. It takes time and money as well as energy and commitment to overcome the problems of distance, language, and culture. Feminists have little control over existing institutions with global networks, such as the media, churches, universities, and the state, but sometimes we must utilize such networks even as we try to set up our own.

Since feminists have limited resources for global travel and communication, it is vital that we learn how to be global in consciousness while taking action locally. For this, we must resist the tendency to separate "international" work into a specialized category of political activity that is often viewed as inaccessible to most women. This tendency reflects a hierarchical mode in which the "world level" is viewed as above the "local level." For those whose work focuses primarily on the global aspects of issues, the challenge is not to lose touch with the local arena on which any effective movement is based. For those whose work is focused locally, the challenge is to develop a global perspective that informs local work. For all of us, the central question is to understand how the issues of women all over the world are interrelated and to discern what that means specifically in each setting.

Global interaction is not something that we choose to do or not to do. It is something in which we are already participating. All we choose is whether to be aware of it or not, whether to try to understand it and how that affects our actions. For citizens of the U.S., we begin our global consciousness with awareness of the impact that our country's policies have on other people's daily lives. I learned in the antiwar movement that often the most useful thing that we can do for people elsewhere is to make changes in the U.S. and in how it exercises power in the world.

There are many well-known issues such as military aggression, foreign aid and trade policies, or the possibility of worldwide destruction through nuclear weapons or chemical contamination that we see as global. But there are numerous less obvious illustrations of global interrelatedness, from the present world economy where women are manipulated as an international cheap labor pool to the traffic in women's bodies for forced prostitution. Therefore, any attempt we make to deal with the needs of women in the U.S., such as employment, must examine the global context of the problem. In this instance, that means understanding how multinational corporations move their plants from country to country or state to state, exploiting female poverty and discouraging unionization by threatening to move again. We must use global strategies, such as that proposed by one group on the Texas-Mexico border advocating an international bill of rights for women workers as a way to organize together for basic standards for all. In a world where global forces affect us daily, it is neither possible nor conscionable to achieve a feminist utopia in one country alone.

DEVELOPING GLOBAL CONSCIOUSNESS

When women from different countries interact authentically, sharing our own experiences, while also recognizing that our work has cultural limits, we can learn from each other. As we listen to others' views, we see our ethnocentric biases more clearly and can discover ways to overcome these. For while feminism draws strength from its grounding in the concept of "the personal is political," this also has limitations. Each of our personal perceptions of women's needs and reality have been so shaped by the racism, anti-Semitism, classism, and so on, of our cultures that we cannot depend on our perceptions alone as the basis for analysis and action. We need to learn from other women's lives and views as well.

In discussing global connections with women in the U.S., I often find a tendency toward two extremes—arrogance or guilt. The arrogant stance implies that since this wave of feminism developed early in the U.S. and has been very active here, we are the "leaders" of the world movement and must show others what to do. On the opposite extreme are those who feel so apologetic about being U.S. citizens that they assume that women in other countries always know best and that we have nothing to offer except unquestioning support. Both of these attitudes are patronizing and unproductive and have little to do with real solidarity among women. Instead, we must strive for an openness and equality with other women in which we all learn and teach, as we seek common denominators in our work.

Specifically, this means that we should not negate what feminists here have achieved, but should offer our insights and experiences unapologetically, trusting that other women can discern what is useful to them. Even on issues that many consider taboo or touchy internationally, such as lesbianism, I have found that my personal openness and clarification of what this issue means to women in the U.S. have been accepted—and often even welcomed—when explained without defensiveness. What no woman anywhere wants concerning any issue is for someone else to tell her what it means in her context or what she must do about it in her country. Only through honest sharing can we learn from each other.

As feminism develops around the world, all of us can benefit enormously from the ideas, actions, and creativity that go with that expansion. It can also help us to make breakthroughs in each of our movements at home. This is not unlike what white women are learning from the growing movement of women of color in industrialized countries, which is creating new understandings of feminism. For as each group of women from varying backgrounds defines feminism and its significance for themselves and for the world, our understanding of feminism in all areas grows.

The development of feminism among diverse groups offers greater possibilities for all feminists even as we must respond to its challenges. First we must try to alter our individual behavior and change our movements internally where oppression occurs. But we should not assume that our task is only within the movement, or worse yet, that we can somehow become perfect nonoppressive beings through just talking about the "-isms." The test of our individual changes is in our actions. It can be seen in how we expand the feminist struggle against these oppressions more forcefully in the world, and in how we broaden our approach to feminism. Just as feminism does not mean adding women and stirring them into male theories and institutions without changing those, so, too, understanding global perspectives or the insights of women of color involves altering our approaches and not just adding in an issue or a person here and there.

At this point it seems useful to look at why it is so difficult for many women to think globally. Perhaps the most obvious reason is that most countries are nationalistic, and the information reported through mainstream media and schools is generally distorted by narrowly defined "national interest." What is taught in schools about the Third World is generally separated from the core content, and just as with the separate curriculum of women's history or black studies, this gives the impression that such material is not essential. Another problem stems from the fact that much of what is called "international" is only "North Atlantic"—that is, it only concerns Europe and North America, which contributes to the invisibility of the Third World. These problems can be countered by making ourselves better informed about the world by seeing it from perspectives other than our nation's mainstream.

Information alone, however, is not the issue. Many women feel overwhelmed by hearing about global problems because they do not think that they can do anything with the information. Feminists are often burdened with just trying to cope with "domestic issues" and survival. It is vital, therefore, that we develop a world view or framework for seeing the local-global connections in order that we can grow from this information rather than become numbed by it.

Certainly none of us can possibly hope to know everything in today's world, and global feminism does not mean that we must understand and act on all issues all the time. The point is not to exhaust ourselves trying to be superwomen. Rather, the challenge is to develop a global perspective from the information we do have and learn to apply that to whatever occurs. For this it may be helpful to focus on one particular country or issue and seek to understand that in some depth as part of expanding one's perspective. Once we see the world in greater depth and from various approaches in one area, it becomes easier to question our biases and look at issues differently in another. This is an ongoing process of learning, questioning, and changing that does not occur all in one moment.

I must reiterate here that a global perspective can be developed anywhere. Spending time in another country can be useful because it removes us from the usual context and assumptions of our lives. But this is not necessary to expand one's world view. For example, in most cities there is a diversity of racial and ethnic groups and communities of people who have left their countries for political or economic reasons or to study. We can learn much from them and by understanding diversity better at home.

There are also techniques that can expand one's perspectives, such as seeking to put ourselves, even if only temporarily, in the position of being "the other." For example, I have suggested that heterosexual women act as if they are lesbians for a week: go places only with women and tell important people in their lives, as a way of gaining a clearer view on this issue. Similarly, one can learn from putting oneself in the position of being in the minority—a white at a predominantly black or Indian event, a person who speaks only English in a Spanish-speaking environment, and so on. While any technique has limitations and can become artificial, it can also be useful if one is genuine in trying to expose one's assumptions and grow in one's perception of the world.

A MATTER OF PERSPECTIVE

Beyond techniques and information, the primary task remains one of attitude, approach, and perspective. The point is not that we necessarily change the focus of our work but that we make connections that help to bring its global aspects to consciousness—in our programs, our slogans, our publications, and our conversations with other women. It is when we try to make a hierarchy of issues, keeping them separate and denying the importance of some in order to address others, that we are all defeated.

To use a previous example, if I cannot develop an analysis and discuss openly the ways in which heterosexism supports the international feminization of poverty, without having some women's homophobia prevent them from utilizing this insight, or without having some lesbians fear that I have abandoned "their issue" by working more on global poverty, then work in both areas is diminished. I believe that the path to effective global feminist theory and action is not through denial of any issue or analysis but through listening, questioning, struggling, and seeking to make connections among them.

To work locally with a global perspective does require stretching feminism, not to abandon its insights but to shed its cultural biases, and thus to expand its capacity to reach all people. In this process, we risk what seems certain at home by taking it into the world and having it change through interaction with other realities and perceptions. It can be frightening. But if we have confidence in ourselves and in the feminist process, it can also be exciting. It can mean the growth of a more effective feminism with a greater ability to address the world and to bring change. If we fail to take these risks and ignore the global dimensions of our lives, we lose possibilities for individual growth and we doom feminism to a less effective role in the world struggle over the direction of the twenty-first century.

My visions of global feminism are grand, perhaps even grandiose. But the state of the world today demands that women become less modest and dream/plan/act/risk on a larger scale. At the same time, the realization of global visions can only be achieved through the everyday lives and action of women locally. It depends on women deciding to shape their own destiny, claiming their right to the world, and exercising their responsibility to make it in some way, large or small, a better place for all. As more women do this with a growing world perspective and sense of connection to others, we can say that feminism is meeting the challenge of bringing the global home.

REFLECTIONS ON GLOBAL FEMINISM AFTER NAIROBI

T here seems to be widespread agreement among feminists that the UN conferences in Nairobi in 1985 were generally a success. Many women speak of them as magical or eye-opening events, and certainly the presence of over fifteen thousand women from diverse cultures talking and celebrating together was a historical moment. However, I think we should see this success not as magical or lucky but as an earned success. What happened there was possible because of the hard labor of many women for many years who believed, in spite of great odds, that feminism was possible in their countries and that it could be global, in spite of our conflicts and differences. I see the Nairobi conference less as the end-of-the-decade and more as the culmination of this process that has put us on the threshold of having a truly global feminist movement.

This success is particularly important in light of the media's continual efforts to declare that feminism has subsided. To put that in perspective, I have a file folder at home labeled "Death of the Women's Movement" with articles that go back to 1971. There is another trend fashionable in the United States that Nairobi challenges—blaming feminists for what has not changed

This article in based on several speeches given in the United States in 1985 and 1986.

yet for women, such as the lack of adequate child care. The problem is not that feminists have failed to address such issues, which often have been included in our demands, as illustrated by the 1977 Plan of Action passed by the National Women's Conference in Houston (which had a twenty-five-point plank including child care, housing, minority women, and so on). Rather, the problem is that the forces opposed to feminism and the policies we have proposed have been greater than we expected.

The Nairobi conference helps us to put that opposition in perspective—to see that patriarchy is strong throughout the world and that the U.S. is no exception. It also enables us to see how much feminism has succeeded in changing the agenda for women, if not yet in achieving all our goals. Further, the energy of women present at the conference caused a rebirth of excitement and sense of possibility for many a tired feminist. It reminded us why we are in this movement and rekindled our visions of a changed world.

My sense of the possibilities for feminism came primarily from what I saw reflected in the NGO Forum, but I want to comment on the official UN conference as well. It was significant that well over 80 percent of the delegates from governments were women—considerably more than in 1975 or '80. While they still represented their male-controlled nations, there was great determination among many of these women that something constructive should emerge from this conference. This created a climate of compromise that produced the agreement on the "Forward-Looking Strategies" document that passed unanimously—something that was not possible in 1980.

It is useful for U.S. women to note that this document, which was endorsed by our government, calls for many improvements for women that often involve the very types of programs that Reagan has opposed or abolished in his assault on the rights of women, racial minorities, and the poor within this country. We should utilize this document to demand more responsiveness to women's needs from our government in both domestic and foreign policies.

Returning to the Forum, what excited me was how it reflected the growth of feminism over the decade. This is growth in both the numbers and the diversity of women who are defining what feminism means for their lives. Perhaps the most important way in which Nairobi differed from the Copenhagen and Mexico City conferences was in the visibility of feminist leadership from the Third World. Not only were Third World women and women of color from the West present in large numbers, but also they were taking the initiative in many areas, including the exploration of feminism. This meant that debates over feminism were usually on what we should be doing or how to organize rather than over whether to use the term, as was the case so often in 1980. While many women did not call themselves feminist, there was less hostility toward the word and more assumption of feminist analysis as basic to understanding women's conditions.

In Nairobi, there was also widespread recognition that feminism is a world view that must address all issues and should not separate women's concerns from other matters such as militarism, racism, or the world economy. Third world leadership has helped many women to understand that the various forms of domination that we experience are connected, and that our strategies must address these together rather than separate them into unrelated categories. Thus, women like Maureen Reagan never had a chance when they tried to say that issues like apartheid were not women's issues. This sense of connectedness was particularly clear at a conference held on a continent where poverty and racism so shape the forms of women's oppression.

Such changes in the approach to feminism at Nairobi were possible because of the growth of feminism indigenously at the local level in many Third World countries over the past five years. Everywhere at the Forum the local work being done by feminists was visible: in workshops on women's centers led by feminists in Latin America, in sessions on how to use videotapes with village women, in the Third World women's publications panel where a whole range of materials were on display. My favorite find was a pamphlet from Sri Lanka called "Feminism Is Relevant." In twenty-five pages it answers basic questions about the history and approach to feminism in Asia and promises a second pamphlet on "Biology and Culture" to come. This spirit of women taking on the big questions, indeed taking on the world, animated and energized the proceedings in Nairobi.

Third World leadership and organizing were also visible in the planning that had gone into Nairobi. There were many regional gatherings to prepare for the conferences; perhaps the most ambitious was the Asian Women's Research and Action Network's

(AWRAN) meeting of women from seventeen countries who prepared an alternative report on the impact of the decade on women. There were a number of global networks like DAWN (Development Alternatives for Women in a New Era)—a Third World project creating a feminist dialogue on development that had produced both a book and a program of sessions at the Forum. One could learn of many fascinating future plans, such as the South Asian meeting for feminists working in a Muslim context, which was then held in early 1986. Feminism is so alive in Latin America that even though many were in Nairobi in July, over a thousand women (most of them not at Nairobi) gathered in Brazil only two weeks later for the Third Feminist Encuentro for Latin America and the Caribbean.

Along with the acceptance that all issues are of concern to feminists, we saw a growing recognition that women have vital insights to add to concepts and strategies for change in the world in every area. For example, workshops looking at development from a feminist perspective noted that governments and UN agencies must pay more attention to the informal sector where most Third World women and many of the poor work. Groups addressing violence against women seek a broadening of the concept of human rights, just as Chilean feminists have expanded the idea of democracy with their demand for "Democracy in the Nation *and* in the Home." The Tech and Tools area saw women, particularly Africans, looking at what technologies will lighten women's workload and questioning the effects of technology generally. The slogan, "If it's not appropriate for women, it's not appropriate"* illustrated how women were turning the idea of what technology means for women into an issue of how women look at the whole society.

Another area of growth reflected in Nairobi was how women dealt with our diversity. Women at the Forum were diverse in race, class, culture, religion, sexual preference, age, physical abilities and so on. And there were inevitable conflicts among us especially around the most controversial issues. Nevertheless, in most instances, women sought to learn from these differences, to celebrate those variations that could strengthen us, and at least to

*This slogan was created by the International Women's Tribune Centre, which cosponsored the Tech and Tools Area in Nairobi.

349

try to understand better those that still divided us. While this did not produce immediate answers to tough conflicts like the Middle East, some women were engaged in dialogue about the need for alternative approaches and the difficulty of finding ways, for example, to support Palestinian rights while also working against anti-Semitism.

This more constructive approach was evident in what happened to lesbians, about whom there had been much concern prior to Nairobi. Not only were we not harassed during the Forum as some had predicted, but we held numerous workshops and had informal gatherings on the lawn every day where hundreds of women from all regions exchanged experiences and made plans for future work. There was, of course, homophobia within the Forum and many avoided this issue, but the right of lesbians to participate openly was defended and considerable education on the issue occurred in the sessions, where many came to ask questions and talk.

What happened around lesbianism illustrated the progression of the decade. In 1975, when lesbians raised their voices at the NGO Tribune, it was mostly considered an outrage. Nonetheless, the issue was out and it helped lesbians from different countries to find each other. At the Forum in 1980, there were about six lesbian workshops accepted into the program and considerable networking occurred. However, we were marginalized, since few of the women present ever encountered us or the issue there. In 1985, partially as a result of the fears around the issue, it was made public immediately and more women were aware of our presence. The discussions were also more productive because of the groundwork laid at the previous conferences, and because there has been more discussion of lesbianism among feminists in the Third World. Thus, while we were not everywhere or fully accepted, we were a positive presence in workshops on many topics, on the lawn, at the women's dance organized by lesbians, and in a landmark international press conference where lesbians from around the world spoke publicly, some for the first time. Even at the official UN conference, lesbianism was included in a presentation from the Netherlands and thus made it into UN documents, perhaps for the first time.

I do not want to give the impression that Nairobi was feminist heaven because there were problems and conflicts as well. While there was a generally constructive approach to diversity, women also had difficulty trusting each other. The national, racial, and other conflicts that divide our world were reflected among us even as we tried to overcome them. Many women were justifiably impatient and angry over injustices; dialogue often broke down, although in areas like the "peace tent" considerable attention went to dealing with such conflicts.

A major underlying tension was that while what we were doing in Nairobi and in our projects at home was exciting, it might never be enough to reverse the destructive forces at work in the world. For while feminism is transforming many women's lives and has the potential to affect significantly how society is organized, it is a slow process of change and the sense of urgency is great, particularly in poorer parts of the world. The threats of war and nuclear contamination, poverty and famine, racism and violence against women hung over our proceedings as a reminder of the urgency of our struggle. Yet, in spite of this, there was a pervading optimistic spirit at Nairobi—that if women continued to progress in consciousness-raising and organizing as we had in the past decade, we would be able to alter these forces and begin to see new possibilities in the world.

The question now as the Nairobi events fade into memory is how to keep that spirit alive and bring global consciousness into our everyday lives and work. The three international conferences of the Decade for Women have been tremendously important in advancing the women's movement and creating greater global connections among us. Now, however, we must find ways to continue this process even if there is little support from the UN. We must utilize those inroads into institutions and consciousness that women have made locally, nationally, and globally to move ourselves into the next phase of global feminism. This phase will be one of grounding our work in greater depth and dealing with the complexities of creating structural change.

Far from being out of step with the developments of feminism globally that I describe here, I see the women's movement in the U.S. undergoing a parallel process of growth and change. In both the women of color movement here and in many grass-roots projects, there has been a broadening of the feminist agenda and greater attention paid to our diversity. This has included more efforts at coalition-building both among women's groups and with other forces for change. One example are the Women's Agenda Projects in about ten states from Montana to Pennsylvania that have built coalitions across class and race lines to demand state legislation and budget allocations that directly affect women's lives. While the feminist movement has changed in the '80s, I believe that it is a mistake to see it as in decline. Rather, a wider variety of women who have been influenced by the ideas of feminism are now seeking ways to take that into their lives and to create more profound structural change.

Within the U.S., it is important to utilize the interest generated by the Nairobi conferences to continue expanding the global dimensions of our local work as just discussed in "Bringing the Global Home."* Challenging U.S. policies as they affect the local options of women elsewhere is a vital aspect of this awareness. This is obvious in relation to major controversies such as apartheid in South Africa. But it is also important with regard to less publicized matters such as the Reagan government's denial of funds to aid groups in the Third World that support abortion or the U.S.-funded schools for children of Afghanistan rebels that are closed to girls. To challenge our government's policies and their implications for women worldwide, we must learn more about what is happening beyond the usual press reports.

Nairobi had considerable impact on making women aware of this need and of the value of hearing other women's perspectives. Since then, I have observed women from many parts of the world utilizing what they learned there and making global connections in their work. There are sister projects made possible by the experiences of the decade, such as that between Native Americans in North Dakota and the Lua minority women in Western Kenya. There are conversations about global gatherings on everything from reproductive rights to a women's economic summit.

The challenges that face women in the last years of this century are great, particularly in light of the world economic crisis and the rise of religious fundamentalism in so many regions, including the U.S. Nevertheless, there is an enduring sense that women are organizing for the future, and that we have begun to learn how to do that with a global perspective. I expect that the growth of global consciousness and of feminist activism manifested in the variety of women's struggles present in Nairobi will be the most lasting legacies of the UN Decade for Women.

*See pp. 328–345.